RACISM AND AUSTERITY

Tory Ideology, Migrants, Muslims and the Working Class

Mike Cole

First published in Great Britain in 2025 by

Bristol University Press
University of Bristol
1–9 Old Park Hill
Bristol
BS2 8BB
UK
t: +44 (0)117 374 6645
e: bup-info@bristol.ac.uk

Details of international sales and distribution partners are available at bristoluniversitypress.co.uk

© Bristol University Press 2025

British Library Cataloguing in Publication Data
A catalogue record for this book is available from the British Library

ISBN 978-1-5292-3977-5 hardcover
ISBN 978-1-5292-3978-2 paperback
ISBN 978-1-5292-3979-9 ePub
ISBN 978-1-5292-3980-5 ePdf

The right of Mike Cole to be identified as author of this work has been asserted by him in accordance with the Copyright, Designs and Patents Act 1988.

All rights reserved: no part of this publication may be reproduced, stored in a retrieval system, or transmitted in any form or by any means, electronic, mechanical, photocopying, recording, or otherwise without the prior permission of Bristol University Press.

Every reasonable effort has been made to obtain permission to reproduce copyrighted material. If, however, anyone knows of an oversight, please contact the publisher.

The statements and opinions contained within this publication are solely those of the author and not of the University of Bristol or Bristol University Press. The University of Bristol and Bristol University Press disclaim responsibility for any injury to persons or property resulting from any material published in this publication.

Bristol University Press works to counter discrimination on grounds of gender, race, disability, age and sexuality.

Cover design: Andrew Corbett
Front cover image: Stocksy/Evan Dalen

Contents

Acknowledgements		iv
Introduction		1

PART I Conceptual and Theoretical Issues

1	The Multifaceted Nature of UK Racism	13
2	Austerity: A Flawed Economic Policy or a Deliberate Act of Capitalist Crisis Management and Class Warfare from Above?	25

PART II Racism and the Hostile Environment

3	Theresa May and the Hostile Environment: Preparation, Official Launch and Enactment (2010–2019)	37
4	Boris Johnson and Priti Patel: Personal Rhetoric and Further Draconian Measures (2019–2022)	59
5	Suella Braverman: Hostile Rhetoric and the Escalation of the Hostile Environment (2022–2023)	74

PART III Austerity

6	David Cameron, the 'Age of Austerity' and its Impact (2009–2019)	95
7	Boris Johnson's COVID-19 Economy, Liz Truss's Mini Budget and Their Impacts (2019–2023)	109
8	Rishi Sunak's Fiscal and Industrial Austerity: Cutting Social Expenditure and the War against the Unions (2022–2023)	122

Conclusion: Hostility and Austerity as Interrelated Concepts – Some Examples and Some Solutions	135
Postscript: Election 2024 – Labour Wins, Far-Right Riots and the Tories Elect a New Leader	148
Notes	159
References	188
Index	225

Acknowledgements

My grateful thanks are due to the following for help, advice, comments and support while drafting this book: Mark Blyth, Noam Chomsky, John Clay, Lyka Cole, Dave Hill, Michael Hillard, Clara Mattei, Richard Mcintyre, Peter McLaren, Jonathan Portes, Richard D. Wolff and the anonymous reviewers for Bristol University Press. This, of course, does not imply that they have agreement with all the analysis, nor that they take responsibility for any shortcomings in the final product.

Introduction

Use of endnotes

I would like, at the outset to make a few comments about my use of endnotes. As well as indicating, where applicable, the source of the points I am making (the full references appear in a list at the end of the book), the endnotes can also contain further details and/or suggestions for additional reading. These include recommendations for the development of a deeper understanding of aspects of the theories or issues being discussed in the text, or other related readings. While these may be required reading for students or a resource for those researching the field, for the general reader interested in the main themes and topics of the book, these can be understood, without reading all, or indeed any, of the endnotes.

Why a book on racism, the hostile environment, austerity and the Tory Party?

Racism has been endemic in the Tory Party[1] since the 19th century,[2] whereas the hostile environment, a major new policy initiative in the Tory racism arsenal, is much more recent, having been launched in 2012, though in preparation before that. Austerity has a much longer history, with its intellectual origins dating back to the 17th century, but, in the modern era, it became official Tory policy in 2010. While hostility and austerity are distinguished in the book for analytical reasons, they are not mutually exclusive. First, hostility, as in the 'hostile environment', is also austere; and austerity is itself inherently hostile. Second, 'migrants' are on the receiving end of austerity as well as hostility; and the working class are treated with hostility as well as subject to austerity. Third, in referring to 'migrants', I have in mind 'immigrants' and 'would-be immigrants'. Certain first-generation 'immigrants' and their offspring – in particular the Windrush generation – are also on the receiving end of the hostile environment. Ongoing Islamophobia, of course, impacts Muslim communities and is exacerbated by the effects of the hostile environment. Fourth, my use of the term 'working class' encompasses *all* workers, including, of course, people who are first-generation immigrants onward. Fifth, there are working-class *communities* that are part of the working class and consist of a wide constituency of people living in communities defined by their class position in society: families, others living together and people living alone. Some of these will not be in the labour market and some will be unemployed and looking for work. Some will be homeless and not able to work, some will be homeless and working.

So, the reason I felt the need for a book on racism, the hostile environment, austerity and the Tory Party is the wide and massive effects that Tory rule over 14 years has engendered. These effects are discussed in detail throughout the book. I return to the effects of the interrelated two-pronged offensive of the hostile environment and austerity in the Conclusion to the book.

Marxism as an explanatory theory

Throughout the book, *where relevant*, I adopt Marxist theory as my main form of analysis. This is because I believe that, more than any other theory, it best explains economic and political processes in capitalist society.[3] I stress 'where relevant', because it is not my contention that everything is explained by Marxism. In the words of Friedrich Engels, Karl Marx's collaborator and co-writer:

> According to the materialist conception of history, the *ultimately* determining element in history is the production and reproduction of real life. Other than this neither Marx nor I have ever asserted. Hence if somebody twists this into saying that the economic element is the *only* determining one, he transforms that proposition into a meaningless, abstract, senseless phrase.[4]

'We make our history ourselves', Engels continues, 'but, in the first place, under very definite assumptions and conditions'.[5] 'Among these', he concludes, 'the economic ones are ultimately decisive. But the political ones, etc., and indeed *even the traditions which haunt human minds also play a part*' (emphasis added).[6]

Let me say at the outset that, for some readers, the term 'Marxism' will immediately ring (loud) warning bells. This is because the term has been thoroughly misunderstood and deliberately manipulated and denigrated by those whose wealth and privilege feel threatened by it.[7] From a Marxist perspective, in capitalist societies class exploitation is the component that defines capitalism and without which it could not exist; and racism of various forms is omnipresent. In the UK Tory Party, class warfare from above[8] is the norm and racism integral.[9] The hostile environment policy, a major component of Tory racism addressed in the book, and austerity consist of what I have called a two-pronged attack on 'migrants' and 'would-be migrants', Muslims and the working class, and working-class communities in general. I need to re-emphasize that my use of the term 'working class' encompasses *all* who need to sell their labour to survive, including, of course, many people who are first-generation immigrants onward and a large number of Muslims.[10] There are working-class *communities* that are part of the working class and consist of a wide constituency of people living in locations defined by their class position in society: families; others living together; and people living alone. Some of these will not be in the labour market and some will be unemployed and looking for work. Some will be homeless and not able to work, some will be homeless and working.

Marxism is reflected in the subtitle of the book, in that in referring to 'Tory ideology' I am using the concept of 'ideology' in a Marxist sense. Marx argued that the ideas of the ruling class are in every epoch the ruling ideas.[11] In other words, because the capitalist class owns the material resources of society, it also tries to maintain control, in general successfully, albeit contested to varying degrees, over the ideas. Thus, not only is capitalism presented as a natural system, it is also lauded as independent from social class and as eternal.[12] From such a perspective, it follows that if a hostile environment is *necessary* to prevent 'illegal immigration' (and increasingly 'legal migration'), which we are told is not fair to British people; and if austerity *needs* to be imposed on the working class to keep the (capitalist) system working properly, then so be it, there are no alternatives. From the perspective of the ruling class, 'ideology' is something that *others* are guided by, not they themselves. For the Tory Governments addressed in the chapters of this book, it is only those who oppose racism and the hostile environment and austerity (for example, the left in general, 'lefty human rights lawyers' and militant trade union leaders and their supporters) who are spurred on by 'ideology', not the ruling Tory elite and the rest of the ruling class and their supporters.

Summary of chapters

The book has three parts: 'Conceptual and Theoretical Issues'; 'Racism and the Hostile Environment'; and 'Austerity'. Part I has two chapters, and Parts II and III contain three chapters each. The book ends with a Conclusion and a Postscript, the former with the title, 'Hostility and Austerity as Interrelated Concepts: Some Examples and Some Solutions'; the latter entitled 'Election 2024: Labour Wins, Far-Right Riots and the Tories Elect a New Leader'.

I begin with Chapter 1 of Part I, which is about the multifaceted nature of UK racism. In the introduction, I challenge the view that racism is just a 'Black and White' issue. I move on to a discussion of the wide parameters of UK racism and the Marxist concept of racialization that is an ideological process whereby people are categorized (falsely) into the scientifically defunct notion of distinct 'races'. I then look at racialization and common sense, distinguishing the latter from good sense. Racism serves the 'divide-and-rule' tactics of capitalism. The next section of the chapter is on types of racism, where I argue that racism can be unintentional as well as intentional; that it can be direct or indirect; overt as well as covert. It can be dominative as well as aversive. It can also become (more) apparent given certain stimuli. I also stress that 'seemingly positive' attributes ascribed to a person or persons will probably have racist implications. Racism can be based on genetics or biology, or it can be based on culture or on a combination of both. I then look at different types of racism that I categorize as colour-coded; non-colour-coded; and hybridist, giving examples of each. I move on to some pivotal definitions around 'asylum', making the point that 'irregular immigrants' are not 'illegal'. Next, I provide some definitions of a 'refugee' and an 'asylum seeker'. I go on to point out that racism can be personal, collective or institutional. I conclude the chapter by suggesting that analysing the plethora of different forms of racism in the UK is important in at least four respects. First, I insist that it can come from anyone, or any combination of individuals, towards anyone, stressing that being Black or of Asian origin, for example, does not give immunity from being racist towards others. Second, it is important to bear in mind that 'racial' and cultural identities are interrelated. Third, considering multiple forms of racism, and relating them to historical and contemporary changes in capitalism and accompanying economic and political processes and practices, not just to physical appearance in an ahistorical context, gives us a much clearer understanding of racism and how to combat it. Fourth, to reiterate, racism exists far and beyond what White people do to Black and Asian people. I give as an example the 2023 survey, 'Racism and Ethnic Inequality in a Time of Crisis'.[13] I point out that the findings do not indicate that the majority of people in the UK are intentional racists, citing the 2023 European Social Survey that provided some degree of optimism, rather that there is a hard-core of active racists. I conclude the first chapter with some fairly detailed historical snapshots of the profusion of Tory racism dating back to the 19th century, thus exemplifying the long history of multifaceted racism in the UK and providing a backdrop to Part II of the book.

Chapter 2, the second conceptual chapter, is a consideration of whether austerity is a flawed economic policy or a deliberate act of capitalist crisis management and class warfare from above. The introduction to the chapter is a brief consideration of the history of the ideology of austerity. It is argued that its intellectual origins began in the last decade of the 17th century with John Locke. Locke, together with John Hume and Adam Smith who both followed him in the 18th century, produced austerity by default[14] on account of their pathological fear of government debt and stress on 'parsimony, frugality, morality'.[15] However none made a specific case for it. Liberal economists built on the work of the three in the 19th century.

These included David Ricardo, who argued that the state should police private property but not redistribute it, and John Stuart Mill, who tried to find a middle path between the claims of the masses and the protection of individual rights. I move on in the main part of Chapter 2 to look at whether austerity is a flawed economic policy, addressing the arguments of economists, working as journalists and in academia, who wonder why austerity continues to dominate government economic policy. Drawing on the seminal work of Clara Mattei, I then address the second option in the chapter's title, whether austerity is better considered a deliberate act of capitalist crisis management and class warfare from above, taking a detour through mainland Europe and Britain after the First World War when revolution was in the air. I next show how austerity came to the rescue of capitalism, as explained by Mattei's analysis of fiscal and industrial austerity. I then discuss Marxism as in direct contrast to austerity theory. Towards the end of the chapter, I analyse a statement from an individual that encapsulates the thinking of an entire social class and verifies the conclusions that I have come to. I end the chapter by noting that from a Marxist perspective, the (*immediate*) solution is to tax the rich instead of imposing austerity on the working class.

In the introduction to Chapter 3, I address some political controversies surrounding the concept of 'hostile environment'. I begin the main part of the chapter by noting the return of racism to the heart of electoral politics as the country edged towards the 2010 General Election that resulted in a Coalition Government under the premiership of Tory David Cameron. While Cameron was clearly supportive of the hostile environment, it was Theresa May who was its driver. The chapter, therefore, focuses on her time as Home Secretary and then as Prime Minister. The preparation for the hostile environment consisted of speeches that displayed rhetoric of hate, blame and threat by both May and Cameron. The hostile environment was launched by May in 2012 and was followed by major and draconian changes in family migration rules. There was also Cameron's creation of the 'hostile environment working group' and May's notorious 'Go home or face arrest vans'. This was followed by the Immigration Acts of 2014 and 2016 that further restricted immigration. May's premiership from 2016 to 2019 witnessed the Grenfell Tower disaster, primarily affecting working-class people of colour and the 2018 White Paper on Immigration that has been called the 'biggest single attack on migration rights in a generation'. This legislation centred around May's and Cameron's ideological and political obsession with reducing net annual migration to below 100,000. The hostile environment was not confined to migrants and prospective migrants but had a wider reach impacting, for example, Muslims, in the context of rampant Islamophobia in the Tory Party and the Windrush generation whose rights as British citizens began to be drastically eroded.

The introduction to Chapter 4 notes how, during May's premiership, Sajid Javid, who replaced Amber Rudd as Home Secretary, unsuccessfully tried to replace the term 'hostile environment' with 'compliant environment'. The chapter proper begins with a discussion of Johnson's own up-front colour-coded colonialist and imperialist racism prior to his premiership. This was mainly revealed in his journalism where he made derogatory comments about 'Black kids' and attacked reforms undertaken in response to the murder of Black teenager Stephen Lawrence. He also published an article by a scientific racist. In addition, Johnson made racist remarks about Black people in the ex-colonies when Foreign Secretary. I also address his infamous Islamophobic comments about Muslim women. His premiership saw the end of free movement to the UK from the European Union and the European Economic Area, and, with the hardline right-wing Priti Patel as Home Secretary, the intensification of the hostile environment. This included the Nationality and Borders Act and the Police, Crime, Sentencing and Courts Act that had implications for both colour-coded and non-colour-coded racism. Johnson's time as Prime Minister also saw the fomenting of the plan to offshore people seeking asylum to Rwanda. The chapter also provides updates on the Grenfell Tower disaster and the Windrush scandal. With respect to the former, there is the revelation that the Government in 2002 knew that the tower's plastic-filled panels burnt 'fast and fierce'. The latter address the Windrush compensation scheme that encapsulated a litany of flaws and a progress report that found Priti Patel's Home Office had failed.

I discuss in the introduction to Chapter 5 how Suella Braverman revealed her cruel stance on people seeking asylum when she wrote about her dream in a *Telegraph* front page at Christmas 2022, announcing the first deportation flights to Rwanda. In the next section of the chapter, I address the nature of the relationship between British Asians and the Tory Party, before moving on to point out that Braverman, who has referred to herself as a 'child of the British Empire', instantly ramped up the rhetoric of the hostile environment on being reappointed Home Secretary. I then look at Sunak's plans for people seeking asylum in small boats, before returning to Braverman's cruel rhetoric and her confrontation with a Holocaust survivor. In a propaganda exercise, she visited Rwanda to promote the forthcoming draconian Illegal Migration Act. She also made racist remarks about 'grooming gangs', rebuked the police for seizing 'gollywogs' from a pub and claimed, without evidence, heightened criminality among small boat arrivals. Braverman was also accused of breaching the barristers' code over racist language. She went on to refuse a more humane asylum support scheme. Referring to the Windrush scandal, I go on to discuss a Home Office commissioned report that locates the scandal in the context of immigration legislation of the 20th century. I then make some more references to Islamophobia in the Tory Party. I move on to the *Bibby Stockholm* migrant barge, the use of which has been described as 'cruel and inhumane'. The Illegal Migration Act of 2023 is then critiqued. The final parts of Chapter 5 address anti-Gypsy, Roma and Traveller (GRT) racism, and Braverman's attacks on the European Convention on Human Rights and the Human Rights Act. I conclude the chapter by discussing the case of a Tory MP accused of racially abusing an activist and the sacking of Braverman for accusing the police of being biased towards pro-Palestinian protesters during the Israel–Gaza war.

In the introduction to Chapter 6, I provide a timeline of the global economic crisis of 2007–2008. I next refer to a brief resurgence of Keynesian economics in an attempt to stabilize the financial system. However, when Britain entered recession, austerity came to the rescue, with the ruling class claiming there was no alternative and David Cameron, then Tory Leader of the Opposition, popularized a new 'age of austerity'. Cameron became leader of the Coalition between Tories and Liberal Democrats, after a hung Parliament, following the 2010 General Election. An extreme and callous fiscal austerity was unleashed. The following year there were uprisings in London and elsewhere, sparked by the killing by police of Mark Duggan, a Black man in his twenties. I then address the impact of austerity that entailed widespread poverty and misery and the Government trying to get people into wage labour at all costs. I follow this with a critique of 'Universal Credit'. Austerity's impact on health is then addressed, including its effect on life expectancy with respect to social class. Austerity also involved dismantling the broader social safety net. I conclude that the rich got richer in the decade after 2010, and the poorest, women and minority ethnic communities bore the brunt.

In Chapter 7's introduction, I point out that, once again, Keynesian policies were briefly enacted, this time to deal with COVID-19. The UK's ability to utilize its Welfare State, however, was constrained by the effects of the 'age of austerity'. After a brief discussion of Chancellor Rishi Sunak's first budget, I turn to the increase in inequality during COVID-19 and Boris Johnson's premiership, focusing on Tory patronage with respect to personal protective equipment and VIP lanes. Items from the latter were much more expensive and Tory donors and associates were given preferential treatment. At the same time, the 'test and trace' system was a failure, despite an eye-watering budget. I then look at Johnson's demise, largely because of 'Partygate', before looking at Liz Truss's brief time as Prime Minister, which included her disastrous mini budget that led to higher mortgage interest rates, higher rents and homelessness.

The last chapter contains an appraisal of the strikes that confronted Sunak's premiership. I then note that, as soon as he became Prime Minister, he signalled austerity and went on to enact both extensive industrial austerity by waging war against the unions and fiscal austerity: cutting social expenditure. Given the centrality of social class in his efforts, I dwell briefly on Sunak's own class background. Chancellor Jeremy Hunt's autumn budget of 2022 has been described by *Guardian* senior economics commentator, Aditya Chakrabortty, as constituting 'the third wave of austerity since 2010'. Before considering Hunt's March 2023 budget that I characterize as 'get the workers back to work' and 'billions for the rich', I discuss the first national nurses' strike and the eruption of widespread strike action at the start of 2023. Sunak's (anti-) Strikes (Minimum Services Levels) Act of 2023 was a continuation of anti-union legislation started by Margaret Thatcher. Five years after a United Nations report, another revealed that extreme poverty had increased. I conclude Chapter 8 and the book with Hunt's autumn statement in 2023 that amounted to more painful austerity than ever.

In the Conclusion, I examine the interrelationship between hostility and austerity, giving examples from the book of how this has panned out in practice. I do this with respect to the ways in which the hostile environment has exacerbated the effects of the Tories' implementation of austerity and how austerity has worsened the lives of those already impacted by the hostile environment. With respect to the former, I focus on the Windrush scandal and detention centres; and to the latter, its general impact, including the increase in inequality among minority ethnic communities and an upsurge in racism. I give, as a specific example, the Grenfell Tower fire disaster. As far as solutions are concerned, some immediate solutions are to stop all austerity measures; to provide safe routes to claim asylum and ensure citizenship for those who need asylum; and to provide further compensation to end the Windrush scandal. A longer-term solution, I argue, is socialism. I then briefly expand on what I mean by this. Only socialism, I believe, has the potential to end poverty, deprivation and despair for good. In the meantime, it is essential to immediately and urgently address the needs of the working class in general who have most felt the brunt of 14 years plus of effects of Tory austerity.

In the Postscript, I begin with the July 2024 General Election that resulted in the defeat of the Sunak Government in a landslide victory for the Labour Party, with Keir Starmer becoming the first Labour Prime Minister in 14 years, since Gordon Brown was defeated by Cameron in May 2010. I move on to the London rally held by far-right activist, Tommy Robinson, that was followed by far-right riots that were sparked by deliberate misinformation concerning the killing of three little girls. The riots occurred in a number of UK cities and went on for seven days. I explain how the riots were organized outside the UK and how this manifested itself in the UK. Left-wing social democrat MP, John McDonnell, has described the events as classic fascist mobilization, having demagogues at the pinnacle of the pyramid, active fascists in the middle, and a mass of disgruntled and impoverished working-class people at the base. I then discuss the antiracist response that also took place across the UK. The Starmer Government rightly responded robustly to the far-right riots and the terror and damage to communities that they caused. Lengthy prison sentences were rapidly imposed by the courts. I conclude the Postscript with an assessment of Tory MPs' and Tory members' choice of a leader to replace Rishi Sunak. That leader is Kemi Badenoch. Way to the right of Rishi Sunak, Badenoch is a culture wars warrior who has been accused of Islamophobia, who supports the Sewell Report that denied institutional racism, and whose hero is an American fiscal conservative economist. Badenoch immediately appointed Robert Jenrick, advocate of leaving the European Convention on Human Rights, as Shadow Justice Secretary.

Note on use of language

I have tried to make my own language inclusive and to use appropriate contemporary nomenclature. Given that some of the people quoted in the book are of earlier times, it is inevitable that some of the language is not inclusive. In addition, some people quoted may have chosen not to use inclusive language for ideological reasons, perhaps considering it 'woke'. I have not commented on language used, since no doubt readers who believe in an inclusive society will themselves spot the use of language that is inappropriate in the second decade of the 21st century.

PART I
Conceptual and Theoretical Issues

1

The Multifaceted Nature of UK Racism

Introduction

In April 2023, Labour MP Diane Abbott wrote a letter to *The Observer* in response to an article in that newspaper by Tomiwa Owolode, entitled 'Racism in Britain is not a black and white issue. It's far more complicated'.[1] Here is the letter in full:

> Tomiwa Owolade claims that Irish, Jewish and Traveller people all suffer from 'racism'. They undoubtedly experience prejudice. This is similar to racism and the two words are often used as if they are interchangeable. It is true that many types of white people with points of difference, such as redheads, can experience this prejudice. But they are not all their lives subject to racism. In pre-civil rights America, Irish people, Jewish people and Travellers were not required to sit at the back of the bus. In apartheid South Africa, these groups were allowed to vote. And at the height of slavery, there were no white-seeming people manacled on the slave ships.[2]

Hours after her remarks were published, Abbott apologised and claimed they were made in error and that an 'initial draft' of her thoughts had been sent for publication by accident. Nevertheless, she had the Party Whip suspended and an investigation was launched.[3]

An anonymous letter to *The Observer*'s sister newspaper, *The Guardian*, captured the absurdity of Abbott's claim with particular respect to antisemitism:

> No, my ancestors did not have to sit on the back of the bus in pre-civil rights America, and were allowed to vote in apartheid South Africa, but I find both facts irrelevant. ... My family came to the

UK from Białystok, Poland, a city where more than 99% of Jews were exterminated.[4]

The letter-writer went on to point that throughout that person's life in the UK, antisemitism has been experienced in many forms, 'from casual "cheap Jew" comments to Nazi insignia brandished in my face. To compare those experiences to the struggles of redheads is incomprehensible'.[5] The anonymous person also said of Abbott that although she is 'a symbol of hope and resilience, a Black woman who has defied the odds', to trivialize the struggles of Jewish people is inexcusable. The letter-writer concludes that while her apology is insincere and her 'initial draft' excuse 'laughable', she hopes that Abbott is able to learn from this experience. 'She is clearly a good person with her heart in the right place.'[6] Also commenting on Abbott's remarks in a *Guardian* article, Aditya Chakrabortty reminds us that Abbott, Britain's first Black woman MP, came up through the Labour movement's 'Black Sections' in the 1980s. It was open to all groups who experienced racism as a result of colonialism, and included not only African-Caribbeans but also Bengalis and Cypriots.[7] At the time, 'Black' was an all-inclusive term. Chakrabortty also points out that Irish immigrants in 19th-century America have been described by Keenan Malik as 'n****rs turned inside out'.[8]

Theoretically, Abbott's viewpoint finds its expression in that form of Critical Race Theory (CRT) (one of CRT's main tenets is that 'race' rather than social class is the primary form of oppression in many countries)[9] known as 'black exceptionalism'. As founders of and leading exponents of CRT, Richard Delgado and Jean Stefancic put it: '[e]xeptionalism holds that a group's history is so distinctive that placing it at the center of analysis is, in fact, warranted', which they dispute.[10] CRT, in fact, has a number of varieties.[11] Black exceptionalism is, of course, explicit in Abbott's analysis. She appears to believe that anti-Black racism is the only real form of racism, all other forms being 'prejudice'.

Even in everyday language in the UK, racism goes beyond viewing racism as being only or primarily directed at Black people but is still often limited to the way White people view and/or treat people of colour, both individually, collectively and institutionally.

The parameters of UK racism and some key related Marxist concepts

In fact, people are on the receiving end of racism because of a variety of perceived 'identities', including nationality, perceived 'race', religion, skin colour, ethnicity, culture or a combination of these.[12] For these reasons, it is essential to adopt a broad concept of racism rather than a narrow one based on skin colour and/or imagined biological inferiority alone. In order to understand how different people become on the receiving end of racism, it is useful to look at the concept of 'racialization', particularly its Marxist variant.[13]

Racialization

Racialization is an ideological process whereby people are categorized (falsely) into the scientifically defunct notion of distinct 'races'.[14] The Marxist concept is distinct from other interpretations of racialization in that it is based on the premise that, in order to understand and combat racism, we must relate it to varying historical, economic and political factors. Specifically, the Marxist concept of racialization makes links to patterns of migration that are in themselves determined by economic and political dynamics.

'Common sense' and 'good sense'

From a Marxist perspective, any discourse is a product of the society in which it is formulated: '[O]ur thoughts are the reflection of political, social and economic conflicts and racist discourses are no exception'.[15] Dominant discourses tend to directly reflect the interests of the ruling class, rather than 'the general public'. The way in which popular consciousness reflects on racialized 'others' is via 'common sense'. 'Common sense' is generally used to denote a down-to-earth 'good sense' and is thought to represent the distilled truths of centuries of practical experience, so that to say an idea or practice is 'only common sense' is to claim precedence often over the arguments of left intellectuals and can be used to try to foreclose discussion.[16]

The Italian Marxist, Antonio Gramsci, made a distinction between common sense and good sense. The former 'is not a single unique conception, identical in time and space. It is the "folklore" of philosophy, and, like folklore, it takes countless different forms. Its most fundamental characteristic is that it is ... fragmentary, incoherent and inconsequential'.[17] Good sense, on the other hand, for Gramsci is exemplified by Marxism. As Diana Coben has argued, good sense, for Gramsci, 'may be created out of common sense through an educative Marxist politics'.[18] Gramsci believed that ' "everyone" is a philosopher, and that it is not a question of introducing from scratch a scientific form of thought into everyone's individual life, but of renovating and making "critical" an already existing activity'.[19] Therefore, access to Marxism is not something that is just for an intellectual elite. To paraphrase Gramsci, he believed that everyone is an intellectual but, in capitalist societies, not everyone has the function of 'intellectual'.[20]

Whereas for the Tories and other sections or upholders of the ruling class, and crucially those who have adopted Gramscian 'common sense', it is common sense to restrict immigration to protect *British* workers' jobs and to keep education, free health and so on for British people, and to not make the UK overcrowded. From a Marxist perspective, on the other hand, good sense is to critically examine the economic and political context in which decisions are made, and especially, whose interests they serve. It is also to explore the possibilities of a world beyond capitalism where wealth is shared, with plentiful employment opportunities for all, worldwide, where people would not need to migrate northwards. With the Global South increasingly poorer than the Global North, such movement will increase. In addition, and, unless we address climate destruction seriously, it will become inevitable.[21]

Divide and rule

Racism serves the 'divide-and-rule' tactics of capitalism in diverse ways and directs workers' attention away from their real enemy and towards their racialized sisters and brothers. This was recognized by Marx towards the end of the 19th century:

> In all the big industrial centres in England there is profound antagonism between the Irish proletariat and the English proletariat. The average English worker hates the Irish worker as a competitor who lowers wages and the standard of life. He feels national and religious antipathies for him. He regards him somewhat like the poor whites of the Southern states regard their black slaves. This antagonism among the proletarians of England is artificially nourished and supported by the bourgeoisie. It knows that this scission is the true secret of maintaining its power.[22]

While Marx was writing at a time when racialized Irish workers served this 'divide-and-rule' function, in the period under discussion in this book, it is mainly the hostility towards other racialized people, particularly people trying to cross the English Channel in small boats that serve 'divide and rule': 'austerity is inevitable and "illegal immigrants" make it worse for you!' (see the section 'Some pivotal definitions around asylum' in this chapter).

Types of racism

Racism can be unintentional as well as intentional (the former can sometimes cause as much harm and distress as the latter). The difference between these two forms of racism depends obviously on intention and is summed up by the epithet: you do not have to be a racist (intentional) to be racist (which can be unintentional).[23] Racist pronouncements, intentional as well as unintentional, are often introduced with 'I'm not racist but …'. Racism can be direct (open and spelt out) or indirect (rules for everyone that are racist for some); it can be overt as well as covert. Racism can be dominative (direct and oppressive), as well as aversive (exclusion, cold-shouldering[24] and avoidance of interaction).[25] Racism can also become (more) apparent given certain stimuli, such as large numbers of people gathering in a competitive and sometimes angry atmosphere. Crowds at UK soccer matches are an obvious example. During the 2023–2024 season, 'Kick It Out', an organization that fights racism and other forms of discrimination and promotes inclusion, received reports of a 47 per cent rise in racist abuse across all levels of the game.[26]

It should also be stressed that 'seemingly positive' attributes will probably (ultimately) have racist implications, as in 'they are good at sport' that may also have the subtext that 'they' are not good at much else or at something else. Also, 'seemingly positive' can be used to contrast what a group used to be like with what they are like now.

Racism can be based on genetics, a belief that some genes are inferior to others – biological or scientific racism;[27] or culture, thinking that some cultures are not as good as others – cultural racism, or it can be a combination of both.

Racism related to skin colour is the most recognized and discussed form of racism in the UK. I refer to this as colour-coded racism. Directed towards Black and Asian communities, it has its origins in the British Empire and dates back at least to the 18th century.[28] Racism, however, is not necessarily related to skin colour. When it is not, or is possibly not, I use the terms 'non-colour-coded racism' and 'hybridist racism': the first to describe racism that is *not* related to skin colour; and the second to refer to racism that is *not or not specifically or not necessarily* related to skin colour.

Examples of non-colour-coded racism are anti-Irish racism, antisemitism, and anti-Gypsy Roma and Traveller racism, all of which have a long history in the UK.[29] A newer form of non-colour-coded racism is xeno-racism,[30] that form of racism that is directed at White Central and Eastern European workers and their families.[31] Xeno-racism dates back to the turn of the century[32] with one of the first groups to experience xeno-racism in the UK being the Poles,[33] and other Eastern European workers when Poland joined the European Union in 2004, along with the Czech Republic, Estonia, Hungary, Latvia, Lithuania, Slovakia and Slovenia.

Finally, 'hybridist racism' I use to encompass Islamophobia and anti-asylum-seeker racism. Those on the receiving end of Islamophobia are not by any means a homogeneous group, since 'Muslim' includes people of many nations and colours, who speak many languages and whose only common denominator is religion and religious culture, and even here, there are different varieties of the Muslim religion and associated cultures. Thus, Islamophobia is often triggered by modes of dress or appearance, rather than skin colour. As Ambalavaner Sivanandan put it, 'the victims are marked not so much by their colour as by their beards and headscarves'.[34]

To conclude this section of the chapter, it is crucial to add that in moving beyond the simplistic notion that only White people can be racist towards specific people of colour and the examples given as to why this is important, should not serve to underestimate the fundamental historical and ongoing significance of colour-coded racism.

Some pivotal definitions around 'asylum'

Given the 'discourse of derision'[35] during the timespan of this book surrounding the issue of 'asylum' that emanates from sections of the media and from the mouths of some politicians, and the hysteria that this helps to generate, along with physical attacks on innocent people seeking asylum, it is instructive to provide some key definitions.[36]

Irregular immigrants not 'illegal immigrants'

The Tory Governments referred to in this book refer repeatedly to 'illegal immigrants', particularly when referring to people attempting to cross the English Channel in small boats. Irregular migration is the practice of crossing an international border without official permission from the authorities. Irregular migration is not synonymous with illegal immigrants because irregular travel in order to seek asylum is *not* a crime.[37]

Refugee

According to Article 1 of the 1951 United Nations Convention Relating to the Status of Refugee, a refugee is a person who:

> owing to a well-founded fear of being persecuted for reasons of race, religion, nationality, membership of a particular social group, or political opinion, is outside the country of his nationality, and is unable to or, owing to such fear, is unwilling to avail himself of the protection of that country.[38]

Asylum seeker

An asylum seeker is a person who has applied for asylum and is waiting for a decision as to whether or not they are a refugee. In other words, in the UK an asylum seeker is someone who intends to ask or has asked the Government for refugee status and is waiting to hear the outcome of their application. There is no such thing as a 'bogus' or 'illegal' asylum seeker: 'Everybody has a right to seek asylum in another country. People who don't qualify for protection as refugees will not receive refugee status and may be deported, but just because someone doesn't receive refugee status doesn't mean they are a bogus asylum seeker.'[39]

In the words of Kofi Annan, former Secretary-General of the United Nations: 'Let us remember that a bogus asylum-seeker is not equivalent to a criminal; and that an unsuccessful asylum application is not equivalent to a bogus one.'[40] Thus, it needs to be stressed again and again that asylum seekers are simply people waiting for a decision on whether they have refugee status, and refugees are extremely vulnerable people who have left their country because of well-founded fears for their safety should they remain there. People seeking asylum are not criminals or illegal or scroungers, but some of the most desperate of the worldwide victims of racism and exploitation, often as the direct or indirect result of the aftermath of colonialism by Western capitalist nations.

I refer to racism directed at those seeking asylum as hybridist because of the diversity of origin of their home countries. In the year to September 2022, the main applicants came from Albania (12,000), Afghanistan (5,600), Iran (5,800), Iraq (2,800) and Syria (2,600).[41]

Racism can be personal, collective or institutional. In 2023, there were a large number of instances of institutional racism in the UK,[42] for example, in the criminal justice system,[43] in schools,[44] in the fire service,[45] and in cricket.[46]

Why is all this important?

Why is all this important? This brief incursion into the plethora of different forms of racism that characterize the UK both historically and in the present is not merely analytical in intent. It is also important in at least four other respects. First, anyone or any combination of individuals can be racist towards anyone or any combination of individuals who is not/are not considered to be the same nationality, to be part of the same perceived 'race', to have the same religion, skin colour, ethnicity or culture, or a mixture of these. People can also be racist towards people who are racialized for the same reasons that they are. It is patently untrue, for example, to claim that people who have been subject to entrenched institutional racism for centuries or decades cannot be racist towards others. Thus, for example, Asian people can be racist towards Black people and vice versa, Asian people can be racist towards asylum seekers or other Asian people, and so on.

Second, it is important to bear in mind that 'racial' and cultural identities are interrelated. For example, Jewish people can be Black and/or Asian and/or Central and Eastern European and/or asylum seekers; Central and Eastern European people can be Black and/or Muslim; members of Gypsy, Roma and Traveller communities can be Muslim and/or Asian, and so on.

Third, considering multiple forms of racism, and relating them to historical and contemporary changes in capitalism and accompanying political processes and practices (for example, controls on immigration and deportations), and to economic and political developments in capitalist societies from imperialism and colonialism to the present, and not just to physical appearance in an ahistorical context, gives us a much clearer Marxism-informed understanding of the phenomenon of racism, and crucially, makes us better equipped to combat it.

Fourth, to reiterate racism exists far and beyond the commonplace notion that it is related only to perceived biological or cultural inferiority and confined to what White people think of, or the way they treat, or what they do to Black and Asian people.

The 2023 Racism and Ethnic Inequality in a Time of Crisis Survey

The results of a survey of more than 14,000 people across 21 ethnic groups, the biggest and most comprehensive in the UK for more than a quarter of a century, were reported by Nissa Finney et al in 2023.[47] They found 'strikingly high' levels of exposure to abuse across a wide range of minority ethnic groups, as well as a high prevalence of racism and inequality of outcomes in education, the workplace, housing and interactions with the police. More than a third of people from ethnic and religious minorities experienced 'racially' motivated physical or verbal abuse.[48] The report concluded that 'Britain is not close to being a racially just society'.[49] Its detailed evidence of discrimination and unfairness directly challenges the findings of the Boris Johnson Government-commissioned Sewell Report on 'racial disparities' published in 2021, which the survey argues downplayed the existence and impact of structural and institutional racism in the UK. Thus, the survey found that almost one in six people from minority ethnic and religious groups said they had experienced a racist physical assault prior to the pandemic. This increased to more than one in five Jewish people and more than one in three Gypsy, Traveller and Roma people, while more than a quarter of all respondents from minority ethnic groups had experienced racial insults, and 17 per cent said their property had been damaged by racist attacks. Nearly a third said they had experienced racism in a public place, and one in six said they had suffered racism at the hands of neighbours.[50] Other findings included: 'Nearly a third of people from ethnic and religious minority groups reported racial discrimination in education (29%) and employment (29%), and nearly a fifth said they experienced discrimination when looking for housing.' More than a fifth of all minorities reported experience of discrimination from the police, though this rose to 43 per cent of Black Caribbean groups and more than a third of Gypsy, Traveller and Roma groups.

Minority ethnic minority groups were more likely to live in overcrowded housing – 60 per cent of Roma families were overcrowded and a quarter of

Pakistani and Arab people – and far more likely than White British people to be without access to outdoor space at home.[51]

The findings do not indicate that a majority of people in the UK are *racists*, rather that there is a hard-core of *active racists*, that the UK is an *institutional* racist society, and that people are affected by this and sometimes think or act in racist ways.

The 2023 European Social Survey

The European Social Survey, which has sampled attitudes every two years since 2001, reported in 2023 that the majority of the British public now hold positive views about the impact of immigration on the UK,[52] despite all the negative rhetoric from the Tories and some other politicians. Views on immigration and its economic and cultural impact, it found, had undergone 'a complete about-turn' over the past 20 years, becoming significantly more favourable after 2016. The survey asked people to rank out of ten whether immigration was bad or good for the economy, whether cultural life was undermined or enriched, and whether it made the country a better or worse place to live, with ten being the most positive.[53]

For the first time a majority of respondents interviewed in the year 2021/2022 thought immigration was very positive for the UK economy (59 per cent giving between seven and ten), that it enriched the country's cultural life (58 per cent), and that it made the country a better place to live (56 per cent).[54]

In the previous poll, just 17 per cent were very positive about the economic benefits, 33 per cent thought it culturally enriching, and 20 per cent thought it made the UK a better place to live (2016: 44 per cent, 46 per cent and 39 per cent). In 2002 less than one in ten respondents believed the UK should admit 'many' immigrants of a 'different race or ethnic group to the majority'; by 2022 this had increased to more than a third (34 per cent). The proportion believing no immigrants in this category should be allowed to enter the UK dropped from 15 per cent to 3 per cent over the same period.[55] The UK element of the European Social Survey conducted face-to-face interviews with 1,149 people between August 2021 and September 2022.[56]

A profusion of racism in the Tory Party: some historical snapshots

As I stressed in the Introduction to this book, racism has been endemic in the Tory Party since the 19th century. Here, I present a brief summary to exemplify some of the theoretical analysis in the chapter and as a foretaste of what is to follow in Part II of the book.[57] Beginning with the premiership of Benjamin Disraeli, Britain's first and so far only Prime Minister of Jewish origin, he was on the receiving end of antisemitism from the very beginning of his political career. However, this did not stop him being up-front about his own racism that included non-colour-coded anti-Irish racism: 'The Irish hate our order, our civilization, our enterprising industry, our pure religion. This wild, reckless, indolent, uncertain and superstitious race have no sympathy with the English character.'[58] Disraeli also exuded colour-coded racism with respect to Britain's colonies that also stemmed directly from his steadfast conviction the 'great Caucasian race' was superior.[59] Railing against 'the falsity of that pernicious doctrine of modern times, the natural equality of man',[60] he worried about the consequence of 'the Anglo-Saxon' 'race' were 'citizens ... to mingle with ... negro and coloured populations'.[61] During his premierships, Disraeli was able to consolidate Britain's imperial portfolio.[62]

After Disraeli's death in 1881, there were challenges from other imperial powers that led to a scramble for Africa. The turn of the century also witnessed a significant rise in antisemitism in Britain, following the Russian pogroms, that was exacerbated by some Tory MPs, most notably William Evans-Gordon, who, with other East End (of London) Tory MPs, galvanized some of the poor working-class population into angry street marches, calling for an end to Jewish immigration,[63] arguing against 'the settlement of large aggregations of Hebrews in a Christian land',[64] and stating that 'east of Aldgate one walks into a foreign town', 'a solid and permanently distinct block – a race apart, as it were, in an enduring island of extraneous thought and custom'.[65] In 1905, the Tory Government of Arthur Balfour passed the 1905 Aliens Act, the first modern immigration law that restricted Jewish immigration.[66] As Balfour put it, 'some of these persons are a most undesirable element in the population, and are not likely to produce the healthy children ... but are afflicted with disease either of mind or of body, which makes them intrinsically undesirable citizens'.[67]

While acknowledging his wartime resistance to the Nazis, it should be stressed that Winston Churchill was keen to fight and kill for the Empire when he was younger.[68] He also regarded Kenyans as '[l]ight-hearted, tractable if brutish children ... capable of being instructed'.[69] Churchill hated Asian people too. In 1902, he referred to the Chinese as people as inhabiting 'great barbaric nations who may at any time arm themselves and menace civilized nations'.[70] But, he believed, '[t]he Aryan stock is bound to triumph'.[71] As Colonial Secretary in the 1920s, Churchill opined that Indians in East Africa were 'mainly of a very low class of coolies, and the idea that they should be put on equality with the Europeans is revolting to every white man throughout British East Africa'.[72] Churchill was also anti-Irish and once said that allowing Ireland to become independent was akin to offering a country up to a miserable gang of human leopards in West Africa.[73] During his post-war premiership, he was responsible for atrocities in the colonies, while domestically he was intent on restricting immigration from the Caribbean and the Indian subcontinent.[74] Churchill retired in 1955.[75]

From that year until 1968, there was a last fling of the imperial dice under the premiership of Anthony Eden, anti-Irish racism and Enoch Powell's notorious 'rivers of blood' speech, during which he referred to a conversation with 'a middle-aged, quite ordinary working man' who told him that within a couple of decades, 'the black man will have the whip hand over the white man'.[76] The premierships of Harold Macmillan saw an ongoing loss of colonies and further domestic racism, while that of Edward Heath introduced the 1971 Immigration Act, a major milestone in racist immigration control. Heath's time as Prime Minister coincided with the 'Troubles' in Northern Ireland for which he had a policy of internment without trial of those suspected of being involved with the Irish Republican Army.[77]

Margaret Thatcher's 'racecraft' was her attempt to normalize racism. In her infamous 'swamping' remarks, made in 1978, she said:

> [I]f we went on as we are then by the end of the century there would be four million people of the new Commonwealth or Pakistan here. Now, that is an awful lot and I think it means that people are really rather afraid that this country might be rather swamped by people with a different culture and, you know, the British character has done so much for democracy, for law and done so much throughout the world that if there is any fear that it might be swamped people are going to react and *be rather hostile to those coming in*.[78]

Mary Lou McDonald, who has served as President of Sinn Féin since 2018, and Leader of the Opposition in Ireland since 2020, said of Thatcher at the time of the hunger strikes that she was the 'quintessential hate figure'.[79] In a reference to Thatcher's refusal to grant the prisoners any privileges, McDonald notes the 'malice with which she approached a situation that was hugely politically fraught, but was also hugely human, and to see the men die, one after the other'.[80] Lest we are tempted to deduce that Thatcher's contempt for the prisoners was merely 'political', in a June 1988 conversation with former Taoiseach Charles Haughey, Thatcher said (note her use of 'your people' juxtaposed with 'our people', and the racist stereotype concerning why Irish people come to England): 'Your people come over to us. I wish they wouldn't. They come looking for housing and services.'[81] Thatcher's anti-Irish racism was also revealed to former Labour Northern Ireland Secretary Peter Mandelson who she told, the only time she ever spoke to him: 'I've got one thing to say to you, my boy you can't trust the Irish, they are all liars, liars, and that's what … you have to remember, so just don't forget it.'[82]

John Major who became Prime Minister after Thatcher is often referred to as a multiculturalist, whereas in reality, I have argued,[83] it might be more accurate to describe him as a preserver of 'British culture'. For example, in 1993, he declared:

> Fifty years from now Britain will still be the country of long shadows on county grounds, warm beer, invincible green suburbs, dog lovers and pools fillers and – as George Orwell said – 'old maids bicycling to Holy Communion through the morning mist' and if we get our way – Shakespeare still be read even in school. Britain will survive unamendable in all essentials.[84]

2

Austerity: A Flawed Economic Policy or a Deliberate Act of Capitalist Crisis Management and Class Warfare from Above?

Introduction

Mark Blyth has provided a very useful, concise and succinct analyses of the history of austerity. Focusing on philosophers John Locke and David Hume and economist Adam Smith, he begins with its classical origins in the 17th century.[1] Blyth sums up his discussion of the three by noting that none of them make an argument for austerity: Locke sets up liberalism to limit the power of the state at all costs; Hume sees no point in the state because the merchant class is the productive class to whom the money should flow; and Smith sees a role for the state but struggles to find it.[2] In so doing, with their pathological fear of government debt, and the pre-condition of 'parsimony, frugality, morality',[3] they produced austerity by default.[4]

Liberal economists built on the work of Locke, Hume and Smith in the 19th century. David Ricardo was on the side of 'can't live with the state' and instead favoured a highly competitive economy of small firms producing a very low average rate of profit.[5] The state should police private property but not attempt to redistribute it. In Ricardo's words, even if 'the condition of the laborers is most wretched',[6] the state should take no action to compensate them. John Stuart Mill, on the other hand, tried, in his *On Liberty*, to find a middle road between the claims of the masses and the protection of individual rights, and his *Principles of Political Economy* spelt out what he thought was legitimate state activity.[7] In chapter 7 of Book V of the latter, Mill argued that although taxes would be better, as long as government borrowing did not compete for capital that would drive up the rate of interest, debt issuance was acceptable.[8]

When the British Liberal Party sided with Mill, viewing the state as an instrument for managing and reforming capitalism, New Liberalism, mainly a British movement of the late 19th century, was born. The long-term consequences of this transformation of British Liberalism were dramatic and included universal pensions, unemployment insurance and the intensification of industrial regulation that all followed in the early 20th century.[9] Twenty years later, Blyth concludes, its heirs were 'the great social and economic reformers of the 1930s and 1940s' that included John Maynard Keynes and William Beveridge, who laid the foundations of the Welfare State.[10]

Anton Hemerijck has identified three phases of the development of the Welfare State from 1945 onwards.[11] The first is 'class compromise' between the capitalist class and the working class, to provide welfare, but importantly to forestall socialist ideas. The second is neoliberalism in the 1980s and 1990s. While this phase continues, a third developed in the mid-1990s, characterized by what became known as the 'social investment paradigm'.[12] This recognized new circumstances such as globalization, deindustrialization and new social risks, associated with these vast economic and social changes, and focused on labour market and life course transitions, and the intervention of governments to make these as smooth as possible, as well as the raising the quality of human capital and capabilities, while maintaining strong minimum income universal safety nets as buffers to ensure social protection and economic stabilization.[13]

Is austerity a flawed economic policy?

Moving on to the present, outside the ranks of members of the (Parliamentary) Tory Party and their supporters and defenders, there is a growing consensus among economists, both those working as journalists and those who are academics, that austerity does not work. Typical of the former is Richard Partington, the *Guardian*'s Economics Correspondent. On 2 July 2023, he wrote: 'For more than a year Britain has been trapped with the highest inflation rate in four decades.'[14] Rather than seriously trying to sort this out, he went on, 'the past month's economic developments have turned the country to panic' as '[a]cross the economy the fallout from 13 consecutive interest rate rises in less than two years grows clearer by the day'. Partington then refers to the millions of mortgage holders who are subject to a surge in borrowing costs (see Chapter 7). With interest rates expected to hit 6 per cent by Christmas, he concludes, 'this trickle of bad news could rapidly become a flood'.[15] The problem, according to Partington, however, is not rising interest rates, but that 'despite the lessons of the 2008 financial crisis' (see Chapter 6), 'austerity economics is back with a bang in the name of fighting inflation'.[16] It is a cure far worse than the disease, he says.[17]

Other economists are concerned about the risks of austerity, including Andy Haldane, the former Bank of England Chief Economist, who, although he went against the grain to call for higher rates in early 2021, now advocates a pause.[18] His reason for caution is that the main impact from previous interest rises is yet to be felt. This is largely due to the fact that most people buy at least a two-year fixed rate mortgage, meaning there is a lengthy delay, typically of about 18 months, before monetary policy bites.[19] According to the Resolution Foundation (in its own words, 'an independent think-tank focused on improving living standards for those on low to middle incomes'),[20] 'a typical borrower will be hit with a £2,900 annual rise in their repayments ... sucking a total £15.8bn of spending power out of the economy by 2026'.[21]

'In the face of persistent inflationary pressures', Partington argues, 'the focus should be on bolstering the productive capacity of the economy, not dismantling it'.[22] 'Instead of panic over short-term inflation risks', he concludes, 'there is a need for cool heads to prevail. A scorched-earth approach to tackling inflation would be too heavy a price to pay'.[23]

Blyth is a good example of an academic who makes the case that austerity does not work. He is the William R. Rhodes '57 Professor of International Economics at the Watson Institute for International and Public Affairs at Brown University. In his book, which I draw on in the introduction to this chapter, he focuses on the United States and Europe, his essential argument being that austerity does not work in the sense of achieving its objectives of reducing debt and boosting economic growth.[24] Nevertheless, it has been repeated relentlessly through history. After analysing both the intellectual and the natural history of austerity, Blyth observes of states' adoption of austerity policies: 'If doing the same thing over and over again while expecting different results is the definition of madness, then repeated rounds of austerity in country after country' is madness.[25]

Or is austerity a deliberate act of capitalist crisis management and class warfare from above?

Clara Mattei, in her key 2022 text on austerity, *The Capital Order*,[26] retorts to Blyth's assertion that ends the previous paragraph, by summing up one of the central themes of her book: 'if we view austerity ... as a response, not just to *economic* crises (e.g. contraction of output and heightened inflation) but to crises *of capitalism* ... we can begin to see method in the madness: austerity is a vital bulwark in defense of the capitalist system' (emphasis added).[27]

To his credit, Blyth has responded with exemplary good grace:

> A decade after austerity tore British society apart, the UK government stands ready to do so again. Given that it didn't work the first time

around, one wonders why they want to try it again. This is where Mattei's explanation illuminates brightly: if we think of austerity not as an economic policy, but as a form of capitalist crisis management for moments when the lower orders start to question the governing classes' preferences, then its repeated dosage – despite its damages – makes much more sense.[28]

The First World War, the crisis in capitalism and revolution in mainland Europe

Mattei provides an historical backdrop to illustrate her thesis. The First World War, she argues, heralded the most severe crisis of capitalism to date. The war mobilizations in Europe had shattered belief in capitalism's inevitability as states' showcasing of economic planning signalled that the end of capitalism seemed possible or even likely.[29] In other words, this collective anti-capitalist awakening was facilitated by the exceptional governmental measures taken during the war to confront the enormities of the production effort, thereby temporarily interrupting the accumulation of capital by the owners of private industry,[30] and challenging what had been, until then, 'the untarnished realm of the market'.[31]

> As governments collectivized key industries – munitions, mines, shipping, and railways – they also employed workers and regulated the cost and supply of labor. State interventionism not only allowed the Allies to win the war; it also *made clear that wage relations and the privatization of production – far from being 'natural' – were political choices of a class-minded society.* (emphasis added)[32]

After the war, empowered workers in Europe consolidated collective power through unions, parties, guilds, and rank-and-file institutions to control production.[33] The extent of politicization among large sections of the working class meant that their opinions on economic questions could no longer be ignored.[34] In October 1917, the Russian Revolution overthrew the monarchy and the Russian Empire.[35] And as Rob Sewell, writing for *In Defence of Marxism*, explains, a revolutionary wave swept throughout Europe, as millions of battle-weary troops, along with workers, under the impact of the 1917 October Revolution, rose up to challenge the capitalist system.[36] As Sewell points out, the war itself was not ended by the defeat of Germany, but by the German Revolution that began on 3 November 1918. Following the example of the Russian workers, they overthrew the monarchy and established workers' and soldiers' councils all over Germany. There was unprecedented upheaval throughout Europe, mounting inflation and the winds of revolution blowing from Hungary and Bavaria, as well as Russia.

After the Russian Revolution, there were short-lived Soviet Republics in those countries (Bavaria did not become part of Germany until 1949).

The Hungarian Soviet Republic

As Marxist theoretician and political activist, Alan Woods, writes in *In Defence of Marxism*, Hungary had been ruled by Austria since 1687. After a failed attempt to throw off the Austrian yoke in 1848, oppression of Hungary reached its peak, and 14,000 Hungarians were executed.[37] According to Woods, the only time most peasants were able to wear boots was in the army, where they were subject to racist abuse and physical violence from the drill sergeant.[38] On the eve of the revolution, Hungary constituted the least developed half of the Austro-Hungarian Empire, but for that reason, tensions were nearly reaching boiling point, and peasants were becoming a revolutionary ally of the working class. There was ferment in the factories, and a general strike in January 1918 that sparked mass meetings attended by soldiers. In June, there was a further strike, prompted by workers being shot. Soviets, or Workers' Councils, sprang up and demanded 'peace, universal suffrage, all power to the soviets'.[39] The strike was called off by the leadership, but a new explosion took place in the autumn, the state apparatus disintegrated and collapsed under its own weight, and power 'had passed to the streets'.[40] On 29 October 1918, Hungary was declared a republic. The following day, there was an uprising in Budapest of workers, soldiers, sailors and students.[41] While the revolutionaries lacked a Bolshevik Party able to steer a pre-revolutionary situation towards socialism, they certainly knew what they did not want: rule by an oligarchy, the monarchy, feudal land relations, and oppression and racism.[42] This was, of course, enough to strike terror in the hearts of the ruling class. On 21 March 1919, the Hungarian Soviet Republic was proclaimed. On 1 August, just 133 days later, the Republic was brought to an end with the entry of the counter-revolutionary White Romanian army into Budapest. Had the Hungarian proletariat succeeded, Woods argues, 'the isolation of the Russian Workers' Republic would have been brought to an end'.[43]

The Bavarian Soviet Republic

In Bavaria, Kurt Eisner, a member of the Independent Social Democratic Party, formed in April 1917 by left-wing members of the Social Democratic Party, was arrested later in 1917, and charged with inciting a strike among munitions workers. Eisner was put in prison for nine months until October 1918.[44] In that month, German sailors mutinied and set up councils based on Russian Soviets, which by 6 November had spread to all major cities and ports.[45] Eisner called for a general strike and, on 7 November, having marched through Munich with a few hundred supporters, occupied the Parliament and declared the Bavarian Soviet Republic.[46] Eisner made it clear that this revolution was different from the Bolshevik Revolution, that all private property would be protected by the new Government, and that his programme would be based on democracy, pacifism and anti-militarism. He was soon forced to join a Coalition Government with the Social Democratic Party. The living conditions of the Munich workers and soldiers were rapidly deteriorating, and in the election in January 1919, Eisner received only 2.5 per cent of the total vote.[47] In its short lifetime the Republic had to fight not only against open counter-revolution, but also against the results of its own inexperience.[48]

The brief experience of the Bavarian Soviet Republic, Woods argues, which lasted from 7 April until 1 May 1919, 'was an indication that the flood-tide of revolution was spreading from East to West with what seemed at the time an irresistible urge'.[49] Had the Hungarian workers' state managed to consolidate itself for just a few months longer, Woods concludes, 'the flames of revolution would have engulfed Vienna and Berlin, where the working class was already in a state of revolutionary ferment.'[50] Woods believes that the triumph of the German revolution would have changed the whole course of human history. Instead, the Hungarian Revolution of 1919 entered the annals of history as yet another heroic episode like the Paris Commune of 1871.[51]

Britain

Britain's Chief of the Imperial General Staff, Field Marshal Henry Wilson, wrote in his diary on 9 November 1918, that at a Cabinet meeting, Liberal Prime Minister Lloyd George informed colleagues that the French Prime Minister Georges Clemenceau was worried that Germany may collapse and 'Bolshevism gain control'. He went on, 'Lloyd George asked me if I wanted that to happen or if I did not prefer an armistice. Without hesitation I replied "Armistice." The whole cabinet agreed with me'.[52]

There was talk, however, of a fresh war – against Soviet Russia – but the troops were desperate to return home, sickened by the carnage of the trenches. Suddenly, there was mutiny and, according to Sewell, 'the spectre of revolution hung over Britain'.[53] Mutinies spread, and on 9 January 1919, 1,500 soldiers marched on Downing Street to confront Lloyd George and the Cabinet. Lloyd George was prepared to meet them, but was advised against it by Wilson who declared that the soldiers' delegation 'bore a dangerous resemblance to a Soviet. If such a practice were to spread, the consequences would be disastrous'.[54]

Mattei quotes Willie Gallacher, a leading shop steward at the time, as saying, 'the order of industry, which previous to the war seemed destined to last forever, is now tottering in every country of the world'.[55] On 31 January 1919 there was a mass strike in Scotland in support of a 40-hour week, and fearing a Communist insurrection, the British army sent tanks onto the streets of Glasgow. The leaders of the strike were arrested and Gallacher was imprisoned for five months.[56]

Austerity to the rescue

It was amidst these revolutionary threats that economists turned to austerity. The austerity counteroffensive, as Mattei argues, successfully disempowered the majority:

> Austere governments and their experts implemented policies that either directly (through repressive pay and employment policies) or indirectly (through restrictive monetary and fiscal policies that depressed economic activity and raised unemployment) subjugated the majority to capital – a social relation in which a majority sells their capacity to work in exchange for a wage. Austerity shifted resources from the working majority to the saver/investor minority, and in so doing enforced a public acceptance of repressive conditions in economic production. This acceptance was further entrenched by experts whose economic theories depicted capitalism as the only and best possible world.[57]

This served to quell revolutionary sentiments and establish social order in Europe.[58] In the case of Britain, at the time the most advanced capitalist country in Europe, she explains, two axioms were adopted: produce more and consume less, thus confirming the death knell to any hope of progressive change.[59] Mattei quotes Tory Chancellor of the Exchequer Austen Chamberlain, articulating, in 1920, the severity of what this meant for the working class:

> There is £45,000,000 for the bread subsidy. Nothing would give me greater satisfaction than to deal with that … the sooner we get rid of these subsidies the better. I agree that they conduce to conceal the real facts of the situation from the country and that they put a most onerous burden upon the State and on the national finances … the sooner they are got rid of the better.[60]

Mattei explains that by 1922, wage levels in industry were one third of their levels in 1920. The state denounced labour militancy and buried welfare resources.[61] The British response to the crisis of the 1920s and 1930s remained resolutely austere. As Blyth explains, by the mid-1920s, the postwar slump had become a full-blown recession. The Treasury's argument, following Hume and Smith, was that to borrow money in order to finance spending, the Government would have to offer better terms than private capital. This would eventually lead to more unemployment. Tory Chancellor of the Exchequer, Stanley Baldwin, put it in 1922 thus: 'Money taken for government purposes is money taken away from trade, and borrowing will thus tend to depress trade and increase unemployment.'[62] In 1925, the then Chancellor, Winston Churchill, restored the gold standard which meant that the pound was back at its pre-war parity.[63] To keep the pound strong, interest rates were raised, which hurt business. Mine owners responded by announcing they intended to reduce wages and introduce longer hours. Miners had had enough, and in 1926, the Trades Union Congress began a General Strike that lasted nine days and was the largest industrial dispute in Briain's history. The strike was followed by draconian industrial austerity in the form of the Trades Disputes Act, passed the following year, that banned mass picketing and sympathy strikes. The Act was repealed in 1946 but reintroduced in the Employment Act 1980 by Margaret Thatcher,[64] and extended by Rishi Sunak in the Strikes (Minimum Service Levels) Act 2023 (see Chapter 8).

Fiscal and industrial austerity

Following the publication of her book, Mattei was interviewed in *The Nation* by Daniel Steinmetz-Jenkins, an academic who runs regular interviews for the magazine. In it, Mattei expands on her interpretation of austerity that she describes as 'a tool of class'.[65] She underlines the arguments in her book that austerity can be fiscal (for example, the state cutting social expenditure and/or imposing regressive taxation), monetary (for example, interest rate hikes) and industrial (for example, attacks on unions), all of which are to maintain capitalist social relations and preserve economic subjugation, and are tools of the upward redistribution of wealth and the calcification of social and economic class.[66] Austerity views the working class as 'unproductive' and in need of discipline to force down wages in favour of the savers–investors, viewed as the productive class.[67]

Marxism

All of this is, of course, in direct contrast to Marxism, a basic tenet of which is that it is the working class who are the productive class, and the capitalist class, the parasitic class. From a Marxist perspective, capitalism relies for its very existence on the extraction of surplus value from workers who have to sell their labour power to survive: capitalists pay them less than the value they produce, with the value added by workers' labour appropriated as profit by and for the capitalist when goods are sold.⁶⁸ For Marx and Marxists, wealth should be redistributed downward, so that it is shared by all in a post-capitalist socialist society.⁶⁹

The primacy of private property, capitalist wage relations and economic pain

Thinking about austerity in class terms stands in contrast to dismissing it as simply bad policy. This raises important questions: 'How do we explain austerity's resilience in shaping advanced capitalist societies? Why is it still around? Can it be reduced to stupidity or corruption?'⁷⁰ Mattei concludes her interview with Steinmetz-Jenkins:

> A more convincing historical explanation is that capital requires constant protection. And austerity is particularly effective not in stabilizing economies, but in calcifying class relations. After all, austerity has historically never been about curbing inflation and budget control; its manipulations of aggregate demand have always been a means to a deeper end. Austerity secures the best possible conditions for profits to soar, while the majority – the politically underserved – are forced to relinquish all fledgling projects of economic democracy. People are compelled to 'live harder' through lower wages and lower consumption.⁷¹

Austerity thus lays bare an undeniable truth: for capitalism to survive, workers need to be disciplined into accepting the 'two pillars of capital accumulation – the primacy of private property and wage relations'.⁷²

Mattei further points out in a *Guardian* article that austerity inevitably involves pain, a fact readily admitted by the capitalist class and its representatives. She gives as an example the US Federal Reserve Chair, Jerome Powell, who, announcing in September 2022 his fifth highest interest rate in nine months, avoided the word 'austerity' and instead 'described the process of resettling the economy – through the introduction of increased unemployment and possible recession – as a necessary form of "economic pain"'.⁷³ This formulation has been part of the austerity vocabulary at least since 1920, when, at the first international finance conference in Brussels, Robert Brand, British civil servant, business person and aristocrat, argued that for the post-First World War economy to recover, 'the answer is a very painful one and yet a very simple one. We must all work hard, live hard, and save hard'.⁷⁴

The point is, however, that neither the pain nor the gains are shared. It is always the working class that has to sacrifice, through welfare cuts, unemployment and lower wages, and the capitalist class that gains, via greater profits. This is exemplified in Part III of this book.

Multimillionaire confirms austerity a deliberate act of capitalist crisis management and class warfare from above

'There are certain times when an individual makes a statement that encapsulates the thinking of an entire social class', writes Patrick Martin on the *World Socialist Web Site* (*WSWS*).[75] He is referring to multimillionaire property developer Tim Gurner's remarks, widely shared and condemned on social media, that the 'problem' with COVID-19 was that 'people decided they didn't really want to work so much anymore ... and that has had a massive issue on productivity'.[76] Focusing on building workers in his US$10 billion construction business, Gurner complained that they 'have definitely pulled back on productivity. They have been paid a lot to do not too much in the last few years, and we need to see that change'.[77] 'There's been a systematic change', he went on, 'where employees feel the employer is extremely lucky to have them, as opposed to the other way around. So it's a dynamic that has to change'.[78] Then, he revealed his plan to discipline workers who, from a Marxist perspective, perfectly reasonably want an easier life under capitalism, and have less of the surplus value from their labour power taken away by people like Gurner.[79] Confirming Mattei's assertion that austerity inevitably involves pain, Gurner stressed, 'We need to see pain in the economy', in the form of 'massive layoffs' that lead to 'less arrogance in the employment market'.[80] 'We need', he concluded, 'to see unemployment rise – unemployment has to jump 40 to 50 percent, in my view'.[81] As Martin explains, worldwide, there are 220 million people unemployed. If Gurner got his wish this number would grow by another 88 or 110 million.[82] Apparently, Gurner has an estimated wealth of nearly $600 million.[83]

The simple answer to my question asked in the title of this chapter is therefore that austerity, rather than a flawed economic policy, is a deliberate act of capitalist crisis management and class warfare from above. From a Marxist perspective, while the ultimate objective is socialism (see the last section of the Conclusion to this book), an immediate solution in capitalist economies is to raise taxes on the wealthy, rather than impose austerity on the working class.

PART II

Racism and the Hostile Environment

3

Theresa May and the Hostile Environment: Preparation, Official Launch and Enactment (2010–2019)

Introduction

In March 2022, Tory Cabinet Minister Michael Gove claimed that the 'hostile environment' approach to immigration rules was 'invented under a Labour Home Secretary'.[1] Gove repeatedly banged on the dispatch box as he said to MPs that he had 'had it up to here with people trying to suggest this country is not generous', as he trivialized and attempted to deny the hostile environment with the phrase, 'all the stuff about hostile environments'.[2] As Elaine McCallig explains, writing for *Indy 100*, Gove's tantrum was in response to comments from Labour MP Tanmanjeet Singh Dhesi who told the Commons that as with previous refugee crises, the Government's response to the Ukraine crisis, that followed the Russian invasion of that country the previous month, has been 'quite frankly, been pathetic, revealing the true extent of the callousness within this government's hostile environment policy'.[3]

When asked for comments about Gove's claim about the 'invention' of the hostile environment, Sarah Turnnidge, writing for *Full Fact*,[4] points out that neither his Department, the Department for Levelling Up, Housing and Communities, nor Conservative Campaign Headquarters nor the Labour Party responded to the query.[5]

There have been several other attempts to claim that the Labour Party invented the hostile environment, that, in fact, amount to little more than that certain Labour politicians have used the term in various different contexts. For example, in previous decades it was used by the Home Office to denote dangerous overseas locations, and in the wake of the 9/11 attacks to describe the Government's desire to make the UK a hostile environment for terrorists.[6] *Full Fact* found the following examples of 'hostile environment' being used under Labour Governments:

- In May 2007, it was used by then Immigration Minister Liam Byrne, when announcing a policy of fining firms for employing people without the right to work in the UK: 'We are trying to create a much more hostile environment in this country if you are here illegally.'
- In February 2010, it was used repeatedly in a Border Agency (part of the Home Office) strategy document for 'enforcing our immigration rules and addressing immigration and cross border crime' with a Foreword by then Immigration Minister Phil Woolas. The document includes 'hostile environment' four times, with respect to reducing immigration-related crime.
- There are claims Alan Johnson used the term while Home Secretary, but *Full Fact* were unable to find a specific example.[7]
- In 2009, Labour Peer Lord Brett used the term in relation to people trafficking: 'My Lords, we continue to make the UK a hostile environment for trafficking and to ensure that victims are protected.'[8]

In August 2023, author of *The Windrush Betrayal: Exposing the Hostile Environment*[9] and prolific writer on the 'hostile environment' for the *Guardian*, Amelia Gentleman, revealed that Theresa May, the real initiator of the hostile environment policy, in part blames Clement Attlee, the Labour Prime Minister between 1945 and 1951, for failing to give Windrush arrivals paperwork to show their right to be in the UK, and claims that Labour politicians created the concept of the 'hostile environment' in the decade before she became Home Secretary on 12 May 2010.[10] In a 2018 interview, Labour Shadow Attorney General for England, Emily Thornberry, summed up Labour's use of the term, contrasting this with Tory *policy*: 'The words are used but the culture was not.'[11] I turn shortly in this chapter and in Chapters 4 and 5 to the actuality of the hostile environment under the Tories from 2010 to 2023.

Racism returns to the heart of electoral politics
The 'nasty party'
Despite the long history of racism in the Tory Party,[12] political journalist for the *Telegraph* Rosa Prince points out that, in the years immediately preceding the 2010 General Election, the Tories shied away from putting the issue of immigration at the centre of the party's election campaigning.[13] This was for fear of appearing as the 'nasty party', a term highlighted by Theresa May, when, as newly appointed Chair of the Conservative Party in 2002, she stunned delegates at the Annual Conference by denouncing past sins – still 'unrepentant, just plain unattractive' – admitting: '[L]et's not kid ourselves. There's a way to go before we can return to government. There's a lot we need to do in this party of ours. Our base is too narrow

and so, occasionally, are our sympathies. You know what some people call us: the nasty party.'[14]

This attempt to distance the party from 'nastiness' was ironic given what May was to unleash after 2010, as we shall see in this chapter. It was, in fact, May who demonstrated *par excellence* the truth of the epithet, 'nasty party'. At the time of the 2002 Conference, the party had also been accused of the exclusion of minority ethnic MPs, and in her address, May thus referred in her Conference speech to unnamed colleagues trying to 'make political capital out of demonising minorities': 'At the last general election 38 new Tory MPs were elected. Of that total ... none was from an ethnic minority. Is that fair?'[15] While numerically, this has demonstrably improved, it has done nothing to undermine racism in the Tory Party: quite the opposite, as we shall see in Chapters 4 and 5.

The threat from the UK Independence Party

In the European Elections on 4 June 2009, the racist anti-immigration UK Independence Party (UKIP) claimed a political breakthrough, the party having gained four extra MEPs to take its total number of seats in the European Parliament to 13, the same number as Labour, and having pushed out Labour to take second place in the overall share of the vote.[16] The then UKIP leader, Nigel Farage, denied it was a result of the expenses scandal (a major scandal that emerged in 2009, concerning expenses claims made by MPs and members of the House of Lords over the previous years),[17] and said of the results that Labour's broken promise on a European Union (EU) referendum led to the rout, and called on Labour Prime Minister Gordon Brown to step down since he (Farage) had 'beaten him in a national election'.[18] In Farage's words:

> According to all the experts, this is the second fluke in a row that we have produced. People vote for us because they agree with us. They agree with us that we should be friendly with Europe, trade with Europe, be good neighbours, but not have our laws made there. We have managed to move on from a result five years ago that was considered to be the high water mark. We are up on those elections. We have done extremely well. We have come second nationally. We are very happy people.[19]

UKIP, along with the fascist British National Party (BNP) and the far-right English Democrats got a combined racist vote of nearly one-quarter of the votes (24.5 per cent), not far behind the Tories at 27.7 per cent.[20] By 2010, therefore, the time was ripe to bring immigration back centre-stage. As Prince explains, by then Conservative chiefs felt that voters were 'keen to hear more about limiting the numbers arriving from overseas'.[21] On 10 January 2010, David Cameron, then Leader of the Opposition, stated: 'We would like to see net immigration in the tens of thousands rather than the hundreds of thousands. I don't think that's unrealistic. That's the sort of figure it was in the 1990s and I think we should see that again.'[22] Nicholas Soames, Winston Churchill's grandson, a Tory backbencher and co-chair of an all-party group on immigration, embraced Cameron's intervention. A joint statement from the group read: 'We welcome this statement from the Conservatives and hope the Government will follow suit, and that both parties carry manifesto commitments in this year's general election to keep our population below 70 million.'[23]

The 2010 General Election

Despite a large swing to the Tories, the 2010 General Election in May resulted in a hung Parliament. It was significant in the context of the imminent launching of the hostile environment, in that one of the newly elected Tory MPs was the hard-line, right-wing Priti Patel, who was to become Boris Johnson's Home Secretary in 2019, responsible for ramping up the hostile environment (see Chapter 4). Discussions about forming a Coalition Government between the Tories and the Liberal Democrats went on for five days. When Prime Minister Brown realized that a deal between the other two parties was imminent, he resigned, ending 13 years of Labour government.[24] There then began, in May 2010, six years of ConDem Coalition Government, under the premiership of Cameron who appointed Theresa May as his Home Secretary in the first ConDem Cabinet. It is the way in which the Coalition *condem*ned prospective immigrants, immigrants, former immigrants and their families to lives of misery, along with the austerity that followed the financial crisis of 2007–2008 that was a frontal assault on the working class as a whole (see Chapter 6) that prompts me to use the acronym, *ConDem*.[25]

May's time as Home Secretary, 2010–2016

Preparation for the hostile environment

May's first speech on immigration

May's first major speech on immigration in November 2010 focused on what she perceived as the threat of immigration, and also included an offensive against students and the 'immigrant family'. Beginning with the usual platitude, 'migration has enriched our culture …', she soon set up what was to follow with simplistic scaremongering: immigration 'more than twice the population of Birmingham'; 'public confidence … undermined by … stories of abuse of the system'; 'serious social impacts'.[26]

Directly and assertively, May then alluded to 'the segregation we see in too many of our communities' that 'created community tensions and helped contribute to a society that is not as integrated as we would like', before pledging: 'The public should know that I will take action. I am determined to get the immigration system back under control.'[27]

This callous rhetoric of hate, blame and threat – immigrants create segregation and community tension and we will take action to control them – belies the fact that an alternative to denouncing immigrants and trying to make them pay psychologically and financially to earn the right to be in the UK, is to welcome them in various ways into our communities and to value the various contributions that they make.

Comparing controlling immigration using the 'points-based system alone' (where applicants must reach a points-based score above a minimum threshold to be successful) to 'squeezing a balloon', she spewed further scaremongering, emotive and hostile rhetoric:

> Push down work visas and the number of student visas will shoot up. Clamp down on student visas and family visas will spring up. Bear down on family visas and work visas will explode. With unskilled labour set to zero, all that happened was student visas rocketed by thirty per cent to a record 304,000 in just one year, as some applicants used it as an alternative work route.[28]

Heralding what was soon to crystallize into that part of the 'really hostile environment' that was to divide families, this clergy's daughter, singling out an imprisoned cleric, threatened and warned:

> This summer, we ordered the UK Border Agency to clamp down on sham marriages. They have had significant success, conducting 53 operations and making 118 arrests. Shockingly, this included the arrest of a vicar who was subsequently jailed for staging over 300 sham marriages. As well as tackling abuse of the marriage route we need to ensure that those who come here can integrate successfully into society and play a part in their local community. So … those applying for marriage visas will have to demonstrate a minimum standard of English. This is only right. People coming to this country must be able to interact with the rest of the population.[29]

Cameron follows suit

On 14 April 2011, David Cameron followed suit. He began by talking about what he said the Tories heard on the doorstep on immigration: 'We are concerned about the levels of immigration in our country ... but we are fed up of hearing politicians talk tough but do nothing.'[30] In response, he stated: 'We are determined to be different.'[31] This was followed by denying that concerns about immigration 'were somehow racist'. There ensued the usual 'spiel' about the benefits of immigration, before stating, 'for too long, immigration has been too high' and that 'it has placed real pressures on communities up and down the country. Not just pressures on schools, housing and healthcare – though those have been serious ... but social pressures too'.[32] Cameron then referred to 'significant numbers of new people arriving in neighbourhoods ... perhaps not able to speak the same language as those living there ... on occasions not really wanting or even willing to integrate'.[33] He then referred to 'forced marriages' and 'sham marriages' and 'tightening up the family route'. He concluded with what was becoming the key Tory mantra on immigration: 'net migration to this country will be in the order of tens of thousands each year, not the hundreds of thousands every year that we have seen over the last decade' and made what was to prove to be an impossible pledge: 'No ifs. No buts. That's a promise we made to the British people. And it's a promise we are keeping.'[34]

In 2011 there was an uprising in Tottenham, North London, after Mark Duggan, a Black man in his twenties, was killed by police on 4 August of that year. The unrest spread to other parts of London and of the UK. May's reaction was indicative of the hostile environment that was to be launched shortly. While a report from the charity, the Children's Society, which surveyed 13- to 17-year-olds and adults, found that young people across the UK believed poverty was one of the key reasons behind the August uprisings, and while 66 per cent of adults and 57 per cent of young people believed people had taken part 'to get goods and possessions they couldn't afford to buy', May described those involved as an 'unruly mob' who were 'thieving, pure and simple'.[35] 'One rioter', she went on, 'said the police are always "causing us hell". In my role as home secretary, I can only say: "Good"'.[36]

The hostile environment is launched

In an interview in 2012, May announced her plan to create a 'really hostile environment' (the significance of use of the adverb, 'really', is almost universally overlooked) for so-called 'illegal immigrants', thus putting hostility formally on the agenda in the treatment of large numbers of innocent people that has lasted and was constantly ramped up by the Tories. Shortly after, following up on her 2010 speech, some draconian changes in family migration rules were made. Coming from the party that claims to believe in 'family values', it is informative to quote the changes at length in order to reveal the totality of the founding principles of the hostile environment and to give a foretaste of its cruel and vicious essence.[37]

Family migration rules

- Spouses, civil partners, unmarried partners and same sex partners of people who are British or settled in the UK now have to complete five years of limited leave to remain in this category before they are eligible for indefinite leave to remain. The five years will be made up of two periods of two and a half years each.
- Since October 2013, spouses and partners applying for indefinite leave to remain need to pass both a 'Life in the UK Test' and an English test.
- Spouses or partners who have been married to or living with the British or settled person outside the UK for four years are no longer able to get indefinite leave to enter or remain immediately. They need to wait for five years.
- There must be at least £18,600 per year available to the couple (prior to 2012, there was only a requirement that the couple had enough to live on).
- If the spouse or partner is not already in the UK with an entitlement to work at the date of the application, they are not able to rely on their own predicted income from employment in the UK.
- If the couple are relying on income from employment, then they need to have had the job for at least six months before the date of application.
- The couple can only rely on savings if they have at least £16,000 and have held this for at least six months.
- It will not be possible to rely on offers of financial support from family and/or friends.
- There is a new list of factors that the UK Border Agency (UKBA) will take into account when assessing whether a relationship is genuine.
- Children who are eligible for indefinite leave to enter will continue to have to meet the current requirements of the Immigration Rules.
- Children who are being granted limited leave only (because only one parent is settled in the UK and they are applying with the other parent) have to show that there is an extra £3,800 per year for the first child and £2,400 per year for each additional child.
- The only dependent relatives over 18 who can apply will be parents, grandparents, children and siblings.
- The dependent relative has to show that because of age, illness or disability they require long-term personal care.
- The required care must be unavailable in the relative's home country even with the UK sponsor's financial assistance, because it is not affordable or there is no one to provide it.
- It is not possible to apply under this category from inside the UK.

Human rights and discretionary leave to remain

- People granted leave to remain on human rights grounds will not have recourse to public funds.
- Limited leave to remain on human rights grounds will be granted for two and a half years at once.
- A person will have to complete ten years of human rights-based leave to remain before they are eligible for indefinite leave to remain.
- Leave to remain based on private life in the UK will usually only be a person has lived in the UK for 20 years' residence (for adults), seven years (for children), more than half their life (if they are aged 18 to 25). It may be granted earlier if the person has no ties with their home country.
- The Immigration Rules will set out what the UKBA believes to be in the 'public interest' in Article 8 claims based on private and/or family life in the UK.
- The '14-year rule', whereby people can get indefinite leave to remain after living in the UK for 14 years, is abolished.[38]

Cameron's immigration speech, 25 March 2013

On 25 March 2013, Cameron unveiled a further crackdown on immigration, saying he planned to rein in welfare benefits he believes lure foreigners to live off the British state.[39] His speech must be seen in the context of the lifting of EU freedom of movement restrictions for Romanians and Bulgarians meaning that they could work in Britain from 2014, a prospect that had prompted the right-wing press to warn of the arrival of 'hordes' of welfare-hungry migrants.[40] Cameron once again repeated the meaningless mantra: 'Net migration needs to come down radically from hundreds of thousands a year to just tens of thousands.' The success of the right-wing anti-immigrant UKIP – the party was receiving far more press coverage and a growing number of followers and in late 2012, opinion polls gave it about 14 per cent – added to the pressure for Tory policy change.[41] Farage had said that the unexpected success of his own party had shifted the debate on immigration, bringing it into the mainstream: 'If UKIP had not taken on this immigration debate, the others would not be talking about it at all.'[42] Addressing an audience of students at University Campus Suffolk in Ipswich, Cameron went on, 'when it comes to illegal migrants, we're rolling up that red carpet … and showing them the door'.[43] He said he wanted to stop Britain's welfare system being 'a soft touch' and that all immigrants from the European Economic Area (EEA) will have to wait up to five years for social housing and will be subject to tougher 'reciprocal charging' requirements when using the National Health Service (NHS) – meaning their own country will have to pay.[44]

Referring to Eastern Europe, Cameron continued:

> Now, my view is simple. Ending the 'something for nothing' culture is something that needs to apply in the immigration system as well as in the welfare system. So, by the end of this year and before the controls on Bulgarians and Romanians are lifted, we are going to strengthen the test that determines which migrants can access benefits. And we're going to give migrants from the EEA ... a very clear message. Just like British citizens, there is no absolute right to unemployment benefit. The clue is in the title: Jobseeker's Allowance is only available to those who are genuinely seeking a job.[45]

He said public fears about uncontrolled immigration and the resulting pressure on public services and the rapid pace of change were fair: 'These concerns are not just legitimate – they are right and it is a fundamental duty of every mainstream politician to address them.'[46]

Announcing new measures to make it more difficult for EEA nationals to claim welfare benefits, Cameron said payments would be stopped after six months if recipients could not show they had a genuine chance of getting a job. He also said newcomers would face a much harder test to see if they were eligible for income-related benefits: 'Ending the something for nothing culture needs to apply to immigration as well as welfare. We're going to give migrants from the EEA a very clear message.'[47]

The initial enactment of the hostile environment
Cameron forms 'hostile environment working group'

In July, Sarah Teather, the then Liberal Democrat MP and former Minister for Children and Families in the ConDem Government, revealed to the *Guardian* that an internal working group on immigration was initially named the 'Hostile Environment Working Group', because it was explicitly charged with making Britain a hostile environment for unwanted immigrants.[48] Conceived on the explicit instructions of Cameron, it was renamed the 'Inter Ministerial Group on Migrants' Access to Benefits and Public Services' only following Liberal Democrat objections.[49]

May's 'Go home or face arrest' vans

The year 2013 also witnessed May's infamous 'In the UK illegally? Go home or face arrest' vans, that were sent into six London boroughs with high minority ethnic populations in July and August. Underneath the threatening question was a picture of a handcuff, and to the right the purported number of arrests in that particular borough. Under the main message was the invitation to 'Text HOME to 78070 for free advice, and help with travel documents', and underneath that, 'We can help you to return home voluntarily without fear of arrest or detention'.[50] Simon Hattenstone points out that other Home Office operations over the years were often given simple neutral names taken from nature, rather than being related to the case in question. This particular one, however, was named Operation Vaken.[51] According to Sally Tomlinson, it was named after a poem promoting fascism in 1930s Germany. Posters were also placed in minority ethnic newspapers, and in mosques and temples urging people to 'Go Home'. Detention of immigrants increased, although four in ten appeals against detention were successful.[52]

In September, following the strongest signal yet that from Cameron that the Tories were ready to quit the European Convention on Human Rights, May announced that 'illegal immigrants' would be deported from Britain *before* they get a chance to claim that their human rights are being breached.[53] In the words of Matt Chorley, James Slack and James Chapman in the right-wing, Tory *MailOnline*, in 'shiny patent brogues the Home Secretary … promised to kick out illegal immigrants'.[54] She further stated that the number of grounds for appeals against deportation will be reduced from 17 to four.[55]

Immigration Act 2014

In 2014, there was an Immigration Act. Key aspects of the Act included:

- Limiting appeals against Home Office decisions from 17 to four.
- The right to deport first and hear appeals later in certain circumstances.
- The right to 'respect for family and private life' should not always take precedence over public interest, which should be 'at the heart of [the court's] decisions' in immigration control and deporting foreign criminals.
- Clamping down on those who live and work in the UK illegally and take advantage of our public services; ensuring that only legal migrants have access to the labour market, health services, housing, bank accounts and driving licences.
- Penalties for employers who do not ensure that non-EEA nationals only work as legally permitted.
- Restricting access to free NHS care to those non-EEA nationals with 'indefinite leave to remain' and those granted refugee status or humanitarian protection, thus bringing the NHS into line with Government policy on access to benefits and social housing.
- Temporary migrants seeking to stay in the UK for more than six months to pay an immigration health surcharge on top of their visa fee.
- Landlords required to check the immigration status of their prospective tenants; powers to deal with 'rogue landlords' who rent homes to 'illegal immigrants'.

- With respect to 'removals', create a system where only one decision is made, informing the individual that they cannot stay in the UK, and enabling Immigration Enforcement to remove them if they do not leave voluntarily.
- For illegal migrants held in immigration detention, no bail when the detainee is booked onto a flight in the next few days and there are no exceptional circumstances.
- No multiple repeated bail applications.
- Full rights equivalent to the police for entry clearance officers to take fingerprints before entry to the UK, and to take enforcement action.
- Simplifying the appeals procedure so that instead of appealing to an immigration judge, applicants can contact the Home Office and ask for a simple administrative review to remedy case working errors, thus resolving errors in decisions cheaply and quickly.[56]

The Joint Council for the Welfare of Immigrants (JCWI)'s Saira Grant called the Act pernicious in that it seeks to turn landlords, health workers and other public sector workers into border guards.[57]

May's bid for Tory Party leadership

In 2015 May gave a speech to the Tory Party Conference, in essence a bid for Conservative Party leadership. In the speech, consistent with her established ideological orientation, May used rhetoric of hate and threat in an attempt to win over the Tory faithful, and to scupper UKIP.[58] Then Shadow Secretary of State for International Development, Diane Abbott, tweeted that Theresa May is getting 'down in the gutter with Ukip' to chase votes for her leadership bid.[59] The then Executive Editor, Politics, James Kirkup, at the Tory-supporting online 'broadsheet' *The Telegraph*, stated, 'It's hard to know where to start with Theresa May's awful, ugly, misleading, cynical and irresponsible speech to the Conservative Party conference today.'[60] Paraphrasing her message, Kirkup went on, 'Immigrants are stealing your job, making you poorer and ruining your country. Never mind the facts, just feel angry at foreigners. And make me Conservative leader.'[61] One key point made by May was, 'we know that for people in low-paid jobs, wages are forced down even further while some people are forced out of work altogether'.[62] In actual fact, a review of the evidence by May's own officials concluded: 'There is relatively little evidence that migration has caused statistically significant displacement of UK natives from the labour market in periods when the economy is strong.'[63] Another key assertion made by May was that '[i]mmigration makes it impossible to build a cohesive society'.[64] The evidence at the time, however, as Kirkup points out, was 'that the less personal acquaintance with migrants a person has, the more worried they are about immigration'.⁶⁵ If immigration makes UK society less cohesive, he suggested, that may be partly the result of 'politicians pandering to ignorance and prejudice and wilfully distorting the evidence to persuade people to be angry and afraid'.⁶⁶ Kirkup concluded his comments on the rhetoric of hate in her speech:

> The Home Secretary says she's worried about ... social cohesion. If she really wants to help, she could start by abandoning this cheap and nasty speech and the politics behind it. ... But then ... political ambition is more important than talking responsibly and honestly about immigration, isn't it? What a curious form of leadership.⁶⁷

In her speech, May yet again falsely blamed immigrants for pressures on public services: 'It's difficult for schools and hospitals and core infrastructure like housing and transport to cope.'⁶⁸ In addition, May upped her rhetoric of hate, this time labelling those seeking sanctuary as lawbreakers who contribute nothing to the economy, claiming that a significant number of asylum seekers are 'foreign criminals', and contrary to the vast majority of economists' analyses, summed up her view that 'the net economic and fiscal effect of high immigration is close to zero'.⁶⁹ May dismissed the idea that Britain was a multicultural society: 'It's often said – usually by advocates of open-door immigration – that Britain is by definition a country of immigrants.'⁷⁰ Instead she claimed that Britain has 'until recently always been a country of remarkable population stability'.⁷¹ In reality, Britain is and has always been a multicultural society.⁷²

A foretaste of what was to come

As a foretaste of things to come, in particular what was to befall the Windrush generation (see the penultimate section of this chapter), in June 2015 a Home Office entry clearance officer refused Saleh Ahmed Handule Ali permission to return to the UK from a holiday in Djibouti.⁷³ The family appealed the First Tier and then in the Upper Tribunal of the Immigration Court, but their appeals were rejected.⁷⁴ Ali had arrived in the UK from Somalia with his mother and two younger siblings at the age of nine in 2000 to join his father who had been granted refugee status. The rest of the family were also granted refugee status and Ali was given a travel document in 2004 under the Refugee Convention, valid for ten years.⁷⁵ Diagnosed with TB in 2008, Ali had decided to take a short holiday in Djibouti, hoping that the climate would be good for his illness. While there, he lost his travel document and was unable to return to the UK and has been stranded in Ethiopia undocumented (he went to Ethiopia because there is no British embassy in Djibouti) living hand-to-mouth for 16 years. It later emerged that the Home Office had failed to keep a record of him on its database.⁷⁶

His mother, Shamis Dirya, who sends him money, told *The Guardian*, when the case came to light in April 2024:

> I have been crying for 16 years over the loss of my son. We want the Home Office to bring him back to us. But they are not listening to us. He went to primary school ... [and] to high school here [in Bristol]. He only went to Djibouti for a short holiday.[77]

Immizgration Act 2016

The 2016 Immigration Act that amounted to 'doubling up' on 'hostile environment' policies. Its key changes were:

- Employers who hire illegal migrants and the workers themselves face criminal sanctions.
- Migrants who do not have permission to be in the UK can have certain privileges revoked, such as the seizure of their driving licence and the freezing of their bank accounts.
- It became a criminal offence for a landlord to knowingly rent premises to an illegal migrant, with up to five years in prison for offenders.
- The 'deport first, appeal later' scheme became extended to all migrants.
- Pregnant women could now only be detained by immigration authorities for up to 72 hours (or one week with special permission).
- Arrangements were to be made to relocate unaccompanied refugee children from other countries in Europe to the UK.[78]

The JCWI offered the following overall critique and the implications for the hostile environment:

> [The few concessions] do little to ameliorate the full force of the measures brought in by this Act which will make the UK a more hostile and unwelcoming place. The ... Act ... introduces a vast number of draconian, unaccountable and poorly thought out powers and offences that will have a huge impact on the lives of both migrants and British citizens, particularly those in black and minority ethnic communities. It sets back the progress of integration, and many of the measures that the Government claims are to protect migrants from exploitation, actually increase the risk of this.[79]

May's premiership, 2016–2019

Following the European Union referendum, Cameron resigns

A referendum on whether Britain should leave the EU was held on 23 June 2016, with May and Cameron supporting 'remain'. Immigration was the most prominent referendum issue, with specific countries being singled out for particularly negative coverage – especially Turkey and Albania (both Muslim countries), but also Romania and Poland.[80] The day after the results were declared as 'leave', Cameron announced that he would resign. After a Tory Party leadership campaign, May was declared leader on 11 July. Two days later, Cameron resigned, and May became Prime Minister.

May 'to the right of Thatcher'

At the Liberal Democratic Party's Conference in March 2017, leading member, Tim Farron, laid into Theresa May, who he noted 'took office claiming she would be a social justice crusader. And here she is today, to the right of Thatcher'.[81] May's Government, he went on, is 'a government that is as anti-refugees as Nigel Farage'. 'One of the most despicable things this Government has done', he suggested, 'happened quietly, in a ministerial written statement on the day that Article 50 [the clause to leave the EU] passed the House of Commons', when the 'Home Office quietly confirmed that Britain would stop taking in desperate, unaccompanied child refugees'.[82]

> [This was not] because the crisis was at an end or because we had rescued the thousands of children that the Government had promised, under duress, to help. ... Of the tens of thousands of unaccompanied children fleeing war and destitution, in the end we will take just 350 ... because they calculated that they could get away with it. ... But just to make sure, they sneaked out the news on the same day that Tory and Labour MPs voted Article 50 through. A despicable act, done in a despicable way.[83]

Grenfell Tower

Just before 1 am on 14 June 2017, fire broke out in the kitchen of a fourth-floor flat at the 23-storey tower block in North Kensington, West London, known as Grenfell Tower. Within minutes the fire raced up the exterior of the building and then spread to all four sides. By 3 am, most of the upper floors were well alight. It was the worst residential fire in the UK since the Second World War. Grenfell Tower was clad with plastic-filled panels. The disaster needs to be understood in terms of racism and social class. Of the 72 people who died, a majority were people of colour and working class. In the words of Leslie Thomas QC, who represented bereaved families as well as the survivors:

> The Grenfell fire did not happen in a vacuum. A majority of the Grenfell residents who died were people of colour. Grenfell is

inextricably linked with race. It is the elephant in the room. This disaster happened in a pocket of one of the smallest yet richest boroughs in London. Yet the community affected was predominantly working-class. That is the stark reality that cannot be ignored.[84]

On the day after the fire, May paid a private visit to the site of the disaster, when the building was still smouldering, and chose not to meet with survivors of the fire or the affected community, citing concerns over security. Instead, she met with the emergency services.[85] After the fury among local residents, May paid another visit, this time announcing plans to hold a public inquiry, assuring that all survivors would be housed within three weeks, and said she would leave no stone unturned to find out the truth of how the fire happened.[86]

As Justice4Grenfell points out, the former Grenfell Tower residents 'were portrayed in sections of the media negatively as "immigrants", asylum seekers, refugees, benefit scroungers and subletters'.[87] The organization goes on to suggest that May must take some responsibility for the part she played in this, since it was under her leadership at the Home Office that the 'hostile environment' was created, the catalyst for creating alarm and division in UK society.[88] It further noted that May appointed Sir Martin Moore-Bick to chair the public inquiry, who was once accused by the tenants' solicitor of 'social cleansing of the poor' after he relocated a tenant facing homelessness to a place 50 miles away,[89] while the local Labour MP at the time, Emma Dent, stated that local people had no confidence in Moore-Bick and that he should stand down.[90]

Traumatized families asked for additional diverse panel members – people who reflected their backgrounds. Bereaved families took a petition to Downing Street; others met with May there. Grime artist Stormzy reached out to his social media following to gain 100,000 signatures on the petition.[91] May eventually relented, but only in phase two of the inquiry[92] (this did not open until January 2020). Justice4Grenfell concluded, addressing Theresa May:

> Due to cuts to the fire service and continued deregulation firefighters were left with communication equipment that failed on the night of the fire and a lack of breathing apparatus. Your government should have implemented changes to this with a matter of urgency. You could also look at your party's tardy response to the removal of inflammable materials up and down the country; the installation of sprinklers as a mandatory feature and to the air and soil testing for toxins in our environment … as a final point, please be minded that 72 dead and still no arrests is something no one should be proud of.[93]

As of May 2019, 23 months later, there were still families in emergency and temporary accommodation[94] (for further updates see Chapter 4).

The consolidation of the hostile environment

During May's premiership of 2016–2019, the hostile environment was consolidated, and its impact began to be felt. She pledged to kick out foreign students and to end free movement once and for all, promising, in 2017, to immediately work towards immigration in the tens of thousands by 2022 ad finitum and ad nauseam, a promise that was published in the 2017 Tory Manifesto,[95] but was never fulfilled.

The effects of the hostile environment are witnessed by the existence and growth of the website 'I LOVE MY FOREIGN SPOUSE', a private group, of which I am a member. On 28 November 2017, this, the most popular website for supporting families divided by May's legislation and subsequent policies, had 11,830 members on Facebook. As a demonstration of the hostile environment's ongoing disastrous impact, on 26 April 2024 the group had 22,200 members, almost double.

The 2018 White Paper on Immigration

The 2018 White Paper on Immigration has been described as the biggest single attack on migrant rights in a generation. Its key message was that, post-Brexit, everyone will need the permission of the authorities to come to the UK to work or study. It refers to 'low-risk' countries from which migrants can apply for a visa-free Electronic Travel Authority that will allow them to apply to enter the country without the need for documentary leave to enter/remain for six months. This serves political expediency and reinforces detrimental structural stereotypes about certain cohorts of migrants. The Immigration Law Practitioners' Association notes that it is unclear why some countries are classified as 'low risk' while others are not. High-risk countries are overwhelmingly part of the developing world.[96] Commenting at the time on the White Paper, Ed Lewis, migration campaigner at Global Justice Now, reminded us that '[t]he Brexit result did not require an end to free movement – this is a political choice by the most anti-migrant prime minister in living memory'.[97] In his own words, epitomizing the interconnection between the hostile environment, austerity and colonialism:

> The white paper is the biggest single attack on rights we've seen in a generation. It will create 'Fortress Britain' where migrants come and go at the behest of big business but lack many of the rights which EU migrants have enjoyed to date. It is a recipe for a race to the bottom in terms of worker pay and conditions. As a country that pillaged and exploited the world to gain its wealth – and still does today – it is unconscionable to further close our doors to human beings.[98]

Lewis goes on: 'If people are worried about having their wages undercut by migrants, the white paper makes this more likely. You can only avoid this when you give migrants real rights. The white paper is all about removing rights.'[99]

'Perhaps the most shocking aspect of the White Paper', he argues, 'is that it wants Britain to sign up to dodgy deals with repressive regimes like Turkey or Egypt in the hope those countries will keep refugees and migrants out of Britain'.[100] Such a policy has resulted in thousands of deaths in the Mediterranean and 'slave camps in Libya'. 'On top of this', Lewis points out, 'the government wants to sign up to a version of the Dublin Convention which leaves migrants in already struggling countries like Italy and Greece. … This is truly a charter for making our human rights responsibilities "someone else's problem"'.[101] He then makes links to the source of migrants' needs to migrate:

> Britain is a country that continues to derive much wealth off the backs of other countries around the world. Too often, people are here because of the effects of wars, arms sales, trade deals, tax avoidance and corporate behaviour sanctioned by Britain. It is outrageous to drain other countries of wealth and then refuse to give a place to those who lose out from these policies.[102]

'The freedom to move', Lewis concludes, 'shouldn't just be confined to the rich or middle classes'.[103]

The general impact of the enactment and consolidation of the hostile environment under May's watch was devastating. Its adverse effects are succinctly summed up by Simone Usborne, writing for *The Guardian* in 2018:

> For a doctor in Birmingham, it was the pregnant patient eating less to save money to cover an NHS bill. For a primary school teacher in an inner-city school, it was the moment he sat down with new parents for an uncomfortable conversation about their child's nationality. For a London lecturer, it was the worry that A-level students were being put off university for fear of being deported. In banks, hospitals, letting agencies, schools and lecture theatres, the government's current immigration policy has effectively erected a border within, along which people delivering vital services are coming to terms with unwanted new powers.[104]

As was to be expected, the hostile environment also had a very negative impact on people seeking asylum, with respect to accommodation – vermin-infested housing;[105] detention centres where detainees could find themselves in a small cell with a stranger;[106] along with 'multiple examples of children being detained in adult facilities'.[107] It also had an awful impact on domestic violence and migrant women (such violence doubling between 2012 and 2016).[108] The hostile environment did not just affect migrants. It was confirmed on *BBC* 'Newsnight' in 2019 by Liberal Democrat, Norman Baker, who was a Minister in the Home Office from 2013 to 2014 (when he resigned) during May's tenure as Home Secretary, what many people already suspected or knew, which is that there was 'a conflation of people who were asylum seekers with people who were economic migrants, with people who were here with "leave to remain"' since May 'wanted to exclude as many people as possible from the country, and, those who were here, she wanted to deport if she possibly could'.[109]

A hostile environment for Muslims
Sayeeda Warsi and the 'dinner table test'

It was not only migrants who were on the receiving end of the hostile environment. The years 2010–2019 also witnessed a hostile environment for British Muslims, although this was a continuation of a long-existing Islamophobia in the Tory Party. Why, David Batty asks, writing for *The Guardian*, did May not support fellow Tory Minister Sayeeda Warsi, when, in 2011, Warsi pointed out that Islamophobia had 'passed the dinner table test',[110] meaning that it had become so acceptable to make racist comments about Muslims or Islam that they could be expressed at a middle-class dinner setting. Warsi also extended this to the factory, the school or the street:

> On the matter of portraying Muslims as either 'moderate' or 'extreme' it's not a big leap of imagination to predict where the talk of 'moderate' Muslims leads; in the factory, where they've just hired a Muslim worker, the boss says to his employees: 'Not to worry, he's only fairly Muslim'. In the school, the kids say: 'The family next door are Muslim but they're not too bad'. And in the road, as a woman walks past wearing a burqa, the passers-by think: 'That woman's either oppressed or is making a political statement'.[111]

The then Tory Prime Minister David Cameron distanced himself from Warsi's speech, with his official spokesperson refusing to answer, when asked repeatedly if the Prime Minister agreed with Warsi.[112] Tory MP, Philip Hollobone, on the other hand, who has called for a UK ban on the burqa, claimed that Warsi had not described the reality:

> One of the difficulties with Muslim communities is that a lot of people feel that they adapt least to our way of life. That is a perfectly legitimate concern to raise at the dinner table or anywhere else. There

are other groups who are facing increasing prejudice in Britain today, not least Christians. It would be refreshing if Sayeeda Warsi came out to condemn that at the same time as condemning Islamophobia.[113]

Norman Tebbit, former Tory Chair, stated:

The Muslim faith was not discussed over the dinner tables of England, nor in the saloon bars, before large numbers of Muslims came here to our country. She might consider who is in need of her homilies on prejudice. A period of silence from the baroness might not come amiss.[114]

Mehdi Hasan lays blame on May

On 19 June 2017, Theresa May declared, 'there has been far too much tolerance of extremism in our country over many years – and that means extremism of any kind, including Islamophobia'.[115] May was speaking in the aftermath of the terror attack near a London mosque, in which a man drove a van into a group of Muslim worshippers. The attacker, according to eyewitnesses, shouted, 'I want to kill all Muslims'.[116]

Mehdi Hasan, in an article in *The Intercept*, describes May's statement as 'too little, too late'.[117] 'Why', he adds, 'did innocent blood have to be spilled in order for the prime minister to utter aloud the word "Islamophobia" for the first time?'[118] And where, he goes on, were her earlier warnings about the threat posed to the UK's Muslims by far-right extremists?[119] According to Hasan, in all her years as Home Secretary, May made only the odd, passing reference to the 'hundreds' of anti-Muslim attacks in the UK each year,[120] while obsessing over the threat from 'Islamist extremism'.[121]

Hasan also asks, why, as Home Secretary, May refused to fully engage, or even formally meet, with the Cross-Government Anti-Muslim Hatred Working Group, from which two academics quit in disgust at the lack of support from the Tory Government and from ministers like May,[122] and why she hired Australian political strategist Lynton Crosby – who once urged Conservatives to focus on their core vote rather than 'fucking Muslims' – to run her 2017 General Election campaign?[123] Hasan notes that May, as Prime Minister, allowed former Tory mayoral candidate Zac Goldsmith to stand for Parliament again as a Conservative candidate in 2017, despite his having run an openly Islamophobic campaign against Labour's Sadiq Khan in 2016. Finally, in his critique of May, Hasan asks why she permitted the re-selection of Hollobone and David Davies[124] (the latter had suggested covering the hair is an excuse for sexual violence against women).[125]

Hasan points out that under May's leadership, the Tories selected only three Muslims to stand for Parliament in 2017 in safe seats and, in the words of Tory commentator, Peter Oborne, formerly chief political commentator for the *Daily Telegraph*, the party has 'long given up on policies that appeal to Muslims' and 'is slowly turning into a Muslim-free zone'.[126] Hasan concludes:

> And yet we are now expected to believe that this same Conservative Party will stand up for British Muslims under attack? That Theresa May will lead the fight against rising Islamophobia? … The prime minister's remarks were not only too little, too late. They were the very definition of hypocrisy.[127]

A number of Tories suspended for Islamophobia and other forms of racism

On 1 March 2019, the Tories suspended Councillor Martyn York after a Facebook group that he moderated, the 'Boris Johnson: Supporters' Group', was found to contain a string of Islamophobic and other racist comments.[128] Despite its guidelines telling members not to post hate speech, several referred to Muslims as 'ragheads'.[129] In one comment, the Labour Mayor of London, Sadiq Khan, was called a 'conniving little muzrat', and Muslim Labour MP Naz Shah was targeted with abuse and told to 'piss off to [her] own country' (Shah was born in Bradford).[130] Other disclosures included Dorinda Bailey, a former Tory council candidate accused of Islamophobia, following a post in the group calling for mosques to be bombed. After someone posted that any mosques 'found to preach hate' should be shut down, another user commented: 'Bomb the fucking lot.' Bailey responded, 'I agree, but any chance you could edit your comment please. No swearing policy.'[131]

With respect to anti-Black racism, there were also comments in the group telling an African soldier to 'piss off back to Africa' and calling for Labour MP Fiona Onasanya to be 'put on a banana boat back home'.[132] A non-specific racist comment described immigrants as 'cockroaches'.[133] York was subsequently suspended from the party.[134]

Four days later, Peter Lamb, a Tory council candidate, resigned from the party over his past tweets – including one in 2015, in which he said that Islam is like alcoholism: 'The first step to recovery is admit you have a problem.'[135] Lamb had been suspended from the party and was reinstated after apologising for the comments, but quit again on 5 March 2019, following calls by Warsi for him to go.[136]

Also in March, there was a damaging revelation that the Tory Party had suspended a further 14 of its members after a series of Islamophobic comments were posted on a pro-Tory Facebook page, the 'Sir Jacob Rees-Mogg Supporters Group'.[137] As Alex Wickham explains, writing for

Buzzfeed, while not affiliated to the Tory Party or Rees-Mogg, the page is used by Tory Party members. There were comments from people such as 'I am a member and will not be voting for Islam to lead this country',[138] '[a] practicing Muslim should not be allowed to work in any of the emergency professions' and '[I want to] get rid of all mosques'.[139] Others said, 'Islam must be banned from Europe', 'they are here to destroy us' and '[n]o Muslim PM for me'. Another member said Javid was a 'trojan horse', while yet another called for praying Muslims to be thrown off a bridge.[140] Other postings included 'no Pakistani [should become Prime Minister]'.[141]

Warsi was dismissive of May and the then Party chair Brandon Lewis' response to Islamophobia in the party, saying May 'doesn't listen' and that Lewis had failed to show leadership on the issue.[142]

The Windrush scandal

An extraordinary event came to light in 2018 and became known as the Windrush scandal. British subjects, mainly from the Caribbean, who had arrived in the UK before 1973, were detained, denied legal rights, threatened with deportation and some actually wrongly deported. Until the onset of the 'hostile environment', no Government had set out comprehensive policies to ensure that the Windrush generation had their legal status fully documented. However, the subsequent introduction of policies requiring people to 'prove their right to be in the UK' in order to access essential services led to 'thousands of people being placed in a precarious position through no fault of their own'.[143] As the Home Affairs Select Committee pointed out: 'People have lost their homes and their jobs and been refused healthcare, pensions and access to social security. Not only did they not have documentation which proved their legal status in the UK but it was ... made very difficult for them to gain it.'[144] During its inquiry, the Committee heard how:

> [V]ulnerable people did not understand why they were told they did not have the necessary documentation – since they considered themselves British – or what they should do about it. ... Many more tried unsuccessfully to prove their rights only to come up against the barrier of Home Office bureaucracy and poor decision making.[145]

Moreover, some could simply not afford the fees.[146] The Committee also expressed a concern that 'a target-led approach may have led immigration enforcement office to focus on people like the Windrush generation, who may have been easier to detain and remove than those less vulnerable, for example by detaining individuals such as Paulette Wilson and Anthony Bryan who clearly presented no risk of absconding'.[147]

End game: the fall of Theresa May

May's first stated goal on entering Downing Street in 2016, nonsensical for a Tory, was to be driven not by the interests of the privileged few but by 'ordinary working-class families'.[148] Her second goal was to deliver Brexit to the British people. Toby Helm succinctly summarizes what this second goal was to entail: it 'was to consume almost all her time and energy and, in the end, bring her leadership of the country to its disastrous finale'.[149] In the words of one ally, a Tory Minister at the time: 'Over time she became defined not by her achievements but by her ability to hang on and survive everything that went wrong.'[150] From the point of view of her survival, less than a year into her time at Number 10, as Helm observes, May had made 'arguably her worst ... decision of all, to call a snap election in the hope of winning her own mandate to deliver Brexit, only to lose the Tories their majority and leave her dependent on the Democratic Unionist party to get legislation through the Commons'. But somehow, he goes on, 'she staggered on, setting new standards for defiance with every month that passed'.[151]

In the end, she was forced into opening talks with her arch-rival, then Leader of the Opposition, Jeremy Corbyn. At the same time, the prospect of EU elections left her party in open revolt, and Nigel Farage and Brexit Party stood ready to exploit the Tories' and May's woes. Then Labour pulled the plug on the cross-party negotiations, and the last hope of a Brexit deal passing through Parliament disappeared. In typical stubborn fashion, she tried one last ploy, offering Corbyn a vote on whether to hold a second referendum. That was a non-runner. As one Government Minister said: 'She is dead now. It is just a case of when the life support machine is switched off.'[152]

May delayed making an announcement of her resignation until after the EU elections. But once she did in May 2019, Boris Johnson, the early favourite to enter Number 10, set out his stall without delay, insisting that under his leadership Brexit would happen in Autumn 2019, no matter what: 'Playing to the hard-Brexit wing of the Tory party at Westminster and the 100,000-plus Tory members who ... [would] ultimately choose ... the new leader, Johnson said at a meeting in Switzerland: "We will leave the EU on 31 October, deal or no deal".'[153]

4

Boris Johnson and Priti Patel: Personal Rhetoric and Further Draconian Measures (2019–2022)

Introduction

In April 2018, Home Secretary Amber Rudd resigned after a series of revelations in *The Guardian* that she had inadvertently misled Parliament over her role in the unjust treatment of Windrush generation migrants.[1] *The Guardian* revealed that in a leaked 2017 letter to Theresa May, Rudd had told May of her intention to increase deportations by 10 per cent – at odds with her denials that she was aware of deportation targets,[2] but clearly in line with the hostile environment. Rudd was replaced by Sajid Javid who, presumably in a vain attempt to tone things down, referring to 'the hostile environment', declared, 'I don't like the phrase hostile. So the terminology is incorrect and I think it is a phrase that is unhelpful. ... It is about a compliant environment and it is right that we have a compliant environment'.[3] The new term has understandably been largely ignored, given that 'the hostile environment' has established itself as a most accurate description of the state of play in the Tory Party of entrenched racism going forward: the hostile environment was here to stay. Two months after his intervention, Javid paused a range of hostile environment policies in order to stop people who have lived in the UK for more than 30 years being 'erroneously impacted by compliant environment measures'.[4] These included sharing data from HM Revenue and Customs, the Department for Work and Pensions, and the Driver and Vehicle Licensing Agency with the Home Office, thus temporarily halting these combative measures that were introduced under May's watch as Home Secretary.[5] The pause was only for three months.

The Home Office had already issued documentation to over 2,125 people who had contacted a Windrush hotline, confirming the right to live in the UK. Of these, 1,394 were born in the Caribbean, 93 in India and 638 in other countries.[6] Javid pointed out that 584 people had been granted citizenship through the Windrush scheme in June of 2018. Labour MP, Yvette Cooper, then Chair of the Home Affairs Committee, called for a hardship fund for Windrush victims to be set up immediately. Javid replied that some funds were available but did not make it clear how they could be applied for.[7] As we shall see in this chapter and the next, the hostile environment was to intensify in various ways under Prime Ministers Boris Johnson and Rishi Sunak and their respective Home Secretaries, Priti Patel and Suella Braverman.

Boris Johnson becomes Tory Party leader and Prime Minister

On 24 July 2019, Boris Johnson became Tory Party leader and Prime Minister, after winning a convincing victory over Jeremy Hunt in the leadership race.[8] Johnson was seen as the best person to beat the 'formidable electoral challenge' from Nigel Farage's Brexit Party.[9] He had, as we have seen, promised to get Brexit done, deal or no deal. Johnson's premiership was almost immediately welcomed by Donald Trump, then US President, who tweeted: 'He will be great!'[10]

Significantly, Johnson immediately appointed Patel as Home Secretary. A convinced anti-immigration Thatcherite, after being unsuccessful in the 2005 General Election, the then Tory Party leader, David Cameron, had recommended Patel for his 'A-List' of prospective candidates, designed to increase the inclusion of minority ethnic and female Tory MPs to improve the Tories' image. By 2019, she had been Tory MP for Witham, Essex for nine years. A committed Eurosceptic, Patel had been a leading figure in the Vote Leave campaign for Brexit.

Johnson's own up-front colour-coded colonialist and imperialist racism

Johnson's personal racism, both historically and in the present, is seemingly derived from scientific racism (a totally discredited, but still being promulgated, 'thesis' that Black people and others who are not White, have lower IQs than White people and that this biological 'fact' accounts for their inferior intelligence, morals, and so on),[11]

Prior to his premiership

Johnson's own colour-coded racism is well known and dates back at least to 1999, when in a piece for the *Spectator*, the right-wing Tory-supporting magazine, of which he was editor, he wrote that under the Government of the architect of New Labour, Tony Blair, young people 'have an almost Nigerian interest in money and gadgets of all kinds'[12] (Colonial Nigeria was ruled by the British Empire from the mid-19th century until 1960 when it achieved independence).

The following year, in an article written for the *Guardian*, Johnson said that seeing a 'bunch of black kids' out and about set off alarm bells in his head. They were 'shrieking in the spooky corner by the disused gents' and he stated that I 'cannot rule out that I have suffered from a tiny fit of prejudice'.[13]

Also in 2000, Johnson attacked antiracism reforms undertaken in response to the murder of Black teenager, Stephen Lawrence, and said Britain should 'axe large chunks of the anti-racism industry'.[14] He went on to level an attack on the author of the Stephen Lawrence Inquiry Report, William Macpherson: 'Heaven knows why Macpherson made his weird recommendation, that the law might be changed so as to allow prosecution for racist language or behaviour "other than in a public place" [such as the home]'. He also said he could not understand how Macpherson 'was prevailed upon to say that a racist incident might be so defined in the view of the victim "or any other person"'.[15]

In 2002, this time in a *Daily Telegraph* column, mocking Blair's globetrotting and again denigrating ex-colonies, Johnson wrote:

> What a relief it must be for Blair to get out of England. It is said that the Queen has come to love the Commonwealth, partly because it supplies her with regular cheering crowds of flag-waving piccaninnies; and one can imagine that Blair ... is similarly seduced by foreign politeness. They say he is shortly off to the Congo. No doubt the AK47s will fall silent, and the pangas will stop their hacking of human flesh, and the tribal warriors will all break out in watermelon smiles to see the big white chief touch down in his big white British taxpayer-funded bird [the Congo was a Belgian colony from 1908 until its independence in 1960].[16]

In the same year, when he was a Tory MP and editor of the *Spectator*, Johnson said that colonialism in Africa should never have ended, and he downplayed Britain's role in the slave trade. He also argued that Africans would not have grown the right crops for export without British direction.[17]

Publishes an article by up-front scientific racist

So, what informs Johnson's obvious up-front colour-coded racism? The likelihood of it being derived from scientific racism became apparent in 2003, when as editor of the right-wing *Spectator* magazine, Johnson published an article by Taki Theodoracopulos. After enthusing that Enoch Powell was right,[18] Theodoracopulos described young Black people in gangs in Birmingham as 'black thugs, sons of black thugs and grandsons of black thugs ... [who] were allowed to immigrate after the war, multiply like flies, and then the great state apparatus took over the care of their multiplications'.[19] In another article in the *Spectator* in 2008, still under Johnson's editorship, Theodoracopulos wrote: 'Orientals ... have larger brains and higher IQ scores. Blacks are at the other pole.'[20] In 2018, unambiguously parading the extreme nature of his scientific racist worldview, Theodoracopulos wrote an article commemorating D-Day in which he praised the Nazi defence forces and asked readers to sympathize with them.[21]

As Foreign Secretary, dishes out insults

In Ankara in September 2016, then Foreign Secretary in May's Government, Johnson had been filmed being asked whether he would apologise for writing a crude limerick about the Turkish President that included a line that he had 'sowed his wild oats with the help of a goat'.[22] Johnson replied with typical bluster that 'nobody has seen fit to raise it'.[23]

In January 2017, Johnson was accused of 'incredible insensitivity' after being caught on camera reciting part of a colonial-era Rudyard Kipling poem in front of local dignitaries while on an official visit to Myanmar.[24] Johnson was inside the Shwedagon Pagoda, the most sacred Buddhist site in the former capital Yangon.[25] The opening verse to the poem, 'The Road to Mandalay', which he started uttering, contains the line, 'The temple bells they say/Come you back you English soldier'.[26] Johnson's impromptu recital was so embarrassing that it prompted the UK ambassador to Myanmar, Andrew Patrick, to stop him.[27] Fortunately, Patrick managed to do this before Johnson could get to the line about a 'Bloomin' idol made o' mud/Wot they called the Great Gawd Budd' – obviously a reference to the Buddha.[28] Johnson had taken part in a ritual involving pouring water over a golden statue of what he described as 'a very big guinea pig',[29] after which he approached a 42-tonne bell, rang it with a wooden stick and spontaneously started reciting Kipling's poem. When told reciting the poem was probably not a good idea, his patronizing colonial racism came further to the fore: 'What?' Johnson replied. 'The Road to Mandalay?' 'No', the ambassador said sternly. 'Not appropriate.'[30] 'No?' Johnson replied, looking down at his mobile phone. 'Good stuff.'[31] As Social Affairs Correspondent for the *Guardian*, Robert Booth, points out, 'Kipling hardly knew Myanmar at all and only travelled there for three days in his 20s, but his poems and short stories about the place helped forge the image of the country in the imagination of colonial Britain'.[32]

During his premiership

Michael Mansfield, the barrister who represented the Lawrence family at the Macpherson Inquiry, said of Johnson in 2019: 'This is a man who is deeply prejudiced and obviously I'm horrified about the possibility that he may remain prime minister. He is fundamentally sexist and racist.'[33] But remain he did, and his premiership was also witness to his up-front colour-coded racism. For example, he hired Andrew Sabisky as an aide, through his advisor Dominic Cummings. Sabisky had written on the latter's website in 2014: 'One way to get around the problems of unplanned pregnancies, creating a permanent underclass would be to legally enforce universal uptake of long-term contraception at the onset of puberty. Vaccination laws give it a precedent.'[34] In February 2020, Johnson's Deputy Official Spokesperson refused several times to disassociate Johnson from scientific racism. Then Tory Transport Secretary Grant Shapps claimed that Sabisky's comments were 'not my views and those are not the views of the government'.[35] Tellingly, the Deputy Official Spokesperson said Shapps was speaking only for himself when he made that statement.[36] This would seem to confirm the worst about Johnson's own views on 'race' and eugenics.

Institutional racism denied

So, given these many obvious instances of his own colour-coded racism firmly in the public domain; and in the face of his association with known racists, a fascist sympathizer and eugenicists; and his refusal to disassociate himself from scientific racism; and despite centuries of institutional racism in the UK, both inside and outside the Tory Party, Johnson found himself in the position of having to investigate racism (in Government-speak, 'race and ethnic disparities') in the UK. This was in the light of the murder of George Floyd in the United States, and the ensuing Black Lives Matter protests. He could have chosen to start from a fresh slate, he could have chosen to admit to some mistakes in the past. Johnson's solution, however, was to seize upon a trusted ally, Tony Sewell, who had led Johnson's Mayor's Education Inquiry into London schools in 2012, when Johnson was Mayor of London. Sewell, a long-term commentator on 'race' and education and member of the Tory Party, had been criticized in the past for claiming that 'the mantra "institutional racism" [is] a hurdle'.[37] In 2010, he had claimed that 'much of the supposed evidence of institutional racism is flimsy'.[38]

Sewell was accordingly appointed Chair of the Commission on Race and Ethnic Disparities (CRED) in July 2020. Commission members were recruited by Director of the Number 10 Policy Unit since 2019, Munira Mirza, who used to be one of Johnson's Deputy Mayors. According to Rajeev Syal, Rowena Mason and Lisa O'Carroll, writing for the *Guardian*,

Mirza was a prominent critic of Theresa May's 'racial disparities audit for public services', apparently commenting that the 'scene was being set for another bout of political self-flagellation regarding the subject of race in Britain'.[39] In 2017, she wrote that 'anti-racism is becoming weaponised across the political spectrum'.[40] Mirza has also 'cast doubt on the existence of institutional racism and condemned previous inquiries for fostering a "culture of grievance"'.[41]

Totally unsurprisingly, therefore, the CRED report, published in March 2021, concluded that the claim that 'the country is still institutionally racist is not borne out by the evidence'.[42] For his part, Sewell said that although the report did not deny that racism exists in Britain, but there was no evidence of 'actual institutional racism'.[43]

Late in 2021, Katharine Birbalsingh, the headteacher of Boris Johnson's favourite school (he praised the rote learning), Michaela Community School in North London, was appointed as Social Mobility Commissioner. Birbalsingh rose to prominence at the 2010 Tory Party Conference with a speech about Britain's 'broken' education system and was applauded for claiming that underachievement by Black pupils was due partly to 'the chaos of our classrooms, and, in part, to the accusation of racism [against teachers]'.[44]

Her response to the Sewell Report is predictable. She tweeted: 'It is always acceptable in our woke culture of 2021 to mercilessly attack black conservatives. They have "betrayed" their leftist masters by daring to think for themselves, when they should be grateful. THAT is institutionalised/cultural racism. And it is everywhere.'[45]

Johnson calls a snap General Election

Johnson lost his working majority on 3 September 2019, when Phillip Lee crossed the floor of the House of Commons to join the Liberal Democrats[46] and 21 Tory MPs voted against the Government in order to enable Parliament to take control of the order paper and to debate a backbench bill designed to prevent a no-deal Brexit.[47] For this, they were expelled from the party. Two days later, Johnson's brother and fellow Tory, Joe Johnson, announced his intention to resign, because he had 'been torn between family loyalty and the national interest', adding 'it's an unresolvable tension and time for others to take on my roles as MP and Minister'.[48] On 7 September, Amber Rudd announced that she was resigning as Secretary of State for Work and Pensions and Minister for Women and Equalities, and leaving the Conservative Party.[49] Two days later, Parliament was prorogued, giving anti-no-deal MPs less chance to stop a no-deal Brexit.[50] Johnson managed to get an agreement with the European Union (EU) for a revised Brexit withdrawal agreement that replaced the Irish backstop (a device designed by the Theresa May

Government to try to prevent a border with customs controls between the Republic of Ireland and Northern Ireland)[51] with a new Northern Ireland Protocol.[52] However, this failed to get support from Parliament.

The end of free movement

Johnson called for a snap General Election on 12 December, resulting in a Tory landslide, with Johnson winning 43.6 per cent of the popular vote – the highest percentage for any party since Thatcher's first election victory in 1979 and giving him a majority of 80.[53] Many of the Tory gains were in long-held Labour seats, that had registered a strong Leave vote in the 2016 EU Referendum described as the 'red wall'.[54] Although a wide manual working-class support for Brexit is well known, this is still somewhat surprising in that Johnson, even more than most other Tories, epitomized the class arrogance and social privilege of Britain's upper-middle-class.[55] In the words of Julie Hyland, writing on the *World Socialist Web Site*, 'This is a man whose experience with the "lower classes" extends only to giving orders.'[56] Johnson said he would work 'flat out' and lead a 'people's government', while Jeremy Corbyn, who, out of the two, I would describe as the real people's contender, said he would not fight another election as Labour leader. He was replaced by someone very much to the right of Corbyn, Keir Starmer.

Johnson now had the mandate he wanted to formally implement the withdrawal from the EU. He formed a Cabinet that he described as a 'Cabinet for modern Britain',[57] but which was more accurately viewed as an 'ethnically diverse but ideologically homogeneous statement of intent'.[58] On 31 January 2020, Britain left the EU, heralding the beginning of the end of free movement to Britain from the EU and the European Economic Area (including Iceland, Liechtenstein and Norway) (it actually ended on 31 December 2020, after a transition period).

The policies of the Johnson Government, 2019–2022: the hostile environment is intensified

Hostile environment polices took on a new dimension, ten years after its launch by Theresa May in 2012 (see Chapter 3). The most significant legislation passed under Johnson's premiership included the Nationality and Borders Act and the Police, Crime, Sentencing and Courts Act (2022).

The Nationality and Borders Act (2022)

Having achieved the end of free movement from the EU, the Johnson Government focused its efforts on trying to halt immigration by attempting to stop movement across the English Channel into the UK. These attempts were accompanied by a series of 'moral panics' about the increase in the numbers of people coming to seek asylum in the UK, and served as a prelude to the Nationality and Borders Bill. Originally passed by 298 votes to 231 in the House of Commons in December 2021, it was described by Home Secretary Patel as the most significant overhaul of asylum system in over two decades. According to the Johnson Government, the Bill sought to:

- increase the fairness of the system to better protect and support those in need of asylum;
- deter illegal entry into the United Kingdom, thereby breaking the business model of people smuggling networks and protecting the lives of those they endanger;
- remove more easily those with no right to be in the UK.[59]

In the words of Amnesty International, Patel's 'attempt to paint this bill as targeting ruthless criminal gangs is a cynical distraction from her true intent', which is 'to simply, and at whatever the cost, punish, penalise and deter people who seek asylum. The xenophobia that underpins this Bill is plain. It is as ruthless to victims of repression, torture and exploitation as it is exploitative of the racism and prejudice they face'.[60]

After several months of 'ping-pong', the 'to and fro' amendments to Bills between the House of Commons and the House of Lords, the Act became law in April 2022. The United Nations High Commissioner for Refugees warned that Patel's Act could 'dramatically weaken' international systems for protecting those fleeing war and persecution, while Oxfam described it as a 'devastating blow for families fleeing conflict and persecution', and Médecins Sans Frontières (Doctors Without Borders) branded it 'despicable'.[61]

Offshore them!

Offshore processing of asylum seekers clearly reveals the Government's sinister plans and intent: allowing the UK to send people seeking asylum to a so-called 'safe third country' and to submit claims at a 'designated place' determined by them Home Secretary. In a scarcely believable, even for Johnson and Patel, development of the hostile environment, the former appeared on TV screens at a press conference in Kent (the county most affected by so-called 'illegal Channel crossings') on 14 April 2022 to announce plans to send 'unauthorized' asylum seekers on a one-way air ticket to Rwanda, 4,500 miles away in East Africa, with those who are rejected by the Rwandan Government being deported.

The scheme involved an initial down-payment of £120 million to the Rwandan Government in return for accepting 'tens of thousands of asylum seekers'. At the same time as Johnson's appearance at the press conference,

Patel was in Rwanda sorting out the deal. Syal reports that in the Rwandan capital, Kigali:

> Patel was shown pristine accommodation that will be used to house people flown from the UK. The guest house has 50 rooms over four floors that can accommodate a maximum of 100 people. Two more blocks will be built that will provide a maximum capacity of 300. In a press conference with Rwanda's foreign minister, Vincent Biruta, Patel said: 'Our world-leading migration and economic development partnership is a global first and will change the way we collectively tackle illegal migration through new, innovative and world-leading solutions.'[62]

It has since been revealed that in the 'guest house', bedrooms are around 3.5 metres by 3.5 metres with two beds in each, and there are just 12 toilets and five showers for 100 people.[63]

In the words of Chief Executive of the Refugee Council, Enver Solomon, 'Boris Johnson's administration in England has chosen to ... offshore people seeking asylum to Rwanda; to treat them as no more than human cargo to be shipped thousands of miles away so they are out of sight and out of mind'.[64] Solomon points out that the people the Government is seeking to offshore 'are not all illegal economic migrants, as it claims, but are mainly those who have escaped bloodshed and terror ... exercising their right under the UN refugee convention, which the UK was a founding signatory of, to seek asylum in a country of their choosing'.[65]

In a display of breath-taking hypocrisy, Theresa May, the architect of the hostile environment that split up thousands of families (see Chapter 3), including my own,[66] attempted to seek assurance from Patel in the House of Commons that 'families will not be broken up'.[67] In the interchange between May and Patel, the latter said she understood the scheme was only for young men but did not tell the Commons if women and children would be sent to Rwanda.[68]

The Police, Crime, Sentencing and Courts Act (2022)

This was an attempt to criminalize effective protest. It was introduced in March 2021, sponsored by Patel, and passed in April 2022. The Act includes the following measures:

- Making it a criminal offence for protesters to cause 'serious distress, serious annoyance or serious inconvenience' without 'reasonable excuse' – carrying a penalty of up to ten years in prison.
- Allowing the police to impose restrictions on marches if 'noise' could cause 'serious disruption' to a nearby organization or Government department.
- Police power to contain a crowd for an indefinite period.

Colour-coded racism

The severe maximum ten years' prison provision also includes damage to memorials that was in response to the toppling of the statue of slave trader Edward Colston as part of the 2020 Black Lives Matter protests following the murder of George Floyd[69] – true to form, Patel had described the protests as 'dreadful' and also said that she opposed taking the knee, a symbol of support for antiracism.[70] This part of the Act is not only blatantly aimed at Black people, but also criminalizes antiracist protesters in general. The Act also introduced what the Government refers to as 'Serious Violence Reduction Orders'. This entails 'new stop and search powers' even though it has been shown that this disproportionately affects Black communities.[71]

Non-colour-coded racism: Gypsy, Roma and Traveller communities

Alongside colour-coded racism and the serious threat to civil liberties in general, George Monbiot argues correctly that we must not forget 'something else buried in this monstrous bill'.[72] He is referring to the part of the Act that turns trespass from a civil into a criminal offence, allowing the police to arrest people who are Gypsies, Roma and Travellers (GRT) and confiscate their homes if they stop in places that have not been designated for them, as well as to move them on and to issue heavy fines.[73] This is because the Act creates a new offence of residing on land without consent in a vehicle and broadens police powers to seize caravans and other property.[74] As Monbiot points out, under the Act, in another unbelievable use of incarceration as a punishment, any adult member of the communities can be put in prison for up to three months.[75] 'Given that authorized sites and stopping places cannot accommodate the GRT people who need them', Monbiot goes on, 'this is a deliberate attack on a vulnerable minority'.[76] It is also a manifestation of blatant non-colour-coded racism.

The role of Lee Anderson in the Act

The year before the passing of the 2022 Police, Crime, Sentencing and Courts Act, in June 2021, top Tory MP, Lee Anderson, later to be made Deputy Chairman [sic] of the Conservative Party by Prime Minister Rishi Sunak (in February 2023) had contrasted some familiar attributes ascribed to GRT communities with common racist tropes that provide 'official' justification for the sort of non-colour-coded racism that is core to the Act. While the familiar ascribed attributes *could be seen* as positive, they are actually patronizing and crass, while the racist tropes serve to criminalize whole communities. Thus, Anderson had suggested that some of the Gypsy encampments seen in his Ashfield constituency are not the traditional, old-fashioned Gypsies sat there playing the mandolin, flogging lucky heather and telling fortunes. The Travellers I am talking about are more likely to be seen leaving your garden shed at 3 o'clock in the morning, probably with your lawnmower and half of your tools. That happens every single time they come to Ashfield.[77]

Sarah Sweeney, Policy Manager of Friends, Families and Travellers, said he should step down:

Anderson assumes all Travellers to be criminals and by that token would have all Travellers locked up – simply for existing. This is an extremist view and Anderson should be ashamed of himself. Politicians should be working to identify solutions to support communities to live happily alongside one other – not fanning the flames of racial tension. Lee Anderson should resign – he is clearly not fit for a role in parliament.[78]

Anderson, however, defended his remarks, claiming anyone calling for his resignation 'needs to take a journey into the real world'.[79] He went on: 'Come to places like Ashfield and speak to residents who have to put up with the destruction, the anti-social behaviour and increasing crime every time an illegal camp sets up in the area.'[80] Anderson then revealed his direct personal input into the Police, Crime, Sentencing and Courts Act and its intentional targeting of GRT communities:

For the last few weeks I've been sat on the Police Crime Sentencing and Courts Bill committee, and we've been talking about travellers this week. This new legislation will actually sort this problem out, it will give police and local authorities greater powers and once a traveller camp sets up they can get them straight off. Anybody who thinks it's a good idea to have these camps in Ashfield, feel free to email me your full address, dimensions of your lawn or back yard, and I will send the next encampment to your house.[81]

Earlier that week (week beginning 7 June 2021), Anderson had contributed to the colour-coded racism around 'Black Lives Matter', a movement that aims to highlight colour-coded racism and to promote 'racial' inequality, when he vowed to boycott England games during Euro 2020 if the team continued to take the knee before kick-off: 'For the first time in my life I will not be watching my beloved England team whilst they are supporting a political movement whose core principles aim to undermine our very way of life' (see Chapter 1 for a discussion of types of racism), In March 2023, Anderson was to defect to Reform UK, a party even further to the right than the Tories, and in July 2024, he became a Reform UK MP and its chief whip (see the Postscript for a discussion of the July 2024 General Election and its aftermath).

Islamophobia

Johnson's most notorious racist remark is probably his reference in a *Telegraph* article to women wearing the burqa as looking like 'letter boxes' or a 'bank robber'. Tell Mama, the organization that monitors Islamophobia, said there was a near four-fold increase (375 per cent) in Islamophobic incidents in the week following his comments when compared with the week before.[82] Of these, 22 involved 'visibly Muslim women who wore the face veil', according to Tell Mama.[83] Johnson's comment, as we have seen, is indicative of a much more general problem of Islamophobia in the Tory Party. In November 2019, Warsi declared the essence of her self-destructive relationship with the Tory Party:

> There is a lot of emotional attachment here. It's like a really painful divorce. It does feel like I'm in an abusive relationship at the moment, where I'm with somebody that I really shouldn't be with. It's not healthy for me to be there any more with the Conservative party.[84]

Grenfell Tower

In its first phase of the inquiry into the fire, it unsurprisingly concluded that the cladding fuelled the fire, while the second phase examined how it could have happened in the first place. As of the end of February 2022, according to Robert Booth, Social Affairs Correspondent for the *Guardian*, a senior official admitted that the Government knew in 2002, 15 years before the Grenfell Tower disaster, that plastic-filled cladding panels burned 'fast and fierce' and he believed they should not be used on tall buildings.[85] Arconic, the company that made the combustible polyethylene-filled panels on Grenfell, targeted the UK market because of less stringent requirements.[86] Taxpayer-funded tests 'showed the cladding panels failed "catastrophically", with flames reaching 20 metres into the air within five minutes'.[87] As well as Grenfell, similar panels went on to be used on more than 400 high-rise blocks. Under a European classification of combustibility, the panels were likely to be ranked as D, which meant they should not be used on tall buildings.[88] The Grenfell Tower final report was published in September 2024. It found that many were at fault for the disaster, which 'was the culmination of decades of failure by central government and other bodies in positions of responsibility in the construction industry to look carefully into the danger of incorporating combustible materials into the external walls of high rise residential building and to act on the information available to them'.[89]

The Windrush scandal
Windrush compensation scheme

Since 2018, a compensation scheme had been 'operating' to recompense the many thousands of British residents who were denied healthcare, housing or the right to work: in theory 'righting the wrongs' of the Windrush scandal.[90] According to Jenna Macfarlane, writing for *The Scotsman*, towards the end of November 2021 it was expected that between £60 million and £260 million would be paid in compensation to around 11,500 people.[91] In that month, a cross-party Commons Home Affairs Committee revealed that it believed responsibility for the scheme should be transferred out of Priti Patel's Home Office, after discovering 'a litany of flaws' in how it was being managed.[92] As of the end of September, Macfarlane points out, 'just 20.1% of the initially estimated 15,000 eligible claimants had applied, 5.8% had received ... [some] ... payment, and 23 individuals had died without receiving compensation at all'.[93] As the Committee put it: 'The treatment of the Windrush generation by successive governments and the Home Office was truly shameful.'[94] As if to add insult to injury, in January 2022 four Windrush generation descendants lost their High Court battle for the scheme for victims to be widened to include them.[95] As Diane Taylor explains in the *Guardian*, rules at the time stated that children who arrived as adults over the age of 18 after 1988 were excluded from the scheme. Moreover, this group did not have a path to citizenship through the scheme even if they had been resident in the UK for many years.[96] Following the victory of the Home Secretary, Damian Gabrielle, one of the four descendants, responded:

> I am absolutely devastated by today's decision. Most of my adult life has been in limbo. For me, the UK is my home. It's where my mum, dad, brothers, sisters and extended family all live. I thought that today would have given me and other Windrush descendants who are in a similar predicament hope. But that has been taken away from us.[97]

Karen Doyle of Movement For Justice, which has campaigned for inclusion of Windrush descendants in the Windrush scheme, said:

> The damage done to the Windrush generation was not just to the individuals. It was damage done to whole families separated across borders. Families who came to rebuild Britain and were subject to brutal discrimination and racism. Many had to leave children behind they would otherwise have brought. Reuniting and offering security to those families now in the wake of the Windrush scandal would have been putting the government's apologies into action. Yet this government continues to fail the Windrush generation and their

families at every stage. We are deeply disappointed in this decision but will continue to fight for the recognition and status of Windrush descendants.[98]

The Home Office response *including the hypocrisy of the last sentence* should come as no surprise to readers. Its spokesperson commented:

We're pleased the court found in the department's favour. The Windrush scheme was designed to recognise the existing status and connection to the UK of members of the Windrush generation and their eligible children. The home secretary and the department remain steadfast in our commitment to members of the Windrush generation.[99]

Windrush Progress Report, 2022: Patel's Home Office has failed

In March 2022, a progress report on the Windrush scandal by Wendy Williams, the then HM Inspector of Constabulary and Fire and Rescue Services, was published. This followed two years after the 2020 *Windrush Lessons Learned Review*, also written by Williams, was laid before Parliament.[100] At the time, Patel accepted all 30 recommendations of the review and promised significant cultural and systemic reform of the Home Office, as she committed the Tory Government to undertake a 'scrupulous' evaluation of the risks and of (hostile environment) legislation. The 30 recommendations required the Home Office to introduce a new mission statement based on 'fairness, humanity, openness, diversity and inclusion' and force a change in culture to recognize that migration and wider 'Home Office policy is about people'.[101]

Given the preceding analyses of the 'hostile environment' in this book, unsurprisingly the progress report found that the Home Office had broken its promise to change its culture, rendering completely hollow Patel's acceptance in full of Williams' recommendations.[102] Two years on, only eight of the 30 recommendations had been fully acted on. In Williams' words, using Javid's attempted change of nomenclature from 'hostile' to 'compliant': 'The failure to complete the review of the compliant environment policy will fundamentally hamper the department's effort to learn lessons and move on constructively.'[103] For example, the Home Office failed to appoint a migrants' commissioner, one of Williams' key measures. In addition, more efforts were needed to increase the number of Black, Asian and minority ethnic people at senior levels in the Home Office.[104] Williams was concerned in particular with the compensation scheme, quoting a small poll of applicants that she had done that revealed that 76 per cent said they had not been treated respectfully by Home Office staff, and 97 per cent did not trust the Home Office to deliver on its commitments. Moreover, about 386 claimants had waited more than a year for their claims to be resolved, including 179 waiting more than 18 months.[105] Williams expands on the implications:

> I met people who were still in severe financial and personal difficulty two years on from my original review. Some were unable to find work after time away from the job market. Others were in temporary accommodation, having to live with families or facing eviction because of unpaid bills. Many still had unmet physical and psychological needs and had experienced a sense of loss and devastation which had fundamentally affected their ability to cope, undermining their sense of identity and feelings of self-worth.[106]

As Gentleman points out, several anonymous Home Office staff interviewed by Williams expressed concern about the scheme. One told her: 'Our approach does not scream "righting the wrongs" or compassion, but "how little can we get away with paying out".'[107] Tellingly, although the Home Office had introduced a training programme to educate staff on the 'legacy of empire and colonialism', only 163 people out of a total of about 38,000 had visited the Windrush learning hub on its internal intranet system.[108]

Johnson resigns

In July 2022, Johnson announced his resignation. Given the preponderance of racism in the Tory Party as detailed in this chapter and in the rest of Part II of this book, readers may not be surprised that it was not racism that brought Johnson's downfall, but a number of quite different issues, many of which were related to the COVID-19 pandemic in 2020 and 2021, not least the 'Partygate scandal'. These are discussed in Chapter 7.

5

Suella Braverman: Hostile Rhetoric and the Escalation of the Hostile Environment (2022–2023)

Introduction

On 6 September 2022, Liz Truss was elected Tory Party leader and hence Prime Minister by the Tory Party membership, having defeated future Prime Minister Rishi Sunak. She immediately appointed hard-line anti-immigration advocate, Suella Braverman, as Home Secretary. Braverman was soon to reveal her cruel stance on the treatment of refugees and people seeking asylum. In the *Independent* on 5 October 2022, the last day of what was to be Truss's first and only Tory Party Conference as Prime Minister, Tom Peck wrote: 'Arguably the most horrifying moment of the entire rolling horror show was when Suella Braverman spoke in a fringe event of her "dream".'[1] It was this: 'I want to see a *Telegraph* front page, by Christmas, of the first deportation flight to Rwanda. That's my dream, that's my obsession.'[2] Peck parodies the implications of Braverman's 'viciousness':

> What a lovely dream. I dream of seeing those desperate people, flown off for a life of misery at my hand. I dream of crushing the lawyers who keep quite correctly pointing out it's illegal and therefore stop it from happening, and 'by Christmas' too. A kind of Christmas present to herself. Cruella de Vil only ever dreamed of cruelty to dogs. Suella de Vil goes one better.[3]

On 19 October 2022, after just six weeks in the job, Braverman resigned as Home Secretary. According to Rajeev Syal, writing for the *Guardian*, reports claimed that this followed a furious 90-minute row with Truss and her new Chancellor, Jeremy Hunt.[4] Syal also reveals that sources close to Braverman said she was angry that they wanted her to announce a new plan to liberalize immigration rules to make it easier for the Office for

Budget Responsibility to say the Government would hit its growth targets.[5] Unable to confirm that the Government would stick to its manifesto pledge that overall migrant numbers would come down (at the Tory Party Conference fringe meeting, Braverman had also said, 'In the 90s it was in the tens of thousands under Mrs Thatcher – net migration – and David Cameron famously said tens of thousands, no ifs no buts. So that would be my ultimate aspiration').[6] Truss' spokesperson responded: 'We have a commitment to control immigration and recognize that, alongside that, economic stability and growing the economy are important.'[7] According to the Government, on the other hand, Braverman resigned on account of her breach of ministerial rules when she sent confidential and market-sensitive policy details using her personal email. The email was aimed at garnering support for official Government policy on immigration.[8] Thatcherite Tory MP Edward Leigh, in a question to the Cabinet Office minister Brendan Clarke-Smith in the Commons, stated that he had 'great confidence' in Braverman's determination to 'meet our manifesto commitments': 'Can the minister assure us this resignation was entirely due to a technical breach of the rules and there was no policy disagreement between the prime minister and the home secretary?'[9] Several other MPs made similar interventions. Clarke-Smith replied by referring them to Braverman's resignation letter where she outlined her reasons, namely a breach of the ministerial code.[10] The day after Braverman's resignation, 20 October 2022, only her 44th day as Prime Minister, Truss also resigned following a disastrous mini budget, a month earlier (see Chapter 7), making her the UK's shortest ever serving Prime Minister.

British Asians and the Tory Party

Rishi Sunak's tenure as Prime Minister, which followed that of Truss, began on 25 October 2022, when he automatically got the job after Johnson and Penny Mordaunt, then Leader of the House of Commons, dropped out of the contest and Sunak passed the 100-nomination threshold, leaving him as the only remaining candidate. This meant that members did not get to vote. Sunak is the first British Asian to hold the office of Prime Minister. This raises the question of how could this happen in this party of entrenched racism? Writing before Sunak's premiership in *TRT News*, the Turkish Radio and Television Corporation public broadcast outlet, Amar Diwakar provides some answers. Referring to leading Tories, Munira Mirza, Sajid Javid, Priti Patel, Suella Braverman and Alok Sharma, as well as Sunak, Diwakar suggests that the party has a strategy of weaponizing certain members of minority ethnic communities, particularly British Asians, since the success of some British Asians within the capitalist economy *appears* to fulfil a narrative of Tory progress on racism and diversity.[11] Diwakar gives the example of

Patel's operationalizing her background, weaponizing her ethnicity, as a defence mechanism to attempt to thwart any criticism of her policies, as she mocked the advocates of 'free movement', a policy that she vowed to end once and for all at the 2019 Tory Party Conference: '[L]et me tell you something, this daughter of immigrants needs no lectures from the North London metropolitan liberal elite.'[12] Arguing in a similar vein, Fatima Rajina, from the Stephen Lawrence Research Centre at De Montfort University, suggests that the Tories have chosen British Asians who won't challenge or disrupt Tory ideology with a tactic 'straight out of the cold colonial book of divide and conquer'.[13] In addition, editor of *Burn Roti* magazine, that promotes South Asian culture, Sharan Dhaliwal, highlights what she sees as a perceived connection between British Asians and the Tories. The tenets of individualism – the idea that anyone can be successful as long as they apply themselves – is deeply embedded within Conservatism and has been deliberately tied to the Asian diasporic experience – albeit not uniformly.[14] Explaining her assertion, from the 1980s onwards, she goes on, the Tories began to court an 'Indian community' to encourage the ideology that because some British Indians were successful, there is evidence of what could be achieved under a free-market Conservative Government.[15] After 30 years of Thatcherism, some British Indians are now staunchly pro-Tory. So, here we have a plausible elucidation of why Sunak became Prime Minister. Sunak was also Britain's first (Tory) Hindu Prime Minister. Given the degree of Islamophobia in the party (as discussed throughout the book, including later in this chapter) it is unlikely that a British Muslim would have been chosen as Prime Minister.[16]

As we see in the chapters in this book on the hostile environment, the presence of minority ethnic politicians at the pinnacle of Tory power has done nothing to stem the tide of entrenched racism in the Tory Party. In fact, the opposite is the reality. This serves to underline my arguments in Chapter 1, on the multifaceted nature of UK racism, that anyone can be racist to anyone, including those now powerful members of minority ethnic communities whose forebears were subject to institutional racism for centuries, both in the former colonies and in the UK.

Braverman reappointed and instantly ramps up the rhetoric of the hostile environment

On becoming Prime Minister (on 25 October 2022), Sunak immediately reappointed Braverman as Home Secretary. Braverman was to play a key role in the intensification of the hostile environment. Firmly on the right of the party, and contemptuous of the left, Braverman supports the withdrawal of the UK from the European Convention on Human Rights and was Deputy Chair of the European Research Group from 2016 to 2017 and then its

Chair until 2018. She once referred to Twitter as 'a sewer of left-wing bile … [where] sensible, moderate voices … get drowned out'.[17]

Braverman has described herself as a 'child of the British Empire', adding: 'My parents were born under the British Empire in their countries, they came to this country with an admiration and gratitude for what Britain did for Mauritius and Kenya, and India, where we have our ancestral origins.'[18] She went on, 'born … in the 1940s … they have nothing but good things to tell me about the mother country'.[19] She believes that, on the whole, 'the British Empire', of which she described herself as being 'proud',[20] 'was a force for good'.[21] While she admits 'awful things' happened in the Empire (because of the culture at that time) she condemns the left's disdain of Empire: 'It's born out of a left-wing apology for patriotism and for Britain: ashamed of our history, fearful of our past, not the ingenuity and the genius of the British people', adding that she gets 'very frustrated with leftie activists who want to decolonise our curriculum and cancel our culture and pull down statues'.[22]

Braverman lost no time in reasserting her commitment to ramping up the rhetoric of the hostile environment. On 30 October 2022, homemade incendiary devices were thrown at the Western Jet Foil Border Force Asylum Processing Centre in Dover, leaving two staff with minor injuries. The police described the firebomb attack as 'primarily driven by an extremist ideology'.[23] The following day, Braverman told Parliament that she was working to stop the 'invasion on our southern coast', in reference to the arrival of migrants and refugees in small boats across the English Channel.[24] In so doing, she came under heavy criticism with her choice of language being described as 'inflammatory' and 'heinous'.[25] 'Let's stop pretending', Braverman asserted, that 'they are all refugees in distress, the whole country knows that is not true'.[26] In November, she was criticized for conditions at a migrants and refugees processing centre at Manston in Kent which were described by Independent Chief Inspector of Borders and Immigration David Neal as 'pretty wretched'.[27] People were sleeping on the floor, some were not given access to telephones and were not allowed to close toilet doors fully. Intended to house about 1,500 people for less than 24 hours at a time, numbers have swelled to more than double that, with one Afghan family saying they had been there for 32 days.[28]

Sunak's 'plans' for people seeking asylum in small boats

Dishonestly claims motivation is 'fairness'

Seven weeks after he became Prime Minister, Sunak made a statement on 13 December 2022 to the Commons on 'illegal immigration' that aligned him with the politics and rhetoric of Braverman. Falsely claiming to have 'fairness' as his 'moral framing', and ignoring the fact that for a large majority of immigrants there are very few safe and legal routes to enter the UK to seek asylum, and those were nearly all for very specific groups, such as those from Hong Kong and Ukraine, Sunak stated it is 'unfair that people come here illegally'. He went on, 'unfair on those with a genuine case for asylum', 'unfair on those who come here legally' and 'above all, it is unfair on the British people who play by the rules'.[29] Treading on dangerous ground, given that he was speaking soon after the firebomb attack on the immigration centre at the end of October, Sunak went on to say: 'So people are right to be angry … because they see what I see … which is that this simply isn't fair.'[30]

Directing concern on 'criminal gangs' rather than desperate human beings, a common ploy by Tory and Labour politicians alike, he went on to address the accusations of cruelty levelled at the Tories' racist immigration policies: 'It is not cruel or unkind to want to break the stranglehold of the criminal gangs who trade in human misery and who exploit our system and laws.'[31] Moreover, according to Sunak, it is not the hostile environment that is the root cause of the misery, but '[h]ostile states [that] are using migration as a weapon on the very borders of Europe'.[32]

We then had another reference to the 'ruthless, organised criminals' and a warning that, unless we act now, it will get worse.[33] Without a thought about the need for proper safe routes in his head, Sunak then announced five new steps, involving more military intervention, and more hostility and surveillance; halting access to bank accounts; putting people seeking asylum in military-type camps; and stopping immigration from Albanians, then the latest targets for xeno-racism.

Sunak then announced his plans. First, he promised a new, permanent, unified Small Boats Operational Command to bring together military and civilian capabilities, and that the National Crime Agency would coordinate intelligence, interception, processing and enforcement, and 'use all available technology, including drones for reconnaissance and surveillance, to pick people up and identify and then prosecute more gang-led boat pilots'.[34] This, he implied, will have a further bonus. It 'will free up immigration officers to go back to enforcement, which will, in turn, allow us to increase raids on illegal working by 50%'.[35] To which I would add, thus intensifying the hostile environment for those already here.[36]

Second, to try to deprive people seeking asylum access to funds, he pledged that since 'it's frankly absurd that today illegal migrants can get bank accounts which help them live and work here … we will re-start data sharing to stop this'.[37]

Third, he stated, because 'it's unfair and appalling that we are spending £5.5 million every day on using hotels to house asylum seekers … we will shortly bring forward a range of alternative sites such as disused holiday parks, former student halls, and surplus military sites'.[38]

Fourth, Sunak argued, there is a need to process claims in days or weeks, not months or years, so 'we will double the number of asylum caseworkers', hoping to abolish the backlog by the end of 2024.[39]

Fifth, he indicated he wanted to stop all immigration from Albania by embedding Border Force officers in Tirana Airport; issuing new guidance for case workers, making it 'crystal clear that Albania is a safe country'; and requiring 'a case worker to have objective evidence of modern slavery rather than just a suspicion'.[40] Sunak said he had already sought and received 'formal assurances from Albania confirming they will protect genuine victims and people at risk of re-trafficking'. This, he claimed, would allow the UK Government to 'return people to Albania with confidence and in line with ECAT [Council of Europe Convention on Action against Trafficking in Human Beings]'.[41] As a result of these changes, the vast majority of claims from Albanians can simply be declared 'clearly unfounded', '[a]nd those individuals can be swiftly returned'. Sunak concluded that 'we'll keep going with weekly flights until all the Albanians in our backlog have been removed'.[42]

On 4 January 2023, Sunak revealed new laws to stop small boats crossing the Channel to make sure that 'if you come to this country illegally, you are detained and swiftly removed'.[43] As Pippa Crerar, *Guardian* Political Editor, comments, Sunak's pledge to stop the boats 'has fudge written all over it', since legislating to crack down on people seeking asylum is easy, but actually making it happen when desperate people are seeking safe haven here is another.[44] This is especially given that there are no safe and legal routes. The most recent attempt to stop the boats was, of course, the Nationality and Borders Act, passed by the Boris Johnson Government under the watch of Priti Patel (see Chapter 4). At the time of Sunak's promise (January 2023), the crossings were at a record high.[45]

Braverman's cruel rhetoric

Confronted by Holocaust survivor

When confronted by Joan Salter, a Holocaust survivor, during a meeting in her constituency on 13 January 2023, Braverman said she would not apologise for her language after Salter told her that her description of migrants as an 'invasion' was akin to rhetoric the Nazis used to justify murdering her family.[46] Salter said:

> I am a child survivor of the Holocaust. In 1943, I was forced to flee my birthplace in Belgium and went across war-torn Europe and dangerous seas until I finally was able to come to the UK in 1947. When I hear you using words against refugees like 'swarms' and an 'invasion', I am reminded of the language used to dehumanise and justify the murder

of my family and millions of others. Why do you find the need to use that kind of language?'.[47]

In reply, Braverman, like Patel, operationalized her background in an attempt to thwart any criticism of her policies. She said she 'shared a huge amount of concern and sympathy' over the 'challenge' of illegal immigration, adding that her own parents were not born in Britain, and owed 'everything to this country and they have taught me a deep and profound love of Britain and British people. Their tolerance, their generosity, their decency, their fair play'.[48] She went on:

> That ... means that we must not shy away from saying there is a problem. There is a huge problem that we have right now ... the scale of which we have not known before. I won't apologise for the language that I have used to demonstrate the scale of the problem. I see my job as being honest with the British people and honest for the British people. I'm not going to shy away from difficult truths nor am I going to conceal what is the reality that we are all watching.[49]

Braverman concluded that she was 'incredibly proud' of the UK's recent immigration record but that 'we have a problem with people exploiting our generosity, breaking our laws and undermining our system. We must accept the enormity of the problem if we've got any chance of solving it'.[50] Braverman's answer was greeted with applause from the audience,[51] clearly overwhelmingly her Tory supporters.

In March 2023, criticizing Braverman's asylum plans, BBC sports commentator, Gary Lineker, tweeted: 'There is no huge influx. We take far fewer refugees than other major European countries. This is just an immeasurably cruel policy directed at the most vulnerable people in language that is not dissimilar to that used by Germany in the 30s.'[52] In the same month, former Shadow Chancellor when Jeremy Corbyn was Labour Party leader, John McDonnell, pointed out that his Hayes and Harlington constituency may have the largest number of people seeking asylum in hotels, that he has met them and some of them have wounds from torture. They have skills, and they could work, he stressed. McDonnell concluded by asking Braverman to tone down her 'inflammatory language' because it is putting them, and the people who represent them, at risk. Braverman failed to respond.[53]

Visits Rwanda in a propaganda exercise

Finally, in the month of March 2023, during the weekend of the 17th to the 19th, like Patel earlier, Braverman visited Rwanda in a propaganda exercise, designed to promote the Illegal Immigration Bill, soon to become an Act.[54]

The previous week, she had used extreme rhetoric to make the following ridiculous claim: 'There are 100 million people around the world who could qualify for protection under our current laws. Let's be clear. They are coming here.'[55] Sunak supported her on the same platform with a 'Stop the Boats' sign. Braverman revealed that in the last year, the UK had handed the Rwandan Government over £140 million to build camps for the deportees.[56] During her visit to the accommodation that Robert Stevens, writing for the *World Socialist Web Site*, described as 'hovels', she told her guide: 'I like your interior designer. I need some advice for myself.'[57] She went on continuing the nonsense by pointing to an architect's plan and asking about desperate impoverished people being deported with nothing but the clothes they would be wearing, 'And if people have a car, they can park their car here?'[58] Predictably, Braverman was accompanied on her visit by the right-wing media, including the *Sun*, the *Express*, the *Times*, *Telegraph* and *Daily Mail* as well as the hard-right GB News.[59] According to Stevens, the left liberal *Guardian*, *Independent*, *Daily Mirror* and *Independent* were banned.[60]

Grooming gangs

In early April, in an article in *Mail on Sunday*, Braverman claimed child sexual abuse grooming gangs in the UK were 'almost all British-Pakistani'.[61] She singled out British-Pakistani men due to 'cultural attitudes completely incompatible with British values' that 'have been left mostly unchallenged both within their communities and by wider society'.[62] In also reducing victims to 'overwhelmingly white girls from disadvantaged or troubled backgrounds',[63] argues Ella Cockbain, research group lead on human trafficking, smuggling and exploitation at University College London, Braverman goes 'well beyond mere dog whistles and into overt racism'.[64] In September 2023, the Press Regulator ruled that Braverman's claims were false, in that her decision to link 'the identified ethnic group and a particular form of offending was significantly misleading' because the Home Office's own research had concluded offenders were mainly from White backgrounds.[65]

Rebukes police for seizing 'gollywogs'

Also in April 2023, it was reported that police officers had taken several 'gollywog' dolls from the White Hart Inn in Grays, Essex, as part of an investigation into an alleged hate crime reported in February.[66] A source close to Braverman suggested her unhappiness had been made 'very plain to Essex police so they are under no illusions', according to *MailOnline*. It quoted the source as saying police forces 'should not be getting involved in this kind of nonsense' and instead focus on 'catching criminals'.[67] Sources at the force said no contact had been made by Braverman over the investigation.[68] The pub's owner, Benice Ryley, said she had displayed the collection of about 30 dolls, donated by her late aunt and customers, in the pub for nearly ten years. She said of the dolls, which are racist caricatures of Black people: 'They're my childhood history, it's a part of our inheritance. I can't see any harm. I don't know how they can find it offensive.'[69] Following the seizure, Ryley assembled a replacement collection as an act of defiance. She commented, 'I'm getting a notice printed saying "We've got gollies on display, if you find this offensive please don't come in." If they don't like them they can walk out the door.'[70] She and her husband denied being racist. When asked about her husband being photographed in a T-shirt from the far-right group Britain First, Ryley replied, 'I don't think Chris is a supporter of Britain First, he was just wearing that shirt because it was convenient at the time.'[71]

Claims heightened criminality among boat arrivals

In late April, asked whether she agreed with the then Immigration Minister Robert Jenrick's view that uncontrolled inflows 'threaten to cannibalise the compassion of the British public', Braverman said:

> I think that the people coming here illegally do possess values which are at odds with our country. We are seeing heightened levels of criminality when related to the people who've come on boats related to drug dealing, exploitation, prostitution. There are real challenges which go beyond the migration issue of people coming here illegally. We need to ensure that we bring an end to the boat crossings.[72]

Asked to explain on what evidence she based her claims of 'heightened levels of criminality', she said she had spoken to several senior police officers. The Oxford Migration Observatory, the academic institute that gathers data on the movement of people, said it was not aware of any recent academic or official statistics examining criminality among refugees who had recently arrived in the UK.[73]

Accused of breaching barristers' code over racist language

In May 2023, it was revealed that lawyers and faith organizations had lodged a complaint with the Bar Standards Board that Braverman, a qualified barrister, had breached the body's code of conduct with 'racist sentiments and discriminatory narratives'.[74] Although not a practising barrister, Braverman is still subject to certain professional rules governing conduct by the Board that regulates barristers in England and Wales, to make sure that barristers 'conduct themselves in an appropriate manner'.[75] Nine organizations, including the Society of Asian Lawyers, the Association of Muslim Lawyers and the Joint Council for the Welfare of Immigrants, wrote to the Board urging it to investigate and take action against what they claim is racist and inflammatory language used by Braverman about British men of Pakistani heritage and people seeking asylum. The letter also stated that Braverman's 'comments are not only highly inaccurate and offensive, but they also perpetuate harmful stereotypes and contribute to a climate of hate and prejudice', and that '[i]t is our view that Ms Braverman's comments incite violence against the British Pakistani and Muslim community as well as refugee communities, fuelling racist sentiments and discriminatory narratives'.[76]

Refuses more humane asylum-support scheme

In August 2023, it became known that after the United Nations (UN) had backed a Home Office-funded pilot which would have dramatically reduced the spiralling costs of the crisis-hit asylum system, Braverman refused to endorse it, despite it being described as 'more humane'.[77] The UNHCR found the scheme cut the cost of accommodating refugees and migrants by more than half when compared with placing them in detention. The savings came through housing people and giving legal and welfare support.[78] Based in Bedford, between August 2022 and August 2023, it had supported '75 vulnerable migrants of 23 nationalities, offering them legal advice, clothing, mental health support, English language learning and GP registration while in the community', leading to 'better outcomes, such as settled status [and] [f]ewer than half of those held in immigration detention centres [being] deported'.[79] Braverman was intent, instead, on overseeing a huge increase in the Home Office's detention estate, which experts estimate would take billions to fund,[80] presumably in preparation for the Illegal Migration Act, discussed later in this chapter. As she stated to Parliament, she intends to pursue 'a programme of increasing immigration-detention capacity'.[81] At the time, the Home Office was paying more than £5 million a day to house people seeking asylum in hotels,[82] another reason for the increase, given the backlash against their use for this form of accommodation.

The Windrush scandal

According to a leaked Home Office commissioned report, the origins of the Windrush scandal lay in 30 years of racist immigration legislation designed to reduce the UK's non-White population.[83] The report, 'The Historical Roots of the Windrush Scandal', focuses on the immigration legislation of the 20th century, rather than on more recent events, such as the hostile environment. Officials, Gentleman points out in May 2023, had repeatedly tried to suppress its stark conclusion for about a year.[84] It describes how 'the British Empire depended on racist ideology in order to function',[85] and sets out how this affected the laws passed in the post-war period, concluding that the origins of the 'deep-rooted racism of the Windrush scandal' lie in the fact that 'during the period 1950–1981, every single piece of immigration or citizenship legislation was designed at least in part to reduce the number of people with black or brown skin who were permitted to live and work in the UK'.[86] 'As a result', it further notes, 'the experiences of Britain's black communities of the Home Office, of the law, and of life in the UK have been fundamentally different from those of white communities'.[87] The report goes on, '[m]ajor immigration legislation in 1962, 1968 and 1971 was designed to reduce the proportion of people living in the United Kingdom who did not have white skin'.[88] There was speculation over whether the report was withheld internally for a year because its conclusions were at odds with the Government's narrative on 'race', epitomized by Tony Sewell's Commission on Race and Ethnic Disparities report, discussed in Chapter 4.

Also in May 2023, Home Office Minister Simon Murray, responsible for compensation schemes, was heckled by people caught up in the scandal during a heated meeting organized by Action for Race Equality in Westminster to draw attention to the slow progress in assisting those affected by the Home Office's mistakes.[89] He claimed that the Government had then paid or offered more than £70 million in compensation, and that the compensation scheme was being constantly improved.[90] Jeremy Crook, CEO of Action for Race Equality, noted that people affected by the scandal were still trapped overseas, unable to return to the UK because they did not have the correct documentation. Several people explained the complex ways in which their lives were ruined by the mistake.[91] For example, one man, who had to give up his career as a teacher after his right to work in the UK was questioned, said he had been offered a 'derogatory sum' in compensation. When he received the offer, he said he had 'wished the floor would open up for me to fall through it'.[92] Another man described how his sister was still stuck in St Vincent because she was unable to trace documents proving that she had the right to live in the UK, and a former psychiatric nurse told Murray she was unable to travel to visit her mother before she died because the Home Office lost her passport twice and then said they could find no record of her: 'I couldn't get to the funeral. They need to sort this out.'[93]

Labour MP Dawn Butler, born in London to Jamaican immigrant parents, rightly told the meeting: 'The Windrush scandal was just an element of a wider state-sanctioned hostility that has been directed at black people for as long as I can remember. The Home Office is not an effective department; it is not competent.'[94] Murray said he was greatly looking forward to June and the 75th anniversary of the arrival of the *Empire Windrush*, 'when we will celebrate the enormous contribution of the Windrush generation'.[95] The campaigner Patrick Vernon said it would be a bittersweet celebration, adding: 'There are thousands of people still locked in the Home Office's maladministration.'[96]

Islamophobia

The Singh Report and Review

Throughout the book, I have referred to Islamophobia in the Tory Party. In July 2023, two years since the publication of his report on Islamophobia among Tories, Swaran Singh said it had taken 'for ever' for officials to focus on the recommendations, with the biggest problem being tackling issues at a local level.[97] Singh said the number of Tory leaders and Chairs since the report – three and seven respectively – had an impact on the party's ability to fulfil the recommendations.[98] His original report, which while it included criticism of the mayoral campaign of Zac Goldsmith (see Chapter 3) and the language used by Johnson (see Chapter 4) for insensitivity, stated that claims of 'institutional racism' were not borne out by evidence.[99] The report had been condemned in 2021 as a 'whitewash' by Tory Muslims including Warsi and Sajjad Karim, who was a Tory MEP for 12 years and chaired the European Parliament's working group on Islamophobia.[100] In the review in 2023, key findings included Singh's observation that the Tory Party had no formal measures in place to handle complaints about 'discriminatory behaviour' of its most senior members.[101] It also found that there had been over 200 complaints relating to some 130 incidents in the three months up to June 2022. Five of these were categorized as bullying or intimidation, three as sexual assault, two referred to criminal activity and one was about a member writing on an 'alt-right' website.[102]

In September 2023, Tory mayoral candidate, Susan Hall, liked tweets praising Enoch Powell, and described Sadiq Khan as 'our nipple height mayor of Londonistan'.[103] Alongside the image were the words 'it's never too late to save your country', a combination once used on the website of the British National Party. Hall also liked a tweet posting the photo with the message: 'It's never too late to get London back!'[104] Before the 2020 US presidential election, Hall had advocated Trump to 'wipe the smile off this man's face' (referring to Khan).[105]

The *Bibby Stockholm*

In July 2023, the *Bibby Stockholm* migrant barge, set to house 500 people seeking asylum, arrived in Portland Port, Dorset, while opposing groups of pro- and anti-migrant protesters gathered at the quayside.[106] A private firm had been given a £1.6 billion contract to manage the barge, alongside other asylum accommodation and travel services, while the Government covered costs for the National Health Service, the police and other public bodies.¹⁰⁷ A Home Office spokesperson stated, 'there will be 24/7 security on site' which 'is designed to be self-sufficient in order to minimise the impact on the local community, with catering, recreational areas and basic health care provision on board'.¹⁰⁸ The local Tory MP, Richard Drax, MP for South Dorset, was not happy, likening the barge to a 'quasi-prison', having voiced concern about its impact on both people seeking asylum and the tourist-dependent local economy.¹⁰⁹ Confirming Drax's 'prison-like' claims, Portland Port said that people staying there will 'not be free to move around the port' and have to stay either on the *Bibby Stockholm* or in an adjacent 'secure compound'. A bus service is to be provided to take asylum seekers to destinations in the local area, with port officials denying that people will be 'dumped' in one place.¹¹⁰

The charity Freedom from Torture described the barge's use as 'cruel and inhumane', warning of a 'catastrophe waiting to happen'. Clinical services manager Ann Salter added: 'The government must abandon this plan immediately, and instead, address the asylum backlog which it has allowed to spiral out of control.'¹¹¹ Downing Street defended the use of the barge, insisting it is a cheaper alternative to hotels, where around 50,000 people were then being accommodated at a cost of £6 million a day.¹¹²

When journalists were given a tour in July 2023, before the residents had arrived, they discovered that the residents will enter the barge via a gangplank, and go through airport-style security and proceed through windowless corridors, so narrow you can trail your fingers on both sides.¹¹³ As Amelia Gentleman put it, the accommodation is in line 'with the Home Office's prevailing dislike of friendly murals and pictures'.¹¹⁴ She is referring to a scarcely believable act of cruelty, even for the Tories. In April, Robert Jenrick, then Immigration Minister, had cartoon murals painted over at an asylum centre for unaccompanied children, some as young as nine, because he thought they were too welcoming and sent the wrong message.¹¹⁵ Staff at the reception centre for small boats arrivals in Kent were understandably horrified by Jenrick's actions, and opposed painting over the murals.¹¹⁶ Back to the *Bibby Stockholm*, people staying there will be greeted by plain, undecorated walls, with a simple laminated A4 sheet stating 'welcome' stuck on the wall of the reception room.¹¹⁷ According to staff, the Home Office requested that the TVs (previously used by construction workers recently accommodated on the barge) should not be wired up.¹¹⁸

Tragically substantiating the warning from Freedom from Torture, about five months after the barge's arrival, a man was believed to have killed himself on board in December 2023. The family of Leonard Farruku, aged 27, had to turn to crowdfunding to bring him back to Albania for burial.¹¹⁹ His sister, Jola Dushku, said, 'If my brother wasn't put in that boat he was going to have a life ahead of him of normality and peace. Such tragedy could not have happened if he was not put there.'[120] Several people onboard the barge pointed out that Farruku had been in a state of distress shortly before he died, shouting and banging on the wall of his cabin.[121] After his suicide, people staying there revealed that conditions had deteriorated since up to 300 people had moved on to the barge.[122] They were concerned about the requirement to go through the airport-style checks and body searches even if they want to step outside for a short period, a worsening of food quality and quantity (shortages for those at the end of the queue).[123]

The Illegal Migration Act 2023: the hostile environment is further intensified in law

The so-called Illegal Migration Act received Royal Assent on 20 July 2023. It was aimed at stopping people crossing the English Channel. It means that anyone who arrives irregularly in the UK by small boat or other means of transport now has their asylum deemed 'inadmissible', without it even being considered.[124] They can be detained indefinitely but should be 'detained and swiftly removed'. They are then either sent to their own country or, if that is not possible, to a 'safe third country'.[125] 'Safe countries' include the 27 EU member states and Iceland, Liechtenstein and Norway, which, like the '27', are part of the European Economic Area; Switzerland which is part of the single market; and Albania – granted EU candidate status in 2014. The Act does not cover children who will not be removed until they are 18 years old.[126] Chief Executive of the Refugee Council, Enver Soloman, notes that directors of children's services tell him it 'will lead to a serious safeguarding crisis as they know children will simply disappear as they approach their 18th birthday, knowing they face expulsion'.[127] They fear, he goes on, that children will be abused by criminal gangs and traffickers.[128] As part of the Act, the Government must also set a yearly cap on the number of refugees to come to the UK via safe and legal routes.

Widespread criticism

The Act received widespread condemnation. According to Jun Pang, Policy and Campaigns Officer for human rights organization Liberty, the Act breaks a large number of international laws, including the European Convention on Human Rights, the Refugee Convention, the UN Convention on the Rights of the Child, the Council of Europe Convention on Action Against Trafficking and the Statelessness Conventions.[129] Soloman described it as a 'watershed moment', one that will go down in history as a milestone like no other.[130] It 'is at variance with the country's obligations under international human rights and refugee law and will have profound consequences for people in need of international protection', UN High Commissioner for Human Rights Volker Türk and UN High Commissioner for Refugees Filippo Grandi have warned.[131] As the UN put it, the Act 'extinguishes access to asylum in the UK for anyone who arrives irregularly, having passed through a country – however briefly – where they did not face persecution. It bars them from presenting refugee protection or other human rights claims, no matter how compelling their circumstances'.[132] In Soloman's words:

> Pause for a moment and consider what that means. These are all people, like you and me. Mothers, fathers, brothers, sisters. They aren't all 'illegals', as the government claims. They are the family from Syria who saw their neighbours killed by bombs. Sudanese people fleeing the brutal war that is raging in their country. Iranians escaping persecution. And Afghans, who made up the largest nationality coming across the Channel in the first three months of [2023].[133]

Soloman went on to point out that he knew from his experience with the Refugee Council that uncertainty and desperation will leave many refugees feeling utterly hopeless and there is likely to be an increase in serious mental health crises, including self-harm and attempted suicide.[134] As reported nearly six months later in the *Guardian*, a total of 23 people seeking asylum are thought to have killed themselves in Home Office accommodation in the four years up to late December 2023, more than double the previous four years' figures, bringing the total to at least 23.[135] During a session of the Home Affairs Select Committee in December 2023, it was admitted that 132 unaccompanied children who had disappeared from Home Office accommodation were still missing.[136]

Channel crossing figures for 2023

From January to the end of November 2023, 29,437 people crossed the Channel, according to the Refugee Council.[137] This is just over a third less than in 2022 because the number of Albanians crossing the Channel in 2023 was significantly lower than in 2022,[138] due mainly to a new 'returns deal' accounting for much of the year-on-year decline in crossings.

Nearly three-quarters (72 per cent) of people who made the crossing in 2023 came from just seven countries: Afghanistan, Iran, Turkey, Eritrea, Iraq, Syria and Sudan, where conflict, persecution and oppression is well documented.[139] Of those, one in five (19 per cent) were from Afghanistan.[140] Analysis of asylum decisions in 2023 (January to end of September) reveals that just over three-quarters (76 per cent) would be recognized as refugees if the Government had processed their asylum applications.[141] Those who crossed the Channel since the passing of the Illegal Migration Act in July

2023 are awaiting removal to Rwanda and could be left in limbo for months and years on end dependent on ongoing legislation and rulings (see the last section of this chapter) and the incoming Government, following the 2024 General Election.

Anti-Gypsy, Roma and Traveller racism

On 3 August 2023, it was revealed that police were probing a Tory cabinet minister's campaign leaflet about a proposed new Traveller site in his constituency, which they had been informed was racist.[142] The leaflet, produced by Welsh Secretary, David T.C. Davies, asked for opinions on council plans 'to establish a number of Gypsy Traveller sites' in Monmouthshire.[143] Travelling Ahead, a group that provides advocacy and advice for Gypsy, Roma and Traveller communities in Wales, said the leaflet was a clear breach of the Equality Act.[144] The group condemned 'dog whistle actions intended to create a hostile environment for Gypsies and Travellers'.[145] The Tory-branded leaflet was entitled 'Gypsy and Traveller site coming to your area soon!'[146] It invited locals to get in touch with the Conservative Party with their views on the matter, asking questions such as: 'Would you like to see a Traveller site next to your house?'[147] Despite this inflammatory language, Braverman thought investigating it was a waste of time, suggesting that leaflets issued by MPs should not warrant a police probe: 'The police should be laser-focused on cutting crime and not investigating legitimate public concern. … The public want to see police out on their streets preventing crime and catching criminals, not inspecting MPs' leaflets.'[148] Travelling Ahead was contacted by residents who it said were 'absolutely horrified' by the leaflet.[149] As Trudy Aspinwall, a project manager for the group, correctly pointed out to *Wales Online*: 'You really would only have to substitute the words "gipsy and traveller" for any other ethnic group and you would see that it is racist.' She went on, 'There is no doubt that this was targeted at gipsies and travellers. They are protected under the Equality Act and there is a duty to not incite hostility or opposition based on race.'[150]

Deputy Prime Minister Oliver Dowden concurred with Braverman that the leaflets were not racist and apportioned blame to the Labour Party, telling *Sky*:

> I think that what David TC Davis was doing was highlighting the failure of the local Labour Council to carry out a proper consultation on this. That is entirely what people would expect their local members of parliament to do. He's standing up for his constituents making their case for them, and I totally support his right to do that.[151]

Five days later, the police decided to take no further action.[152]

Braverman attacks the European Convention on Human Rights and Human Rights Act

On 26 September 2023, Braverman gave a keynote speech on migration to the American Enterprise Institute in Washington, DC, a right-wing think tank. She described migration as 'an existential challenge for the political and cultural institutions of the West'.[153] She also repeated other fundamental components that make up the anti-immigration ideology of the Tory right: the 'misguided dogma of multiculturalism'; that immigrants bring 'drug crime, exploitation and prostitution'; and have 'contempt for our laws', after which she went on to challenge the existence of basic human rights legislation, specifically the European Convention on Human Rights.[154] Also on the 'small boats' issue, she referred to the human suffering caused and laid the sole blame on people smugglers, as always ignoring the immense pain, hardship, misery and suffering inflicted on people seeking asylum by her racist policies.

Braverman then posed the question, 'So why has the international community so far collectively failed to explore any serious reform of the global asylum framework?'[155] 'I think there are two main reasons', she continued. 'The first is simply that it's very hard to renegotiate these instruments. ... The second is much more cynical. The fear of being branded a racist or illiberal'. Responding to the second point, the UNHCR issued a highly unusual statement rebuking Braverman, defending the 1951 refugee convention and highlighting the UK's record asylum claim backlog.[156] Following her speech, the *Times* reported that Downing Street 'backs Suella Braverman's threat to leave the European Convention on Human Rights'.[157]

Buoyed by her performance in Washington and repeating her alarmist rhetoric of previous interventions and her contempt for human rights, Braverman addressed the Tory Annual Conference in early October 2023. She began with a warning that the world was facing unprecedented mass migration. 'The wind of change that carried my own parents across the globe in the 20th century was a mere gust compared [with] the hurricane that is coming', she said.[158] 'Because today, the option of moving from a poorer country to a richer one is not just a dream for billions of people. It's an entirely realistic prospect.' To applause from hundreds of delegates, she contrasted the 'hard-working commonsense majority' with whom the Tories allied with 'the privileged woke minority' who 'will flock to Labour at the next election':

> They like open borders. The migrants coming in won't be taking their jobs. In fact, they are more likely to have them mowing their lawns. They love soft sentences. The criminals who benefit from such ostentatious compassion won't be terrorising their streets. They are desperate to reverse Brexit. For these people, I have a simple

message: 'You are entitled to your luxury beliefs, but the British people will no longer pay for them.'[159]

She also laid into the Human Rights Act:

> The future could bring millions more migrants to these shores, uncontrolled and unmanageable, unless the government they elect next year acts decisively to stop that happening ... [Britain has] ... become enmeshed in a dense net of international rules that were designed for another era ... the misnamed Human Rights Act. ... I am surprised they didn't call it the Criminal Rights Act.[160]

Back to Labour, she added that any attempt to change the laws had led to false allegations that she and the Conservatives were racist.[161]

Natasha Tsangarides, Associate Director at the charity Freedom from Torture, commented on Braverman's speech:

> The home secretary revealed herself to be grossly out of touch with the millions of compassionate people who recognise that human rights are there to protect us all. Despite a cost-of-living crisis and collapsing public services, she continues to use marginalised groups as cannon fodder to win cheap political points.[162]

Tory MP found guilty of racially abusing activist

On 3 November 2023, Tory MP Bob Stewart, a former British army officer who was stationed in Bahrain in 1969 when the country was a British Colonial Protectorate, was found guilty of racially abusing activist Sayed Ahmed Alwadaei during a fractious exchange on the streets of Westminster. Stewart accused Alwadaei, who is living in exile after being tortured in Bahrain,[163] of taking money: 'You're taking money off my country, go away.'[164] Stewart had been attending an event hosted by the Bahraini embassy after which Alwadaei shouted: 'Bob Stewart, for how much did you sell yourself to the Bahraini regime?'[165] Stewart responded: 'Go away, I hate you. You make a lot of fuss. Go back to Bahrain.' He also told Alwadaei, 'Now shut up, you stupid man.'[166]

Speaking about the row, Alwadaei said: 'I feel that I was dehumanised, like I was someone who is not welcomed in the UK. Because of my skin colour, because of where I came from, he feels I am taking money from his country.'[167]

Braverman sacked by Sunak

On 13 November 2023, Suella Braverman was sacked as Home Secretary by Sunak and was replaced by James Cleverly. This dismissal, not of course for her racist rhetoric, came after pro-Palestinian protests in London calling for a ceasefire during the Israeli bombardment of Gaza, following the Hamas attacks on Israel on 7 October. Braverman had written an opinion piece for *The Times*, in which she blamed the police for 'playing favourites' and for taking a lenient stance towards the pro-Palestinian protesters,[168] and for being tougher on right-wing extremists.[169] She described the protesters, overwhelmingly peaceful and motivated by social justice, as 'pro-Palestinian mobs' and 'hate marchers'.[170] Sunak told reporters that Braverman had not run the article by his office, violating the ministerial code. However, while Sunak was under pressure to sack Braverman, he had initially backed her.[171] The day following her sacking, Braverman launched a blistering attack on Sunak, accusing him of betraying both her and the country.[172] In an attempt to appease the right of the party, Sunak appointed Tory MP and presenter for GB News,[173] Theresa McVey, as a Minister without Portfolio, tasked with leading the Government's anti-woke agenda, acting as a 'common sense tsar' (for a Marxist analysis of 'common sense', see Chapter 1).[174]

PART III

Austerity

6

David Cameron, the 'Age of Austerity' and its Impact (2009–2019)

Introduction

What follows is a timeline of the global financial crisis 2007–2008.[1]

- 9 August 2007: French International Banking Group BNP (Banque Nationale de Paris) Paribas becomes the first major bank to acknowledge the risk of exposure to sub-prime mortgage (issued at high interest rates to borrowers with low credit ratings) markets.
- 14 September 2007: Having borrowed large sums of money to fund customers' mortgages, British bank, Northern Rock, needs to pay off its debt by reselling those mortgages in the international capital markets. But, given that the demand had fallen, it faces a liquidity (cash flow) crisis and needs a Government loan, sparking fears that it would soon go bankrupt. Customers queue round the block to withdraw their savings, the first run on a British bank for 150 years. Adam Applegarth, Northern Rock's chief executive, later said that it was 'the day the world changed'.
- 17 February 2008: After the failure of two private takeover bids, Labour Chancellor of the Exchequer in the Gordon Brown Government, Alistair Darling, nationalizes Northern Rock, claiming it to be a temporary measure. It was nearly four years before it returned to the private sector.
- 7 September 2008: The US Government bails out Fannie Mae and Freddie Mac – two huge firms that had guaranteed thousands of sub-prime mortgages.
- 15 September 2008: Heavily exposed to the sub-prime mortgage market, the American bank Lehman Brothers files for bankruptcy, prompting worldwide financial panic.

- 17 September 2008: The UK's largest mortgage lenders, HBOS, is taken over by Lloyds TSB after a huge drop in its share price.
- 30 September 2008: Shortly after becoming the first European country to slide into recession, Ireland's Government promises to underwrite the entire Irish banking system – a pledge it was ultimately unable to uphold.

As part of the worldwide resurgence of Keynesian economics,[2] between September 2007 and December 2009, the then Labour Government made a number of interventions to support the banking sector generally and several banks specifically: along with Northern Rock, the Royal Bank of Scotland, Lloyds TSB and Bradford and Bingley.[3] Altogether, the Government injected £137 billion of public money in loans and capital to stabilize the financial system.

Britain enters recession

Britain officially entered recession on 23 January 2009, when the Office for National Statistics reported that the economy had shrunk through the last two quarters of 2008[4] (back-to-back quarters of contracting gross domestic product [GDP] is the official definition of a 'recession').[5] It was the worst and most destructive economic downturn since the Great Depression of 1929–1939.[6] This news arrived amid a rash of bankruptcies, including Woolworths,[7] a prominent feature of British high streets since 1909 that sold cheap items, including sweets and its own record label that, up to 1980, produced cover versions of 'top 20' pop music. There were also job cuts in the steel. aerospace and biopharmaceutical industries, following a slump in demand.[8] Even Britain's consumption of electricity fell as factories were shut down and families counted the pennies.[9] In April 2009, the G20 (the international forum for the governments and central bank governors from 19 countries and the European Union) agreed on a global stimulus package worth $5 trillion.[10]

The financial crisis and ensuing recession also had a major, albeit temporary ideological impact:

> Everything that the politicians and economists and bankers had told their populations for two decades about the superiority of free markets turned out to be false. Free markets, it appeared, were responsible instead for the devastation of the world economy. The blatant white collar crime[11] revealed in the most respectable banks only added to the ideological turmoil. No longer could the ruling class just dismiss critics of the 'free market' as throwbacks to an old and superseded order. For the first time, criticisms of the neoliberal order were published on a regular basis in the leading organs of the world's press.[12]

Austerity to the rescue once more

Despite this disillusionment, the ruling class, faced with budget deficits that had ballooned to unsustainable levels in the aftermath of the financial crisis,[13] claimed there was no alternative (or TINA, a key ideological mantra also used by Thatcher to justify neoliberal [capitalist] ideology)[14] to austerity, with the counter argument of oppositional groups not carrying enough weight to be taken seriously. In April 2009, the notion of a new 'age of austerity', which had previously been used to describe the years immediately following the Second World War[15] (although, as discussed in Chapter 2, it can be argued that it had its origins in the 17th century) was popularized in the UK by David Cameron, then Tory Party leader when Gordon Brown was the Labour Prime Minister. In his keynote speech to the Conservative Party spring forum, Cameron declared that 'the age of irresponsibility is giving way to the age of austerity'.[16] He was referring to what he perceived as Labour's 'irresponsibility', which he claimed had accelerated Britain's plunge into recession. In future, Cameron warned, the state needs to be careful rather than casual with public money. Cameron's intervention needs to be seen in the context of what Paul Krugman, 2008 winner of the Nobel memorial prize in economic sciences and columnist for the *New York Times*, referred to as 'austerity fever',[17] which gripped elites 'all across the western world'.[18]

As Tom Bramble concludes in his article for *Marxist Left Review* on the crisis in neoliberalism and its ramifications, the ruling class was thus able to impose ruthless austerity as a way out of the crisis. William Tabb argues that the way the ruling class always attempts to solve crises and forestall the development of the socialist alternative is to redistribute the burden to the working class.[19] In Bramble's words:

> Whatever their differences, the ruling classes could agree on one basic point in the aftermath of the immediate crisis: that the working class, as during every capitalist crisis, had to pay for the cost of rescuing the system ... For the first time in many decades, people in the West could expect their children to have a lower standard of living than themselves.[20]

It is worth reiterating at this point that austerity is the ideological and political *choice* of the ruling class. While not solely *its* prerogative, the Tory Party, a party of class warfare from the beginning, has been particularly vicious, cruel and hostile in its austerity measures.

Cameron becomes Prime Minister

As discussed in Chapter 3, the 2010 General Election produced a hung Parliament. After five days of discussions between the Conservatives and the

Liberal Democrats, they formed a Coalition Government. Cameron became Tory Prime Minister on 11 May 2010, heading the *ConDem* Coalition. In a speech on 14 April 2011, Cameron stated that people on the doorstep 'said they wanted a government that didn't just do what was good for the headline or good for their party but good for the long term and good for our country. That's what we're engaged in'.[21] He then went on, conveniently, to link what he claimed was heard on the doorstep to austerity: 'Clearly, cutting public spending isn't popular, but it's right to bring sense to our public finances. People said they wanted a government that actually trusted them to use their own common sense.'[22] Turning to economic growth, he asserted, 'Nothing – nothing – is more important to this government than growing our economy, creating jobs and prosperity across our country.'[23]

Extreme and callous fiscal austerity unleashed

On 20 October 2010, Cameron's Tory Chancellor of the Exchequer, in the *ConDem* Government, George Osborne unleashed what the *Financial Times* referred to as 'the most drastic budget cuts in living memory, outstripping measures taken by other advanced economies which were also under pressure to sharply reduce public spending'.[24] The sweeping cuts in spending and entitlements amounted to £81 billion over four years – the equivalent of 4.5 per cent of projected 2014–2015 GDP.[25] Declaring that 'today is the day where Britain steps back from the brink', Osborne announced a £7 billion fall in welfare support and 490,000 public sector job cuts by 2014–2015. Invoking TINA, Osborne insisted that there is no alternative to austerity, by which he meant making the working class pay for the bankers' crisis of 2007–2008: 'Tackling the budget deficit is unavoidable. To back down now and abandon our plans would be the road to economic ruin.'[26] Osborne also stated twice the utterly ridiculous (especially when applied to a country deeply divided by social class and wealth disparity, with the differential poised to jump even more) Tory mantra, 'We are all in this together.'[27]

As Bill Dunn explains, the lessons of Keynes, briefly remembered in the immediate aftermath of the 2007–2008 crisis, were quickly abandoned.[28] Fiscal stimulus was replaced by austerity, and when this failed, the ruling class logic was to demand more austerity.[29] The results were miserable, even in narrowly economic terms, and the human consequences appalling.[30] Dunn then draws on Marx to discuss the nature of states in capitalist societies in order to understand 'why austerity continues to be pushed'.[31] A basic tenet of Marxism is that states are not neutral social arbiters. Although they are not merely, as Marx and Engels put it in the *Manifesto of the Communist Party*, 'a committee for managing the common affairs of the whole bourgeoisie'[32] (indeed, Marx himself, and Marxists since Marx have qualified this since), it remains, as Dunn puts it, 'a useful contrast to persistent hopes in state benevolence and in the role of enlightened intellectuals within it'.[33] Capitalists have resources with which to influence states, and states need to foster accumulation within their borders, at least needing to protect capitalism's fundamental priorities of private property (see Chapter 2 for a discussion). As Clara Mattei argues, if we view it as not just a response to economic crises, but to crises in capitalism itself, we can see that 'austerity is a vital bulwark in defense of the capitalist system'.[34] Austerity was to continue unabated under the *ConDem* Government and the Theresa May Government that proceeded it on 13 July 2016, despite May's assertion on 3 October 2018 that 'austerity is over' and 'there are better days ahead'[35] right up to the onset of COVID-19, which forced a brief pause, only to resume with a vengeance under the brief Liz Truss Government and that of Rishi Sunak (see Chapters 7 and 8).

The 'flawed economic policy' and 'class warfare from above' interpretations of austerity

Writing from the 'flawed economic policy' interpretation of austerity (see Chapter 2), Larry Elliott, like Partington, an economist writing for the *Guardian*, refers to a calculation by the Progressive Economic Forum that the decade of austerity triggered by Cameron and Osborne in 2010 resulted in more than half a trillion pounds of lost public spending and a weaker economy.[36] Using figures from the Office for Budget Responsibility, Rob Calvert et al argue that the *ConDem* Government could have maintained real-terms growth in public spending at the 3 per cent level inherited from the previous Labour Government and, by accompanying spending increases with matching tax rises, still have reduced Britain's government debt burden by 2019.[37] As they put it: 'After more than a decade of austerity, the UK lives with private affluence – if only for the privileged few – amid public squalor. ... This did not have to be the case, and does not need to be the case in the future.'[38] Calvert Jump commented: 'Austerity was never a necessity but a poor economic choice whose effects are now all too apparent.'[39]

From a 'class warfare from above' perspective, rather than a 'poor economic choice' or a 'flawed economic policy', austerity is a deliberate Tory strategy to make the rich richer and to make the working class and the poor and disadvantaged poorer, as discussed in the rest of Part III of this book (see also Chapter 2).

The London uprisings of 2011

On 5 August 2011, the fiscally unthinkable occurred. The United States had its triple A credit rating[40] downgraded, a major world problem, since the dollar is the anchor of the world's monetary system.[41] Three days later, the Dow lost 635 points, its sixth worse loss ever, in Europe undermining the single currency and raising doubts about the solvency of the whole banking system of that continent.[42] In London, there were uprisings, 'arguably the greatest outbreak of disorder in London since the 18th century'.[43] As explained in Chapter 3 in the context of racism and the imminent launching of the hostile environment, the initial spark for the uprisings was the killing by police of Mark Duggan. We saw May's reaction to taking goods from shops, unlike the majority who in a survey believed that people had joined the uprising 'to get goods and possessions they couldn't afford to buy', which was that an 'unruly mob' were 'thieving, pure and simple'.[44] This was almost identical to Cameron's reaction, when he described it as 'criminality pure and simple'.[45] The uprisings spread to other UK cities.

To get a real explanation, we need to understand the broad social, political and economic context.[46] As Andy Southwark, writing for *Socialist Appeal*, argues, similar conditions create similar results and thus with a Tory-led Government carrying out brutal attacks on the British working class 'it was inevitable that sooner or later we'd see a return to the social unrest that characterised the 80s'.[47] Writing for *The Conversation*, Stephen Reicher et al summarize the findings of their three-year Economic and Social Research Council research project[48] into the events of 2011:

> [T]here is compelling evidence that recession breeds riots, especially when it's seen to hit the most vulnerable hardest. That is certainly true post-2008 when bankers were seen to get off scot-free while the poor lost their services and benefits through austerity. A sense of injustice prevailed … recession affected people's everyday lives. As jobs went, educational maintenance was slashed and youth centres closed. Those in precarious positions – black and poor people in particular – were increasingly found on the streets. They were seen as a danger. They were stopped and searched by the police. Such encounters were experienced as humiliating and led to simmering anger. An abstract sense of injustice took concrete form. The 'other' acquired a face – the police.[49]

Impact of austerity

Widespread poverty and misery

On 16 November 2018, in the *Guardian*, Aditya Chakrabortty wrote: 'Britain's government has today been held up in front of the world and comprehensively damned for the misery and chaos it has inflicted on its own people. Its defining policy of austerity is revealed to the international community as callous.'[50] This is not, as Chakrabortty explains, the judgement of some well-known foe of Cameron or May, but the UN's Special Rapporteur on Extreme Poverty and Human Rights, Philip Alston. The reliability of his report,[51] published on the same day as Chakrabortty's article, is evidenced by the thoroughness of his research: he visited all four countries of the UK and met Government ministers and those directly affected by their policies.[52]

Alston begins his report by correctly noting that poverty in the UK is obvious to anyone and is witnessed by the growth in the number of food banks and the queues outside them; people sleeping rough in the streets; the growth in homelessness; and a 'sense of deep despair'.[53] It is this sense of despair, he suggests, that led the Tory Government to appoint a Minister for Suicide Prevention and Civil Society, 'to report in depth on unheard of levels of loneliness and isolation'.[54] The appointment was made by Theresa May on 10 October 2018.[55] Local authorities, Alston goes on, have been gutted by a series of Government policies. Libraries have closed in record numbers, community and youth centres have been shrunk and underfunded.[56] At the same time, Sure Start children's centres that give help and advice on child and family health, parenting and caring for children, money, training and employment, have been closed.[57] Public spaces and buildings including parks and recreation centres have been sold off.[58] Pub closures meant that the number of premises decreased from 52,500 in 2001 to 38,000 by 2020, and were another loss of sociability.[59]

As a result of austerity, in 2018, 14 million people, one-fifth of the population, lived in poverty, with four million of these more than 50 per cent below the poverty line,[60] and, according to Suzanne Fitzpatrick et al who wrote the report, *Destitution in the UK 2018*, 1.5 million were destitute, unable to afford essentials.[61] Between 2013 and 2017, the use of food banks almost doubled.[62] The Government made no secret of its determination to focus more on individual responsibility, to place major limits on Government support, and to get people into wage labour *at all costs*.[63]

Into wage labour at all costs

> [P]unitive, mean-spirited, and often callous approach ... designed to instill discipline where it is least useful, to impose a rigid order on the lives of those least capable of coping with today's world, and elevating the goal of enforcing ... [unthinking] ... compliance over a genuine concern to improve the well-being of those at the lowest levels of British society.[64]

Key elements of the Beveridge social contract were overturned, and in Alston's words, 'evidence points to the conclusion that the driving force ... [was] ... a commitment to achieving radical social engineering'.[65]

The message to the Tory Government on the title page of Fitzpatrick et al's report underlines the deliberate intentions of the austerity agenda:

The UK Government needs to:
- End the freeze on working-age benefits so they at least keep up with the cost of essentials and do not create destitution.
- Change the use of sanctions within Universal Credit so that people are not left destitute by design.
- Review the total amount of debt that can be clawed back from people receiving benefits, so they can keep their heads above water.[66]

As Alston points out, 'The Government has remained determinedly in a state of denial.'[67] 'Ministers', he explains, 'insisted to me that all is well and running to plan'.[68] If I am right that Osborne's insistence that there is no alternative to austerity means making the working class pay for the bankers' crisis of 2007–2008, then things did indeed run to plan.

Universal Credit

Alston argues that no single programme 'embodies the combination of the benefits reforms and the promotion of austerity programs more than Universal Credit',[69] a Government payment that is supposed to help with living costs for people on low incomes, who are out of work or cannot work, which he describes as 'Universal Discredit'.[70] Many aspects of the design and rollout of the programme, he goes on, have suggested that the Department for Work and Pensions (DWP) is more concerned with making economic savings and 'sending messages about lifestyles than responding to the multiple needs of those living with a disability, job loss, housing insecurity, illness, and the demands of parenting'.[71] An increasing body of research made clear that there are far too many instances in which Universal Credit is being implemented in ways that negatively impact many claimants' mental health, finances and work prospects.[72]

The Universal Credit system has a five-week delay between when people successfully claim and when they receive benefits. This 'waiting period' often takes up to 12 weeks and pushes many who may already be in crisis into debt, rent arrears and serious hardship, meaning that they may need to go without food or heat.[73] As a result, the majority of claimants seek 'advance payments', which in turn must be repaid to the DWP in a relatively short period.[74] Moreover, debts to DWP and to third parties can be deducted from already meagre payments at a rate much higher than is the case with the older benefit system. Alston discovered that the 'rationales offered for the delay are entirely illusory, and the motivation … [is] … a combination of cost-saving, enhanced cashflows, and wanting to make clear that being on benefits should involve hardship'.[75] Recipients are immediately plunged into further debt and inevitably struggle to survive.[76] Even for minor infringements, draconian sanctions are imposed. Endless anecdotal evidence illustrated the harsh and arbitrary nature of some of the sanctions, as well as the devastating effects that resulted from being completely shut out of the benefits system for weeks or months at a time.[77] Alston concludes that sanctions succeed in 'instilling a fear and loathing of the system'.[78] Apparently, about one third of claimants fail in the application process, many owing to digital exclusion,[79] since the system, like everything else in advanced capitalist economies, is increasingly digital only.

Health

Life expectancy and social class

In 2010, when Osborne's unleashed his callous and draconian austerity measures, Michael Marmot, Professor of Epidemiology and Public Health at University College London (UCL), warned that growing inequalities in society would lead to worse health outcomes.[80] Ten years later, with others, he published the Marmot Report.[81] Here are some of the key findings relating life expectancy to social class:

- Since 2010 life expectancy in England had stalled; this had not happened since at least 1900, when life expectancy kept increasing about one year every four years.[82] If health has stopped improving, it is a sign that society has stopped improving.
- More than 80 per cent of the slowdown in life expectancy between 2011 and 2019 resulted from influences other than winter-associated mortality.
- There were marked regional differences in life expectancy, particularly among people living in more deprived areas. For both men and women, the largest decreases in life expectancy were seen in the most deprived 10 per cent of neighbourhoods in the North-East and the largest increases in the least deprived 10 per cent of neighbourhoods in London.
- The more deprived the area the shorter the life expectancy. Inequalities in life expectancy had increased. Among women in the most deprived 10 per cent of areas, life expectancy fell between 2010–2012 and 2016–2018.
- The gradient in healthy life expectancy was steeper than that of life expectancy. People in more deprived areas spent more of their shorter lives in ill-health than those in less deprived areas.
- Poor health is unnecessary and can be reduced with the right policies.
- Large funding cuts had affected the social determinants across the whole of England, but deprived areas and areas outside London and the South-East experienced larger cuts; their capacity to improve social determinants of health had been undermined.

- The national Government had not prioritized health inequalities, despite the concerning trends and there had been no national health inequalities strategy since 2010.[83]

Specifically blaming austerity, Marmot stated:

> Austerity has taken a significant toll on equity and health, and it is likely to continue to do so. If you ask me if that is the reason for the worsening health picture … it is … responsible for … life expectancy flat-lining, people's health deteriorating and the widening of health inequalities. Poverty has a grip on our nation's health – it limits the options families have available to live a healthy life. Government health policies that focus on individual behaviours are not effective. Something has gone badly wrong.[84]

Not least, the 2010 training cuts had at the time left the National Health Service short of 100,000 nurses and doctors.[85]

Underlining the blame that must be attributed to the Tory-led Governments from 2010 to 2020, Jennifer Dixon, Chief Executive of the Health Foundation that commissioned the Review, added that the Government must 'invest in the circumstances in which people live that have powerful impacts on their health and wellbeing, such as poverty, employment, housing and education. The evidence is clear and the solutions are there – what is needed is the will to act'.[86]

Marmot says the worsening of our health cannot be written off as the fault of individuals for living unhealthy lives. People's impoverished circumstances and poor life chances are to blame. The work of UCL's Institute of Health Equity, of which he is the Director, has established that healthy lives depend on early child development, education, employment and working conditions, an adequate income, and a healthy and sustainable community in which to live and work. Austerity had taken its toll over the previous ten years. As a result, the threshold for claiming free school meals was halved.[87] In a Foreword to the report, Marmot writes of the results of ten years of Tory-led Governments in the following areas:

> From rising child poverty and the closure of children's centres, to declines in education funding, an increase in precarious work and zero hours contracts, to a housing affordability crisis and a rise in homelessness, to people with insufficient money to lead a healthy life and resorting to food banks in large numbers, to ignored communities with poor conditions and little reason for hope. … Austerity will cast a long shadow over the lives of the children born and growing up under its effects.[88]

Child poverty soared, in fact, to its highest level since before the Second World War and infant mortality rose for the first time in two generations.[89] The Thomas Coram Research Institute collected children's own accounts: 'I was so hungry, it was like I got hit in my belly, like I got stabbed with a knife', a 14-year-old told the researchers.[90]

Another dimension to healthcare relates to the Food Standards Agency, which in 2020 tested 58 per cent fewer samples, and the National Audit Office (NAO) acknowledged that local authorities were 'failing to meet their legal responsibilities', with staff numbers cut by 45 per cent.[91] At the same time, checks that establish if food is safe and contains what it says on the label were few and far between. The NAO found only 37 per cent of food checks scheduled actually took place.[92]

Dismantling the broader social safety net

As benefits were reduced and became limited, legal aid was dramatically reduced in England and Wales, funding to local authorities slashed, and along with cuts in other public services, social care services were increasingly at breaking point.[93] In addition, the cap on housing benefit created socially segregated areas for low earners.[94]

> By emphasizing work as a panacea for poverty against all evidence and dismantling the community support, benefits, and public services on which so many rely, the government has created a highly combustible situation that will have dire consequences. ... Government officials dismissed such concerns and claimed that Universal Credit would work equally well when a future recession brings high levels of unemployment.[95]

Among the hardest hit were people seeking asylum and migrants. As noted earlier in the book, people seeking asylum are not allowed to work and the derisory level of support they get from the state 'guarantees they will live in poverty'.[96] While a central plank of the austerity programme is to get everyone into work, this does not apply to people seeking asylum. Others particularly vulnerable to the austerity regime are women, children, people with disabilities, people relying on a state pension and people living in rural poverty.[97] Finally, Alston gives the latest statistics relating to the impact of austerity in 2018. Homelessness was up 60 per cent since 2010, rough sleeping up 134 per cent.[98] There were 1.2 million people on the social housing waiting list, but less than 6,000 homes were built in 2017.[99] Food bank use was up nearly fourfold since 2012,[100] and there were then about 2,000 food banks in the UK, up from just 29 at the height of the financial crisis.[101] As Alston points out, not only does the Government not measure food poverty, but a minister dismissed the significance of food bank use as being only occasional and noted that food banks exist in many other Western countries.

Ethnography

What Alston heard on his UK visit in November, 2018

- One of the people severely affected by austerity told Alston how she and her husband used to work and had savings, but one crisis changed her life: 'I needed full time care, and my husband had to leave his job. Suddenly we were living on disability. Then our landlord gave us eight weeks to vacate the apartment. We discovered that no one will let you view a house when you're on disability benefits ... I do not know where I'll be putting my child to bed soon. Should he be made homeless?'[102]
- 'Universal credit has punched us in the face. Before much longer people will turn to crime. People will smash the windows to get what they want. This is going to cause riots' (Denise Hunter, 57, at the West End food bank in Newcastle upon Tyne).[103]
- 'I got hungry because I was smelling the other food. I had to take my eyes away from it. The most unfair thing is the government knows families are going through hard times but they decide not to do anything about it' (John Adebola-Samuel, 12, whose family couldn't get school meals in Dumfries, Scotland, because of their immigration status).
- 'I wash in what I call a birdbath – a little hot water in a basin and have a spruce down. To keep warm I wrap up in layers and layers. I never thought I would be 48 and in this position' (Sharon Morton, 48, at Newcastle Citizens Advice Bureau).
- 'If people don't have enough space at home, you need to be outside and you are exposed to the big world and all sorts of people and pick up bad habits. Anyone offering them a way of making money, they will take it. That's why I think drugs and crime are on the increase' (Sahra Roble, 19, from South Acton in London).
- 'I was 18 [and homeless] and the council said I was not a priority. I was struggling with depression and anxiety and juggling work. I was told that if I stop work and have a baby I would be more likely to get housing' (Tayah, West London).

Toynbee and Walker's research in March 2020

In a *Guardian* article in 2020, Polly Toynbee and Michael Walker researched a number of people to see how they had fared since Cameron's 'new age of austerity' had set in.[104] This was a follow-up their 2011 book, *The Verdict*,[105] in which they compared the promises made by the New Labour[106] Governments of Tony Blair and Gordon Brown, who were in power from 1997 to the first half of 2007, and the second half of 2007 to 11 May 2010, after which Cameron became Prime Minister, with people's own accounts of what they experienced. Once again, they travelled the country and revisited the same people. They noted that each household owed an average of £15,385, not including mortgages; the gap between rich and poor had increased; the young were worse off than their parents at their age; and home ownership had declined greatly, with families living in life-long precarious private renting.[107]

Spending time with the Chief Executive of Ipswich hospital, Toynbee and Walker watched as he begged a senior nurse not to leave. Jenny (not her real name), one of his most dedicated nurses, had turned around his difficult chemotherapy ward, caring for seriously ill people feeling at their worst, where deaths of patients exacted a heavy emotional toll on staff. But, taking a deep breath, she told him: 'I just can't keep going.'[108] According to Toynbee and Walker, her team cried when she told them.

They followed the fortunes of Emma Percy, in Folkestone, Kent. With her husband, Rob, and three children, the family had moved from rented accommodation to rented accommodation, changing the children's schools as rents rose, roofs leaked. They were sometimes living without a functioning boiler all winter long.[109] They were the 'just about managing'. These were one of the groups Theresa May had promised to help four years previous in her first statement as Prime Minister in July 2016, but never got round to it.[110] Emma and Rob did all the striving and aspiring that May had called for, hoping to save for a deposit, but never quite making enough. Their parents own homes; they may never. In the summer, Toynbee and Walker inform us, 'the only holiday they could afford was camping in the grounds of the school where Rob was caretaker'.[111]

In Hastings, East Sussex, Toynbee and Walker go on, 'we watched the closure of another day centre, the building sold by the cash-strapped council'.[112] This was the seventh of these havens for older adults, they point out, to close in the town since 2010. 'As packing cases were being filled with pictures from the walls, we talked to Rose, Mary and Sal, old friends sitting together as they always did, but now for the last time.'[113] Home alone, they conclude, the statistics showed that many more would arrive in A&E malnourished or dehydrated.

The rich get richer and the poorest, women and minority ethnic communities bear the brunt

At the other end of the scale, it is important to stress, the decade's winners won big. In 2020:

- The UK still had more highly paid bankers than the rest of the European Union put together.

- As GDP and pay growth both slowed, profits rose. A third of the UK's billionaires kept their money in tax havens: the May Government backed off from forcing transparency on crown dependencies and tax exiles donated handsomely to the Tory Party's 2017 election costs.
- British business stayed silent, fearing public scrutiny of its stratospheric director remuneration, dysfunctional boardrooms and negligent auditors.
- Total wealth in second homes, buy-to-lets and flats on the Costa climbed to an incredible £941 billion.
- Jeff Fairburn, Chief Executive of the housebuilder Persimmon, got a £75 million bonus, as profits poured into his pockets from a misdirected 'help to buy' subsidy.
- HM Revenue and Customs (HMRC) cut local offices at the expense of precious local knowledge, a Sheffield accountant told us. Amid austerity, 15,600 tax collectors were dispensed with and the NAO reported four million calls to HMRC went unanswered; £35 billion went uncollected.[114]

In March 2018, the Equality and Human Rights Commission published research by economists, Jonathan Portes and Howard Reed, that contained the most detailed and thorough assessment yet of the effects of austerity.[115] Changes to taxes and welfare payments since 2010 had, in fact, hit the poorest hardest.[116] As Portes notes, reinforcing one of the key arguments of this book, the austerity policies were a political choice: 'It was certainly not inevitable that … the most vulnerable groups would have to bear the brunt.'[117] Exemplifying Mattei's arguments that austerity is a 'tool of class' (see Chapter 2), overall, changes to taxes, benefits, tax credits and Universal Credit announced since 2010, argue Portes and Reed, are regressive, however measured – that is, the largest impacts are felt by those with lower incomes, with those at the bottom losing, on average, approximately 10 per cent of net income. Moreover, the changes have markedly disadvantaged women, minority ethnic groups and low-income families with children (all overlapping groups, of course).[118] In addition, the two-child limit[119] and the benefit cap bear most heavily on minority ethnic children.[120]

7

Boris Johnson's COVID-19 Economy, Liz Truss's Mini Budget and Their Impacts (2019–2023)

Introduction

Following the resignation of Theresa May, who had repeatedly failed to get parliamentary agreement on Brexit, Boris Johnson's first premiership began on 24 July 2019, with a promise to get Brexit done, deal or no deal.[1] In order to do this, he was to call a snap General Election, which took place on 12 December 2019 and which he won with a landslide (see Chapter 4). Once Brexit was achieved on 31 January 2020,[2] economic policy making was largely driven by COVID-19, the first documented cases of which were also in January 2020. The gravity of its economic consequences saw many countries, as in the aftermath of the financial crisis 2007–2008 (see Chapter 6), adopt Keynesian-style policies, with governments prioritizing employment and seeking to maintain a baseline of economic performance, supported by the state provision of loans to private firms, corporate equity ownership with high levels of welfare spending.[3] In the case of the UK, the priority after the onset of COVID-19 was for the state to assume responsibility for *guaranteeing* continued private sector activity[4] and to utilize to the full the battered Welfare State and other public services, such as private businesses publicly financed, to try to cope with the pandemic and to forestall the possibility of complete societal breakdown. Daniel Béland et al refer to this form of capitalist crisis management (see Chapter 2) as 'emergency Keynesianism'.[5] Such temporary changes in economic paradigms as well as the return of neoliberal economics and, *in the case of Britain, to severe and callous austerity*, need continuous public legitimation to curtail challenges from alternative economic ideas,[6] socialism being an obvious example. The Johnson Government's ability to use the Welfare State was constrained because of the effects of the extreme form of austerity imposed since 2010 (see Chapter 6). The Trades Union Congress has summarized how the cuts and underinvestment in public services in the decade up to 2020 undermined the UK's ability to provide an effective and coherent response to the COVID-19 pandemic:

- *Safe staffing levels in health and social care* were damaged by many years of pay caps and pay freezes, which impeded recruitment and increased staff turnover. This left both health and social care dangerously understaffed when the pandemic began.
- *Public service capacity* was damaged by steep cuts to almost every part of the public sector. When the pandemic hit, spending per capita was still lower than in 2010 in social care, transport, housing, childcare, schools, higher education, police, fire services and environmental protection. This limited the ability of services to contribute to civil contingencies and to continue essential activities effectively.
- *A strong social safety net* was damaged by direct cuts to social security through benefit freezes, and by reforms that reduced entitlement and narrowed eligibility to fewer people. This increased poverty levels, which meant greater risks of exposure and transmission, and greater levels of vulnerability to more serious health consequences from COVID-19 illness.
- *Robust health and safety enforcement* was compromised by cuts that decimated public health and safety regulators, and confusion over authorities' remit. During the pandemic, instead of raising the number of inspections and enforcement notices, they fell to an all-time low, despite widespread workplace-linked cases of infection.[7]

Chancellor Sunak's first budget

In February 2020, Johnson appointed Rishi Sunak as Chancellor of the Exchequer. Sunak's first budget in March 2020 was effectively rewritten when furlough was introduced by the Johnson Government in the same month. Designed to support employers to retain and continue to pay staff while businesses were closed during lockdown, the Government paid up to £2,500 per month to furloughed employees.[8] The furlough scheme subsidized the wage bill while ensuring the reproduction of the capital–labour relation.[9]

Announcing the scheme, Sunak stated, encapsulated the extent of lockdown: 'We have closed schools. We have told people to stay at home to prevent the spread of infection. We are now closing restaurants and bars.'[10] He continued:

> Today I can announce that, for the first time in our history, the government is going to step in and help to pay people's wages. We're

setting up a new Coronavirus Job Retention Scheme. Any employer in the country – small or large, charitable or non-profit – will be eligible for the scheme.[11]

He went to spell out the cost of the measures:

I am placing no limit on the amount of funding available for the scheme. We will pay grants to support as many jobs as necessary. ... To help businesses pay people and keep them in work, I am deferring the next quarter of VAT payments. That means no business will pay any from now until the end of June; and you will have until the end of the financial year to repay those bills. That is a direct injection of £30bn of cash to employers, equivalent to 1.5% of GDP. ... To strengthen the safety net, I'm increasing today the Universal Credit standard allowance, for the next 12 months, by £1,000 a year. For the next twelve months, I'm increasing the Working Tax Credit basic element by the same amount as well.[12]

These enormous short-run increases in spending saw public debt grow by around 20 per cent of gross domestic product as economic activity collapsed. The lack of supply following the phased post-lockdown reopening and the Russian invasion of Ukraine in February 2022 led to huge leaps in the prices of fuel and food.[13]

Inequality widens even more during COVID-19 and Johnson's premiership

The general picture

The macroeconomic environment shifted dramatically in the UK during Johnson's premiership.[14] In July 2019, inflation was close to 2 per cent; in August 2022, just days before Johnson left office, it was just over 10 per cent.[15] At the same time, workers were taking the biggest hit to their wages since records began.[16] By 2022, inflation, higher taxes and low wage growth meant that workers had seen their living standards decline at the fastest rate in the post-war period.[17] Meanwhile, findings from the High Pay Centre, an independent think tank focused on the causes and consequences of economic inequality, with a particular interest in top pay, revealed that in 2022, CEOs at FTSE 350 companies with over 250 employees were paid 57 times more than the median worker,[18] almost identical to the 2019 ratio of 58:1, pre-COVID-19.[19]

Moreover, Tax Justice UK, a campaigning and advocacy organization that tries to ensure that everyone in the UK benefits from a sustainable, fair and effective tax system, revealed that six companies made £16 billion in excess profits during the pandemic.[20] These ranged across financing, outsourcing, retail, real estate, mining and pharmaceuticals, with one company, the Scottish Mortgage Investment Trust, up over 800 per cent compared to previous years.[21] The Tax Justice UK Report makes clear that these companies are examples of a broader trend where some companies benefited from Government pandemic spending, while others were well placed to profit from economic changes that have been accelerated by COVID-19:[22] 'The covid pandemic has been unprecedented in its impact. Not only did it cause a recession that saw the wealthiest grow richer, whilst others struggled, it also resulted in some companies making what appear to be unprecedented profits.'[23]

I now turn to some specific examples of such companies.

Tory patronage
Personal protective equipment (PPE) and VIP lanes

In January 2022, the High Court ruled that the Johnson Government's operation of a fast-track, behind-closed-doors VIP lane for awarding lucrative PPE contracts worth billions of pounds to those with political connections was unlawful.[24] The judge argued that the VIP lane conferred preferential treatment on bids, speeding up the process, which meant that offers were considered sooner in a process where timing was critical, and VIPs' hands were held through the process. She stated: '[T]here is evidence that opportunities were treated as high priority even where there were no objectively justifiable grounds for expediting the offer.'[25] The Court also noted that the overwhelming majority by value of the product supplied by the companies Pestfix and Ayanda could not be used in the National Health Service (NHS).[26] The Judge refused to allow publication of how much money was wasted by the Government's failure to carry out technical assurance on the PPE supplied by these two companies.[27] The Good Law Project (GLP)[28] and Every Doctor[29] that brought the case commented, probably over-optimistically: 'Never again should any Government treat a public health crisis as an opportunity to enrich its associates and donors at public expense.'[30] The following month, the Government was accused of 'wasting' billions of pounds on unusable PPE and buying kit at inflated prices, after a report revealed the huge scale of losses.[31] The Department of Health revealed in 2022 that £8.7 billion spent on PPE in 2021 had been written off, entailing significant loss of value to the taxpayer.[32] Apparently, about £2.6 billion was spent on PPE 'not suitable for use in the NHS' and another £673 million was spent on kit not suitable for use by anyone.[33] Moreover, another £750 million was spent on excess items that were not used before their expiry date.[34] At the same time, the World Health Organization pointed to 'unnecessary' use in the UK, particularly with respect to gloves.[35]

Michelle Mone

Probably the most high-profile Tory beneficiary of the PPE scandal is Michelle Mone. Having left school at 15, she went on to launch ventures in diet pills, fake tans and cryptocurrency, before founding a lingerie company. In 2015, she was given a life peerage by David Cameron.[36] Cameron was said to have been impressed when Mone, who is Scottish, backed the Union in the Scottish independence referendum.[37] Mone, with her husband, Doug Barrowman, is facing a National Crime Agency investigation into the procurement of £203 million of Government PPE contracts during the COVID-19 pandemic for PPE Medpro via the VIP lane, after Mone approached Gove, using private email addresses.[38]

Items from VIP lane contacts much more expensive; and Tory donors and associates given preferential treatment

In December 2023, internal Government documents, GLP revealed, showed that the unit price paid for items under VIP lane contracts was on average 80 per cent more expensive and up to four times higher, when the Government bought it from firms referred through the VIP lane by Tory ministers, MPs and officials.[39] One example was the cost of PPE delivered by Meller Designs, a fashion company, at the time co-owned by the Tory donor and former Tory minister, David Meller, which was referred through the VIP lane by Michael Gove's office. Meller Designs was awarded six PPE supply contracts worth £164 million during the pandemic. About £8.46 million worth of the equipment supplied by Meller Designs, according to GLP, was later found to be not used in an NHS setting.[40] Shadow Chancellor, Rachel Reeves, commented: 'Billions of pounds of taxpayers' money have been squandered … when it could have been spent in our schools, hospitals and police.'[41]

The preferential treatment also included access to Matt Hancock, Secretary of State for Health and Social Care from 2018 to 2021. Two major donors who had such access are Mustafa Mohammed and Mohamed Amersi. They used it, according to Felicity Lawrence, to promote companies offering COVID-19 services with which they were involved. Amersi also had a phone meeting with James Bethell, a health minister at the time, in which he put forward projects with which he was connected.[42] Mohammed – who had donated £234,000 to the Tories, and his company Genix Healthcare, a further £156,000 – messaged Hancock on 11 June 2020 with a proposal. Within a week he had met the team at the Department of Health and Social Care (DHSC). A legal letter of intent was signed by the DHSC in September 2020, which guaranteed a multimillion-pound payment to Ecolog (a leading global provider of integrated services, technology, logistics and environmental solutions) even if a full contract was not issued.

The following year the DHSC decided it did not want to proceed and gave Ecolog £38 million in settlement for 'mobilisation costs' and some laboratory testing services as well as a 'profit component'. The DHSC confirmed that no services were provided by the company under the full contract. The Director of GLP, which disclosed the information, Jolyon Maugham, commented: 'No one who followed the ongoing scandal that is Covid procurement will be surprised to learn a minister was directly involved in a huge contract award that failed to deliver. What we desperately need is an independent review into how this happened over and over again.'[43]

Mohammed's access to Hancock did not end with Ecolog. He also promoted a company called Oxsed, which had developed rapid COVID-19 tests. Amersi also promoted Oxsed, recommending the company in a phone meeting in June 2020 with Bethell, according to minutes of the meeting. Bethell asked a DHSC team to report on whether the project had any merit.[44]

Test and trace failed despite 'eye-watering' budget

Writing for the *British Medical Journal* (*BMJ*), Elisabeth Mahase has pointed out that MPs have admitted that England's COVID-19 'test and trace' system failed to achieve its main objective, to break chains of transmission and enable people to return to a more normal life. This is despite an 'eye-watering' budget of £37 billion.[45] The House of Commons Public Accounts Committee noted that the contact tracing service was one of the most expensive health programmes delivered during the pandemic, equal to nearly 20 per cent of the entire 2020–2021 NHS England budget.[46] However, after it was set up the UK still had two national lockdowns and significant case numbers: 'Its outcomes have been muddled and a number of its professed aims have been overstated or not achieved.'[47] Although it was named 'NHS Test and Trace' the system was run largely run by two private companies, Serco and Sitel.[48] Mahase points out that the system was widely criticized for its use of expensive consultancy companies, its poor performance in reaching people who tested positive for SARS-CoV-2 and their contacts, and its centralized rather than localized approach.[49] An earlier report from the Public Accounts Committee, she informs us, found that NHS Test and Trace could not show it had made a difference to the pandemic.[50] Moreover, despite a promise by NHS Test and Trace to reduce its reliance on consultants, the number it employed was higher in April 2021 (2,239) than in December 2020 (2,164). The DHSC pays consultants an average of £1,100 a day, though some are paid even more. The report said that NHS Test and Trace did not know what its overall spending on consultants was and that although it estimated that it would have spent £195 million on consultancy in 2021–2022 it also said it would be spending £300 million on its top ten consultancy suppliers alone.[51]

Unused laboratories

Another major issue related to 'test and trace' was capacity and usage of laboratories and contact tracing centres. In 2020–2021, NHS Test and Trace paid £3.1 billion to secure the laboratory capacity to process PCR tests that test for the COVID-19 virus, and £911 million for contact tracing, mainly on call centres. However, only a minority were used.[52] Meg Hillier, Chair of the Public Accounts Committee, summed up the extent of the vast wastage of public money:

> The national Test and Trace programme was allocated eye watering sums of taxpayers' money in the midst of a global health and economic crisis. It set out bold ambitions but has failed to achieve them despite the vast sums thrown at it. The continued reliance on the overpriced consultants who 'delivered' this state of affairs will by itself cost the taxpayer hundreds of millions of pounds.[53]

The demise of Johnson

Partygate

Given the omnipresent racism in the Tory Party and entrenched class war from above, as detailed in this book, both of which are normalized within the party, and institutionalized in the society as a whole, along with the 'personalisation of politics' in recent years,[54] it should not come as a surprise that it was not racism or class that brought Johnson's downfall, but something more to do with a number of scandals. These included questions over who paid for Johnson's holiday in Mustique and for the expensive refurbishments to his Downing Street flat, when he moved in with his new wife, Carrie Johnson. Most of all, there was 'Partygate'. After telling people to stay away from social events such as parties, to 'save lives and save the NHS',[55] reports began to emerge of parties in Downing Street and Whitehall. This was repeatedly denied until photos, videos and emails came to light. Johnson first responded by once again repeating his denial. Then former Press Secretary Allegra Stratton resigned after 'a video was obtained by ITV News showing her joking about a party in Downing Street that was held in December 2020'.[56] Other revelations followed, and Johnson was eventually forced to apologize in January 2022, when he added that he attended one, but as far as he was aware, the COVID-19 rules had always been adhered to.[57] Just days after the Metropolitan Police launched an investigation into 'Partygate', the war in Ukraine began when Russia invaded in February 2022, shifting people's attention away from parties, so that even when it was revealed that Johnson and his wife had been issued a fixed penalty notice for celebrating his birthday in the cabinet room during lockdown, it 'did not create a sense his downfall was imminent'.[58] However, in May 2022 it came to light that a scuffle broke out, one person attending was sick and excessive amounts of alcohol were drunk when workers at Downing Street held a party on 18 June 2020, in the middle of the COVID-19 crisis.[59] Moreover, at another event, Johnson's former Principal Private Secretary Martin Reynolds boasted to colleagues on the WhatsApp messaging service that staff appeared to have 'got away' with drinks events in the Downing Street garden in May 2020.[60]

The final straw

In June 2022, Graham Brady, chair of the 1922 Committee, announced that he had enough letters of 'no confidence' in Johnson's leadership from Tory MPs to trigger a vote among them. Although it was lost, there were more 'no confidence' votes than expected. Under the rules at the time, that meant no further such votes for a year. In addition, Tories feared changing leader in the middle of the Ukraine war, and a cost-of-living crisis did not make it worthwhile. There followed two serious by-election defeats, with Party Chair Oliver Dowden resigning as the votes came in.[61] The final straw came in early July 2022 when it emerged that Chris Pincher had resigned as Deputy Chief Whip, writing to Johnson that he had 'drunk far too much' the night before.[62] Pincher was accused of groping two men at the Carlton Club, in front of many MPs. In the next few days, Downing Street's account of what Johnson knew about allegations around Pincher changed repeatedly.[63] Ministers were sent out to do media interviews pushing the Government line, 'only to find they had been misled by Number 10 and ultimately Mr Johnson'.[64] Sunak, then Chancellor, and Javid, then Health Secretary, resigned their posts, prompting 'a wave of departures from more junior ranks in government'.[65] McGuinness and Rayner conclude:

> The speed with which the situation became untenable was dizzying – most obviously for Mr Johnson himself as he appeared to be almost in denial as his premiership fell apart around him. Few politicians would have been in the position he was and still remained resolute that they would continue. It was the chutzpah and self-certainty that perhaps explains the extraordinary story of his rise to power. But this time, the political magic did not work. The mischievous, blundering, charismatic persona that had once been his strength had become a weakness in the eyes of his MPs. Boris Johnson was no longer seen as the winner the Conservative Party had elected him to be.[66]

On 7 July 2022, Johnson announced his resignation. Just under a year later, in June 2023, he was to resign as an MP, accusing the Privileges Committee that was investigating Partygate of mounting a 'witch hunt' against him.[67] At the following month's by-election in Uxbridge (July 2023), he was replaced by fellow Tory, Steve Tuckwell, who won with a narrow majority.

Liz Truss's 'mini budget', 23 September 2022

Just over two weeks after Liz Truss became Prime Minister, at this time of economic instability, her Chancellor, Kwasi Kwarteng, introduced a 'mini budget' on 23 September 2022. At first the Tory press were ecstatic: 'At last, a true, Tory budget'[68] was the *Daily Mail* front-page headline, while columnist Alex Brummer praised the 'seismic' boldness of Kwarteng's financial planning. Writing in a similar vein, Allister Heath on the front page of the *Daily Telegraph* had gushed on the day after Kwarteng had outlined his plans in late September: 'This was the best budget I have ever heard a chancellor deliver, by a massive margin. The tax cuts were so huge and bold, the language so extraordinary, that at times I had to pinch myself to make sure I wasn't dreaming.'[69]

The mini budget incorporated unfunded tax cuts, the main proposals being the bringing forward of a planned cut in the basic rate of income tax from 20 per cent to 19 per cent; abolishing the highest 45 per cent income tax rate in England, Wales and Northern Ireland; reversing a plan announced in March 2021 to increase corporation tax (a tax on profit from business) from 19 per cent to 25 per cent from April 2023; and reversing the April 2022 increase in National Insurance and cancelling the proposed Health and Social Care Levy. This tax was for the extra health spending caused by the COVID-19 pandemic and designed to deal with the backlog of patients waiting for treatment, as well as to improve social care. After a widespread negative response, the proposed abolition of the 45 per cent tax rate was reversed on 3 October and the plan to cancel the corporation tax increase reversed on 14 October.

This mini budget meant about £45 billion tax cuts for the rich paid for by a vast expansion in borrowing. Writing on 20 October 2022, Partington states, 'Britain has been through the wringer since last month's mini-budget'.[70] 'Not only', he continues, 'was Kwasi Kwarteng's not-so-mini plan the trigger for a domestic financial crisis and higher mortgage costs for millions, it lit the blue touchpaper for his political downfall'[71] (and that of his close friend, Liz Truss). Partington described the mini budget as 'a bumper, ideologically driven occasion'[72] that led to a run on the pound, a gilt market freefall,[73] in other words, a rush to get rid of sterling, with more sellers in the market than buyers.

The Washington-based International Monetary Fund (IMF) launched a stinging attack on 28 September on the UK's tax-cutting plans and called on Liz Truss's Government to reconsider them to prevent stoking inequality.[74] Commenting on the IMF intervention, former US Treasury Secretary, Larry

Summers, proclaimed that such a warning shot from the IMF would be more usual for an emerging market economy than a country like Britain. He told BBC TV: 'It is early days and things could change and economics is not an exact science, but I would certainly say that this has the look right now of a number of unforced errors.'[75] On 17 October, the new Chancellor of the Exchequer, Jeremy Hunt (Truss had sacked Kwarteng ahead of this U-turn, in a desperate attempt to restore her dwindling political authority)[76] announced further changes to the Government's mini budget:[77]

- Basic rate of income tax will remain at 20 per cent 'indefinitely' rather than decreasing to 19 per cent in April 2023).
- Cuts to dividend income (for example, from shares) tax rates will no longer go ahead as planned.
- IR35 off-payroll working[78] reforms (introduced in 2017 and 2021) will remain in place.
- VAT-free shopping scheme for non-UK visitors will be scrapped.
- Freeze on alcohol duty rates will be scrapped.
- The Energy Price Guarantee (this brought bills down to £2,500 a year) will expire in April 2023 rather than lasting two years, with a review taking place to establish the level of support that should continue beyond this date.

Effect on mortgages

Higher interest rates

One year later, in *Mortgage Strategy*, writing about the effect from the mini budget on mortgages, Emma Simon noted: 'With the value of the pound tanking and gilt yields spiking, it became clear that interest rates would have to rise, and rise quickly, which caused immediate pricing issues for lenders.'[79] It was a disaster for those wishing to get a mortgage. South Coast Mortgage Services Director Gareth Davies stated, 'It created market uncertainty, spooked lenders and put the fear of God into many customers.'[80] L&C Mortgages Associate Director of Communications, David Hollingworth, described how banks and building societies 'went into a frenzy of re-pricing, with fixed-rate mortgages being pulled and some lenders temporarily withdrawing altogether'.[81] At one point, almost 1,000 products were removed in one day, with new deals, where available, offered at very high rates. Many of these were short-lived, being withdrawn in just hours as borrowers scrabbled to snap up what deals they could before rates jumped again.[82] At the start of September 2022, Simon points out, the average two-year fixed rate mortgage was 3.66 per cent. By the start of October, ten days after the budget, this had jumped to 5.24 per cent. By the beginning of November, it was 5.9 per cent. There were similar rises in the cost of five-year fixed rate mortgages.[83]

Despite the U-turn in less than a month and Hunt's further reversals, according to Mortgages for Business Development Director Jeni Browne, higher rates and fewer products remained an ongoing problem.[84] Yellow Brick Mortgages Managing Director Stephen Perkins stated that, although we were through the worst of the market instability by 25 October, 'the longer-term implications of decade-high interest rates and a cost-of-living squeeze are only now starting to be felt by most households'.[85] Simon concluded: 'Interest rates will not drop significantly anytime soon, and Perkins warns that the mortgage market faces an ongoing affordability challenge as many thousands more households move off low-cost fixed-rate deals in the next few years.'[86]

Effect on rents

Temporary accommodation

This dire lack of affordable housing means that an ever-increasing proportion of the population is forced to rely on the private rented sector,[87] a sector itself facing rent rises. Figures published by the Office for National Statistics in September 2023 show that private rents in the UK in the year to August 2023 rose at their fastest rate since records began – by 5.5 per cent generally and in London, 5.9 per cent.[88] In July 2023, the Department for Levelling Up, Housing and Communities had shown that the number of households stuck in temporary accommodation in England was at a record high between January and March that year, over 104,000 households, up 10 per cent from 2022, including nearly 65,000 households with children, just over a 10 per cent increase from the same period in 2022. In total, over 131,000 dependent children were living in temporary accommodation.[89]

Homelessness

The total number of households approaching their local council for help either to prevent them becoming homeless, or to help them get out of homelessness, increased by nearly 6 per cent to over 83,000. Again, these figures hit a record high.[90] In addition, people who were in-work and experiencing homelessness continued to increase. Some 19,500 households seeking assistance were headed by someone working, increasing by nearly 9 per cent from the final quarter of 2022 up until the first quarter of 2023. Matt Downie, Chief Executive at Crisis, a campaigning charity that works with homeless people, pointed out that once again, we witness the effect that

> years of no investment in housing benefit, and a shameful lack of social house building, is having by trapping families in temporary accommodation. Not only do people not have the stability and security

of a home, but they're often left to cope in just one room, with no facilities to cook meals or do washing. This is unacceptable. ... Families experiencing homelessness will continue to be commonplace and more and more children will be forced to live in cramped, unsafe temporary accommodation. Households across the country desperately need more social homes as well as investment in housing benefit so that people can afford even the cheapest of rents.[91]

In March 2023, it was estimated that nearly 2,450 people were sleeping on the streets, a 35 per cent increase on 2022. However, this is only a snapshot of the much larger group of people intermittently rough sleeping.[92] In London alone, the Combined Homelessness and Information Network counted 13,325 different people rough sleeping between April 2022 and June 2023, about half of them for the first time.[93] Jasmine Basran, Policy and Public Affairs Manager at Crisis, said: 'Unfortunately, the trends aren't that surprising and reflect that the overall housing crisis has affected all parts of the country, particularly places that aren't traditionally thought of in this way.'[94]

Aneisha Beveridge, Head of Research at Hamptons estate agents, commented that rents for new lettings were increasing fastest, at 12 per cent in the year to August 2023, the largest increase on record. The average asking price was then £1,304. In London, a 17 per cent year-on-year rise had taken the average rent on newly let properties to £2,332 a month. Each passing month, she explained, had ushered in 'a new rental market record',[95] adding that new let rents across Britain had increased more in 2022/2023 than they did between 2015 and 2019.

These rent rises came, of course, on top of increases in the general cost of living, with families not able to keep their homes warm and feed themselves. In a survey of 11,000 people, flatmate finding service, Spare Room, discovered that a third of the UK's private renting households are spending half or more of their take-home pay on rent.[96]

According to the Tory Government's figures, loss of private tenancy, including through the landlord selling or re-letting the property or increasing the rent, was the largest single cause of homelessness in the first three months of 2023, affecting nearly 40 per cent more households than the year before. The number of privately renting households put at risk of homelessness increased by about a quarter. With a lockdown-era ban on such evictions lifted in 2021, over 24,000 households were kicked out of their homes by Section 21 no-fault evictions, about a 20 per cent increase over the previous year.[97]

The major factor driving up rents has been the Bank of England's interest rate rises, increasing the cost of mortgage repayments and prompting landlords to pass on the costs to their tenants or to sell up – reducing the supply of rental properties and jacking up rates even further.

Ben Beadle, CEO of the National Residential Landlords Association, pointed out that while there were no signs yet of a mass exodus of landlords from the market, anecdotally 'more people are selling than buying and more people are saying that they are going to sell than invest', giving the example of someone whose mortgage was increasing from £800 to £1,500, a £700 rent increase that they couldn't pass on to renters.[98]

According to research commissioned by the BBC, there were then 20 viewing requests per available property, up from six in 2019, while property website Zoopla reported that the number of rental properties listed on its site was 33 per cent lower than before the pandemic and had flatlined. Renters have practically no protection against these surging costs. Local Housing Allowance, social support payments available to the poorest households, was frozen in 2016. Analysis from Zoopla found that just 5 per cent of rents advertised across Britain in the first quarter of 2023 could be fully met by LHA payments.[99]

8

Rishi Sunak's Fiscal and Industrial Austerity: Cutting Social Expenditure and the War against the Unions (2022–2023)

Introduction

As noted in Chapter 7, by 2022, inflation, higher taxes and low wage growth meant that workers in the UK had seen their living standards decline at the fastest rate in the post-war period. Starting in June 2022, during Johnson's second premiership and continuing in Liz Truss's brief period in office (6 September to 25 October 2022), a series of strikes took place in the UK, as workers walked out over pay, conditions and threatened redundancies. Paul Nowak, the General Secretary of the Trades Union Congress (TUC), recognizing the Tory Government's decision to go for fiscal austerity, said that instead of recognizing the huge pressure households were under, the Government had chosen to make millions poorer by holding down public sector pay: 'It is little surprise that workers are having to take strike action to defend their living standards. They have been pushed to breaking point.'[1] In May, members of the Rail, Maritime and Transport Union (RMT) at Network Rail and 15 train operators had announced the launching of a campaign of industrial action.[2] RMT General Secretary Mick Lynch, who was to become a central figure in workers' fightback against fiscal and industrial austerity, said when the decision to go ahead with the first strike was confirmed:

> Today's overwhelming endorsement by railway workers is a vindication of the union's approach and sends a clear message that members want a decent pay rise, job security and no compulsory redundancies. Our NEC will now meet to discuss a timetable for strike action from mid-June, but we sincerely hope ministers will encourage the employers to

return to the negotiating table and hammer out a reasonable settlement with the RMT.[3]

Ministers, who were determined to implement industrial austerity – to take on the unions – as well as fiscal austerity had no intention of encouraging a 'return to the negotiating table' and discussing 'a reasonable settlement', and the RMT action began on 15 June 2022. This heralded what was to be a future figure of 2.4 million days of various strikes over 2022 as a whole, the highest annual figure since 4.1 million days taken up with strikes in 1989 at the tail end of Thatcher's Government.[4] On 21 June, over 40,000 rail workers and 10,000 London Underground RMT members took part in the first strike, which was a national one.[5] On BBC TV, the night before, Lynch pointed out that National Rail handed statutory redundancy notices to the union after it briefly left talks to confirm that strikes would go ahead.[6]

In a clear indication that he was ready to see the dispute rumble on rather than give ground, Johnson told a meeting of his cabinet: 'We need, I'm afraid, everybody – and I say this to the country as a whole – we need to get ready to stay the course to head off public sector pay hikes which would plunge the UK into an inflationary spiral.'[7] Claiming to be speaking on behalf of railway workers, as well as the travelling public, Johnson added:

> [B]ecause these reforms, these improvements in the way we run our railways, are in the interests of the travelling public, they will help to cut costs for fare payers up and down the country. But they're also in the interests of the railways, of railway workers and their families, because otherwise if we don't do this, these great, great companies, this great industry will face further financial pressure; it will go bust and the result will be they have to hike up the costs of tickets still further, so that people don't use the railways at all or use them much less than they used to.[8]

One of the 'reforms' being proposed, the closure of station ticket offices was opposed by 60 per cent of the people, according to a YouGov poll.[9] Another is the extremely dangerous company proposal to move to driver-only operated trains. Having no guards on trains poses serious safety considerations and discriminates against disabled and vulnerable passengers.

Johnson accused 'union barons' of causing 'all sorts of unnecessary aggravations' to people trying to get to work and schoolchildren sitting exams, while unions accused Johnson of pursuing a 'race to the bottom' on pay as they realized the Tory Government agenda and that Johnson was setting the scene for months of confrontation with striking workers.[10] TUC General Secretary Frances O'Grady told the *Independent* that the Government's approach would cause 'widespread hardship' among working families and damage the economy by suppressing consumer demand.[11]

Johnson's official spokesperson warned that generous pay rises in the public sector would become 'embedded in the labour market', sending a signal to private companies that to make similar offers would trigger an inflationary spiral that would hit the real value of everyone's pay packet.[12]

But O'Grady said:

> Britain is in the middle of the worst cost of living crisis in generations. The last thing working families need right now is a race to the bottom on pay. Holding down wages in the public sector – to keep pay awards lower in the private sector – will cause widespread hardship. And it will suck demand out of our economy by depressing consumer spending. It's also jarring to hear the prime minister call for nurses, teachers and other public sector key workers to tighten the belts when he's looking to tear up the limits on City bosses' pay.[13]

Setting a precedent for what was to follow, Transport Secretary Grant Shapps kept out of the dispute, suggesting it would mean ministers would undermine and disrupt the process if Government intervened.[14] A press release by the International Transport Workers' Federation (ITF) on 24 June revealed that over 100 global transport unions, from 52 countries, representing 20 million workers, had written to Shapps, urging him to meet with striking UK unions.[15] The letter expressed shock that 'the UK Government is set to impose cuts to railway services and infrastructure projects'.[16] Stephen Cotton, ITF General Secretary, commented:

> The government pumped in millions to keep private companies afloat, the workers kept the system moving. During the pandemic the Secretary of State for Transport praised rail workers as 'true heroes', yet the first reaction we see as we come out of the crisis – as the cost of living crisis deepens and UK inflation hits a 40-year high – is making the same workers take the hit. Grant Shapps must realise that … if he remains unwilling to even speak with national unions, what hope does he think his government will have when it comes to engaging international unions as part of the government's 'Global Britain' agenda? … [S]ustainable economic recovery from the pandemic … must include long-term sustainable funding for National Rail and TfL [Transport for London]. Refusal to come to the table will squander this for the sake of politics.[17]

ITF President Paddy Crumlin added:

> Come to the table and treat the transport workers of the UK with the respect and dignity that he himself has declared they deserve. Or continue to contradict himself and his government and betray the

workers it celebrated months ago and purports to represent to instead line the pockets of the millionaire rail bosses.[18]

Commenting on the success of the strike, Lynch said:

> Today's turnout at picket lines has been fantastic and exceeded expectations in our struggle for job security, defending conditions and a decent pay rise. Our members will continue the campaign and have shown outstanding unity in pursuit of a settlement to this dispute. RMT members are leading the way for all workers in this country who are sick and tired of having their pay and conditions slashed by a mixture of big business profits and government policy.[19]

Numerous other rail transport strikes by the RMT and other unions representing rail workers and London underground and overground workers, as well as bus workers, dock workers, lorry (truck) drivers and shunters, barristers and postal workers followed. Commenting on the strikes in September 2022, a couple of weeks since she became Prime Minister, following the demise of Johnson (see Chapter 7), Truss told striking workers, 'Get back to work', doubling down on her pledge to bring in measures to limit industrial action within 30 days of coming to power, after the plan was halted by a mourning period, and the suspension of strikes in the aftermath of Queen Elizabeth's death on 8 September.[20] Truss admitted that the 30-day deadline may need to be pushed back to as late as the end of November (unbeknown to her, of course, she would be gone by then).[21] Kwarteng, then Chancellor, and Rees-Mogg, then Business Secretary, backed the call for weakening workers' power.[22] It should be reiterated here that, as argued in Chapter 2, from a Marxist perspective, austerity may be seen as a deliberate act of class warfare from above, rather than flawed economic policy.

Sunak becomes Prime Minister and immediately signals more austerity

As we saw in Chapter 5, Rishi Sunak became Prime Minister on 25 October 2022, following Truss' resignation. He automatically got the job after Johnson and Mordaunt, then Leader of the House of Commons, dropped out of the contest and Sunak passed the 100-nomination threshold, leaving him as the only remaining candidate. This meant that Tory Party members did not get to vote. On 25 October, Sunak gave his first speech as Prime Minister. He began by stating, 'Right now our country is facing a profound economic crisis.'[23] He went on to pay tribute to his predecessor, Liz Truss, and her noble aim of improving growth, but immediately followed this with, 'but some mistakes were made',[24] and that he had been elected in part 'to fix them'.[25] He went on to signal more austerity as the fix:

> I will place economic stability and confidence at the heart of this government's agenda. This will mean difficult decisions to come. … There are always limits, more so now than ever, but I promise you this. I will bring that same compassion to the challenges we face today. The government I lead will not leave the next generation, your children and grandchildren, with a debt to settle that we were too weak to pay ourselves. I will unite our country, not with words, but with action.[26]

As we shall see, the reality of his austerity programme involved redistributing wealth by transfer to capitalist enterprise and the already rich, limiting workers' pay, attempting to crush the unions, and neglecting and undermining the Welfare State.

Sunak claimed that the mandate the Tories got at the 2019 election (a landslide victory and a majority of 80 seats) 'unites all of us'.[27] He went on, 'So I stand here before you ready to lead our country into the future. To put your needs above politics.'[28] Sunak concluded, 'We will create a future worthy of the sacrifices so many have made and fill tomorrow, and everyday thereafter with hope.'[29] We will shortly see how all this rhetoric translates into actual policy towards the working class: not unity, but class warfare from above; Tory politics above need; despair rather than hope.

Sunak's class background

Given the centrality of social class in the decision to implement austerity, at this point it is pertinent to dwell briefly on Sunak's class background. A year after the start of his premiership, in October 2023, voters had checked Sunak out, realizing he was an 'upper-class' politician leading the political party which is most out of touch with the general public and which most represents the 'elite'.[30] He had used his 2023 Annual Conference speech on 4 October to claim that only the Conservatives could stand up to 'vested interests' in the country. He also attempted to paint himself as a child of relatively humble beginnings, while Braverman, then Home Secretary, had accused the Labour Party of representing the 'luxury beliefs' of a remote metropolitan elite.[31] In reality, Sunak leads a life of luxury and has a penchant for private helicopter rides. *The Sunday Times* 'Rich List' puts his and his wife's wealth at an immense £730 million.[32] He is married to Akshata Murthy, who is heir to a fortune of billions.[33] Sunak's father was a GP and his mother a pharmacist who went on to buy and run her own pharmacy in Southampton. He had an elite private education at several preparatory schools, before attending one of the UK's most expensive elite schools,

Winchester College (where, as of 2024, fees for boarding pupils are £49,152 per annum.[34] For comparison, the average annual wage is £34.900).[35] Some of Sunak's supporters claimed he attended the elite school on a scholarship, but he confirmed to Channel 4 that he did not receive a scholarship and that his parents paid the fees.[36]

In July 2022, the right-libertarian internet magazine *Spiked*'s chief politics writer, Brendan O'Neill, wrote an article in the Tory-supporting *Spectator* entitled, 'Of course Rishi Sunak doesn't have any working-class friends'.[37] O'Neill is referring to a 2001 clip from a BBC series called 'Middle Classes: Their Rise and Sprall' that had resurfaced. In it, Sunak stated, 'I have friends who are aristocrats, I have friends who are upper class, I have friends who are working class … well, not working class.' O'Neill argues that, 'It's the way he swiftly corrects himself when he says he has working-class mates that has got people going. It's the speediest of self-corrections. It's like he suddenly thinks to himself: "Oh God, no – I don't associate with *those* people".'[38] While O'Neill quite rightly believes that it is the policies that matter, not who you mix with, like all Tories, Sunak's polices serve the interests of the capitalist class, of which he is so proudly a member. As we are about to see, Sunak's love of capitalism and lack of friends who are working class is accompanied by a ruthless assault on that class, as part of the ongoing Tory agenda of fiscal and industrial austerity.

On Sunak's first day in office, 25 October 2022, lorry drivers and shunters, represented by the Unite union, undertook 11 days of strike action.[39] This was a follow-up to strikes in August and September, after dairy company Mülller imposed changes to employees' rosters that would result in working at least one day every weekend. This was after the company had signed an agreement with Unite committing to no roster changes.[40] Strikes continued throughout Sunak's premiership. From June 2022 to December 2023, some 5.05 million days are estimated to have been spent in labour disputes in the UK, the highest total for any 19-month period for more than 30 years, since 5.34 million days were taken up with strikes from July 1989 to January 1991.[41]

Hunt's autunm budget, 2022

On 17 November 2022, Chancellor Hunt presented his autumn budget. Sunak and Hunt sought to put into practice their promises to soothe the markets and return financial credibility to the UK.[42] Hunt set out a £55 billion package of tax hikes and spending cuts. As Chakrabortty reminds us, this heralded the third major wave of modern Tory austerity since 2010, the second being the cuts made by Sunak when Chancellor as the pandemic eased, and each has 'been about disciplining poor people and protecting the rich'. Each has also come with a fresh wave of authoritarianism.[43] Chakrabortty gives the 2022 Police, Crime, Sentencing and Courts Act as an example (see

Chapter 5). As he puts it, 'First they stole our money, then they robbed our right to protest. And now they are taking away our right to strike too.'[44] He goes on, referring to the Strikes (Minimum Service Levels) Act, 'the very same prime minister who just days ago stood on the steps of Downing Street and promised "integrity and accountability" is pressing ahead with legal attacks on the rights of workers to take industrial action – even allowing drafted-in agency staff to break strikes'.[45] Drawn up by the former Business Secretary Jacob Rees-Mogg, the Act eventually became law in July 2023, and allows bosses in health, education, fire, ambulance, rail and nuclear commissioning to sue unions and sack employees if 'minimum service levels' are not met.[46]

Contra the many commentators who make the case that there are nice Tories and nasty ones,[47] Chakrabortty coins a new term for Tory austerity and stresses, correctly in my view, that we are facing new dangers, and should:

> not be fooled that there is a pre-Brexit nice, liberal Toryism trying to get out from underneath the pulverising post-2016 draconian monster. Sunak, who as chancellor made an annual £1,000 cut to universal credit just as the cost of living emergency took grip, is cut from the very same cloth as Braverman, who wants to clamp down on 'tofu-eating wokerati' climate protesters for something as trivial as making too much noise. They are not different breeds of Conservative, let alone rival ideologues. They both protect the interests of the wealthy, the company bosses and mega asset-owners against the rest of us. Picture brutal metal studs embedded in the sole of a shiny black Oxford brogue: that is the form of government we face now. Let us call it *authoritarian austerity* [emphasis added].[48] Austerity is a one-sided class war, conducted in numbers and defended by economists' jargon.[49]

The first national nurses' strike

On 15 December 2022, nurses walked out over pay and working conditions and the state of the National Health Service (NHS). Confirming that the strike, their first *national* strike, was a major challenge to both industrial and fiscal austerity, the Royal College of Nursing (RCN) issued the following statement:

> Today ... up to 100,000 nursing staff are taking part in strikes in England, Northern Ireland and Wales. ... We're campaigning for a pay rise to overcome years of real-terms pay cuts[50] and to protect patient safety by allowing the NHS to recruit and retain the nursing staff it desperately needs.[51]

After pointing out that Tory Health Secretary, Steve Barclay, and other ministers had repeatedly declined to open formal negotiations, and also underlining the fact that the strike was a response to both fiscal and industrial austerity, RCN General Secretary and Chief Executive Pat Cullen stated:

> The NHS is in crisis, the nursing profession can't take any more, our loved ones are already suffering. ... We are committed to our patients and always will be. We're campaigning for a pay rise to overcome years of real-terms pay cuts and to protect patient safety by allowing the NHS to recruit and retain the nursing staff it desperately needs.[52]

Widespread strike action erupts at the start of the new year

At the start of the new year, strike action closed more than half of schools across England and Wales. On 1 February 2023 striking workers from participating unions held rallies in cities including Bristol, Brighton, Birmingham and London, involving teachers, university staff, rail workers, civil servants[53] and actors. The Tory Government was as intransigent as ever.[54] When Sunak was asked if he would negotiate with public sector workers, he replied instead by calling on Labour to condemn the teachers' strikes as 'wrong', telling MPs that children 'deserve to be in school today, being taught'.[55]

At the same time, Mick Lynch told a rally in London: 'We are the working class, and we are back. We are here, we are demanding change, we refuse to be bought, and we are going to win for our people on our terms.'[56] Downing Street's stance remained unchanged by the strikes, with Sunak's official spokesperson offering no new initiatives to unblock a process that, on account of the Government's determination to impose industrial austerity, remained at an impasse.[57]

Hunt's March 2023 budget: get the workers back to work; and billions for the rich

Budget day saw Chancellor Hunt focus attention on £5 billion of childcare spending and £4 billion in pension tax giveaways, when the real story was a more than £80 billion collapse in household incomes by March 2025,[58] the biggest fall in spending power for 70 years as the surging cost of living ate into wages.[59] The budget also focused on prompting those who have left their jobs to return to the workforce, and boosting business investment.[60]

Get the workers working again

Thirty hours of free childcare for working parents in England, expanded to cover one and two-year-olds, were rolled out in April 2024. In addition:

- Families on Universal Credit would receive childcare support up-front instead of in arrears, with the £646-a-month per child cap raised to £951.
- £600 'incentive payments' were for those becoming childminders, and rules were relaxed in England to let childminders look after more children.
- There was a new fitness-to-work testing regime to qualify for health-related benefits.
- A new voluntary employment scheme for disabled people in England and Wales, called Universal Support, was established.
- There were tougher requirements to look for work and increased job support for lead child carers on Universal Credit.
- £63 million for programmes to encourage retirees over 50 back to work, 'returnerships' and skills boot camps.[61]

Billions for the rich

At the same time, business investment is boosted by companies being now able to deduct investment in new machinery and technology to lower their taxable profits, and tax breaks and other benefits for 12 new Investment Zones across the UK, funded by £80 million each over five years.[62] A 'give away' of £4 billion to the richest people in the country is enabled by scrapping the lifetime allowance limit on pension tax benefits – previously set at just over £1 million – and raising the annual pension contribution which can be made before it is taxed from £40,000 to £60,000 – roughly double the average salary.[63]

Sunak's (anti-) Strikes (Minimum Service Levels) Act 2023

The Strikes (Minimum Service Levels) Act 2023 became law in July, following a lengthy fight in the House of Lords,[64] continuing the raft of anti-union legislation started by Thatcher in 1980 with the Employment Act.[65] It should be made clear that the Act is not about preventing disruption to the public in a strike. It is about preventing workers through their unions pushing back, as they had been, particularly since December 2022, against low wages and poor conditions. It is an attempt to curb resistance to fiscal and industrial austerity. The six sectors covered by the Act are health, fire and rescue, education, transport, nuclear decommissioning and border security.[66] Millions work in these sectors, including many of the applauded workers who kept the country running during the pandemic,[67] which shows the Tory Government hypocrisy of all the televised clapping. The sectors involve most major unions. But in making regulations, though the Act requires ministers to consult whoever they believe to be appropriate, it does not require negotiation (or even consultation) with the unions – or even employers – directly affected by the Act.[68]

Commenting on the draconian nature of the Act, Keith Ewing and John Hendy, President and Chair respectively of the Institute of Employment Rights, note that the UK has the most restrictive laws on trade unions in the Western world, but 'never before have our unions been obliged to act as enforcers on behalf of employers and the State, as is now required by the Strikes (Minimum Service Levels) Act 2023'.[69] Self-evidently, they go on, the Act violates the right to strike, a right established by many international treaties which the UK has ratified. Parliament's Joint Committee on Human Rights, they conclude, made this clear at an early stage in the parliamentary life of the Bill.[70] The TUC has reported the Tory Government to the United Nations watchdog on workers' rights – the International Labour Organization – over the legislation.[71] TUC General Secretary, Paul Novak, vowed at the end of 2023, 'when the first worker is sacked for refusing to work on a strike day, we'll fight it in workplaces and on the picket lines. This movement will fight it every single day until it is repealed'.[72] Labour has pledged to repeal the law within 100 days of taking power.[73]

Five years after Alston: extreme poverty has increased

In November 2023, the month after the cap on bankers' bonuses was removed,[74] and five years on from Alston's 2018 report where he discovered for himself the callousness of austerity inflected on the working class by the Tories (see Chapter 6), UN Special Rapporteur on Extreme Poverty and Human Rights, Olivier De Schutter, Alston's successor, visited the UK. Once again, the levels of poverty in the country were denounced.[75] De Schutter told reporters in 2023:

> If you look at the price of housing, electricity, the very high levels of inflation for food items over the past couple of years, I believe that the £85 a week for adults [Universal Credit benefit payment] is too low to protect people from poverty, and that is in violation of article nine of the international covenant on economic, social and cultural rights.[76]

He went on, 'It's simply not acceptable that we have more than a fifth of the population in a rich country such as the UK at risk of poverty today.'[77] De Schutter concluded: 'The warning signals that Philip Alston gave five years ago were not acted upon. There's a huge gap, which is increasingly troubling, between the kinds of indicators the government chooses to assess its progress on one hand, and the lived experience of people living in poverty.'[78] De Shutter's findings five years later were that 'Things have got worse.'[79] He argues that we should aim at creating a much more inclusive economy rather than one 'that creates wealth for the elites and particularly for the shareholders of the largest corporations'.[80]

Another report around the same time as De Schutter's, from the Joseph Rowntree Foundation, entitled *Destitution in the UK 2023* (a follow-up to *Destitution in the UK 2018* also discussed in Chapter 6) painted the devastating picture of the life endured by millions in 21st-century Britain.[81] The report used a definition of destitution that encompassed all those unable to afford to meet their most basic physical needs to stay warm, dry, clean and fed, that had deep and profound impacts on health, mental health and people's prospects, and, of course, also put strain on already overstretched services.[82]

Under the heading 'Accelerating Destitution', the authors write: 'Destitution is no longer a rare occurrence in the UK. Around 1.8 million households were destitute in the UK at some point over the course of 2022. These households contained around 3.8 million people, of whom around a million were children.'[83] Some minority ethnic communities were disproportionately affected by destitution. In particular, the rate of destitution among Black, Black British, Caribbean or African households in the UK was three times their population share.[84] Migrant workers were hugely disproportionately affected. A fifth of those in destitution in 2020 were migrants and almost half a million migrant households fell into destitution in 2022.[85]

The report also noted that between 2017 and 2022 the overall number of households experiencing destitution more than doubled, with this extreme level of poverty having increased by over 60 per cent between 2019 and 2022. Over half of destitute households had a weekly income of less than £85.[86]

The causes are familiar: extremely low incomes, the rising cost of living, high levels of debt and a punitive social welfare system. Significantly, the report concluded that such 'horrifying levels of destitution' are the result of official political choices. Paul Kissack, Chief Executive of the Joseph Rowntree Foundation, commented: 'The government is not helpless to act: it is choosing not to.'[87] The report's authors condemned the abandonment of basic social functions to the third sector: 'relying on charity to fulfil what should be the responsibility of the government is morally unacceptable'.[88]

Also, in November 2023, Human Rights Watch reported that the Trussell Trust, the largest UK-wide food bank network, had given out 16 per cent more emergency food parcels in 2023 than in 2022, and 116 per cent more than in 2018. The main recipients were the burgeoning ranks of the working poor.[89]

Bed poverty

A study by Barnardo's, a charity that helps hundreds of thousands of children and young people across the UK, published in September 2023, revealed that more than one million children in the UK sleep on the floor, share a bed with parents/carers or siblings, or sleep in inappropriate beds and/or without covers.[90] Barnardo's says that 'bed poverty' is increasing. Understandably, it leaves them tired, anxious and finding it difficult to concentrate at school.[91] More than 204,000 families said their children's bed or bedding was mouldy or damp because putting the heating on was too expensive and more than 187,000 said they couldn't afford to wash or dry bedding.[92]

In the words of a mother of two, Shelley Nicholson, 'People take it for granted everyone has a bed.'[93] Whereas for her, a bed is a luxury. Last winter she slept on a sofa in her front room that had no heat, with her daughters sharing a double mattress on the bare concrete floor. On Universal Credit, Nicholson loses about a fifth of her £1,000-a-month post-rent income through benefit deductions and, ironically, the bedroom tax. This applies if you are of working age, 16 up to retirement age, and renting from a local authority, a registered housing association or other registered social landlord. The tax restricts the size of accommodation for which Universal Credit or housing benefit can cover the rental costs, based on the number of people in your household.[94]

Barnardo's points out that up to 70 per cent of the poverty support grants administered by its staff goes to providing beds and bedding for families in poverty.[95] Meagre social-security benefit levels and policies such as the two-child benefit limit that restricts welfare payments to larger families in an attempt to force parents/carers to find work, has failed to increase employment levels, and has left hundreds of thousands of households in poverty.[96] Barnardo's argues that the Government should invest properly in England's threadbare council-run crisis support schemes, which have been 'savaged by austerity'.[97]

Hunt's autumn statement, 22 November 2023: more painful austerity than ever

In what was one of his last economic announcements before the 2024 General Election, on 22 November 2023, Hunt announced tax cuts for workers and businesses worth £20 billion in an 'autumn statement for growth'. This included a reduction in National Insurance from 12 per cent to 10 per cent. For the average worker, this will mean an extra £9 a week. However, as is very often the case, the Tories were giving with one hand but taking back a lot more with the other,[98] as a result of the previously announced freezing of personal income tax thresholds until 2028.[99] For businesses, it entailed a permanent extension to 'full expensing' – a policy that allows companies to claim tax relief on investment, worth more than £10 billion a year.[100] Hunt described this as the 'largest business tax cut in modern British history'.[101] Unsurprisingly, it received a great welcome from UK businesses.[102]

As Partington, Kiran Stacey and Phillip Inman argue, 'Sunak's government has set the country on course for a "more painful" austerity drive after the next general election than during the decade of belt-tightening under George Osborne',[103] since the day after the autumn statement, the Institute for Fiscal Studies (IFS) proclaimed the £20 billion package of tax cuts announced by Hunt was almost entirely funded by swingeing real-terms reductions to public spending planned from 2025, after the General Election.[104] Whereas Osborne made his cuts after a decade of big spending increases, IFS Director Paul Johnson reminds us that Hunt, or his successor, 'will have no such luxury'.[105] Hunt made little provision for the allocation of funding for public services after the current three-year spending review period, which expires in March 2025, also confirming real-terms cuts to public investment – used to finance the building of schools, hospitals and roads – equivalent to £20 billion a year.[106] Echoing multimillionaire Tim Gurner, who complained that his workers had pulled back on productivity (mentioned at the end of Chapter 2), Ben Zaranko, a senior research economist at the IFS, said: 'Unless you can find some magnificent, heroic productivity improvements in those areas, it seems likely the range and quality of public services would have to suffer.'[107]

Conclusion: Hostility and Austerity as Interrelated Concepts – Some Examples and Some Solutions

In the Introduction, I argued that, while hostility and austerity are dealt with in separate chapters of the book for analytical clarity, they are not mutually exclusive, especially if we widen each beyond their restricted associations with the racist 'hostile environment' and a specific economic *policy*, respectively. In the chapters, I have concentrated on how hostility impacted those it was aimed at, as did austerity affect its targets. Hostility, however, as in the 'hostile environment', is also austere; and austerity is itself inherently hostile. The two are interrelated. While this has been demonstrated throughout sometimes implicitly, in the first half of the Conclusion I provide some explicit and clear-cut examples of ways in which the hostile environment inevitably led to austerity and of how austerity hit at those at whom the hostile environment was aimed. With respect to the former, I analyse the hostile environment's impact on the Windrush generation, and at two examples of the dire conditions in detention centres. As far as austerity affecting those targeted with the hostile environment is concerned, I focus on the Grenfell Tower fire and at the upsurge in racism, witnessed by increased inequality and hate crime, specifically on the link between major cuts in welfare payments and this rapid rise. This is, as I argue, exacerbated by the constraints on antiracist and community organizing, also the results of austerity. This again reinforces the reality of the interconnection between hostility and austerity. In the second half of the Conclusion, I explore what might be done immediately to make the UK less austere and hostile for the working class in general and for minority ethnic communities and other racialized people.

Hostile environment policies causing austerity: some examples

The Windrush scandal

I pointed out in Chapter 3 how thousands of legally resident members of the Windrush generation had been placed in a precarious situation through absolutely no fault of their own, that they had lost their homes and their jobs and had been refused healthcare, pensions and access to social security and, crucially, could not understand why they were told they did not have the necessary documentation, when they considered themselves British. I also stressed that a target-led approach by immigration officers led them to focus on the Windrush generation, believing they were easier to detain and remove. I further explained in Chapter 4, when Johnson was Prime Minister, that in January 2022, four Windrush generation descendants were refused the compensation which was promised to their forebears. I also referred again to the austerity people were experiencing, being in severe financial and personal difficulties, with some not able to find work, and others in temporary accommodation, living with family or facing eviction because of bills they could not afford to pay. I concluded my discussion of the Windrush generation in that chapter by mentioning the minuscule number of Home Office staff who attended an online training programme on the legacy of empire and colonialism. Returning to the Windrush scandal in Chapter 5, when Sunak was in office, I provided some details from a leaked Home Office report attributing the scandal to 30 years of racist immigration legislation whose purpose was to limit the UK's population of people of colour, and concluded with a quote from Labour MP, Dawn Butler. In her words, '[t]he Windrush scandal was just an element of a wider state-sanctioned hostility' that had for years been directed at Black people.[1]

In September 2024, the Home Office was forced to release the suppressed Home Office report by a tribunal judge.[2] Wendy Williams argued that 'officials' poor understanding of Britain's colonial history' was one of the causes of people wrongly arrested, detained and deported as well as the other miseries inflicted on them. Diane Abbott, who had tried without success to get it issued in 2022, commented: 'It is a disgrace that the Home Office tried not to release this report. They could have released it at any time and shouldn't have waited for a campaigner [James Coombs] to go to court. It is as if they are trying to bury the whole history of immigration.'[3] She added that she hoped that the report would now be widely read.[4]

Detention centres

Two of the most notorious detention centres are Yarl's Wood and the *Bibby Stockholm*. The former opened in 2001 for adult women and adult family groups awaiting immigration clearance; the latter opened for people seeking asylum when Rishi Sunak was Prime Minister.

Yarl's Wood

In March 2018, under Theresa May' premiership, the then Deputy Leader of the Green Party Amelia Womack wrote about her visit to Yarl's Wood

Immigration Removal Centre: 'I'll never forget my first visit to ... one of our Government's brutal and inhumane detention centres.'[5] She had joined one of the many protests that gathered in front of the building, 'making fleeting moments of contact with the incarcerated women'.[6] She went on, 'while we were separated by bricks and barbed wire, we were united in solidarity'.[7] At the time, over 100 women there were on hunger strike. The incarcerated women were living 'under fear of their guards', 'separated from their families', she continued, and 'never knowing when their hell would be over' because 'unlike every other country in Europe, we lock people up indefinitely, just because of their immigration status'.[8] One woman she spoke to did not know 'if she'd be forcibly removed and deported from the country on one of the charter flights that sporadically take women from the centre with no warning'.[9] Their demands were eminently reasonable requests for basic human rights:

- a 28-day limit to detention;
- adequate healthcare and mental health provision;
- a fair bail process; and
- for the Home Office to recognize rape as torture.[10]

The Home Office refused to meet them.[11]

Three years earlier, when May was Home Secretary, she was accused by the then Shadow Home Secretary, Yvette Cooper, of allowing the 'state-sponsored abuse of women' at Yarl's Wood after a Channel 4 investigation uncovered 'guards ignoring self-harm and referring to inmates in racist terms'.[12] The TV channel filmed Serco guards describing various detained women as 'black bitch', 'animals' and 'evil', with one guard filmed commenting: 'They are all slashing their wrists, apparently. Let them slash their wrists. ... It's attention-seeking.'[13] The previous year, May had extended Serco's contract to run Yarl's Wood despite allegations of abuse, sexual exploitation, rape and self-harm.[14]

The Bibby Stockholm

In Chapter 5, I wrote about the austere conditions on the *Bibby Stockholm* migrant barge under the Sunak Government when Braverman was Home Secretary, including a worsening of food quality and quantity (shortages for those at the end of the queue).[15] Several inmates told the *Guardian* that it was like being in prison.[16] Standing behind 15-foot metal fencing and two sets of guarded gates, with up to six people packed into each of the beige-walled rooms, most cabins featured an austere two-person bunk bed, desk, metal wardrobe and en-suite bathroom, with the door just an arm's length away from the bedframe.[17]

Over 60 charities, including Refugee Action, Refugee Council, Care4Calais and Refugees at Home, had demanded the immediate closure of the *Bibby Stockholm*.[18] In a letter to the *Guardian*, they stated:

> For those on board, the Bibby Stockholm feels like a prison. It is cramped, restrictive and segregated. The barge is no place to accommodate people who have fled violence, persecution and torture, many of whom are traumatised and isolated. They are unable to get the help and specialist support they need. Their mental health has deteriorated and some have felt suicidal. While people on board pay an appalling price, the government is paying £22.5m to operate the barge. These funds should be spent on providing people seeking asylum with safe housing in the community. It is also vital that the government launches an independent inquiry into the death so that lessons are learned and those responsible are held accountable. This country must never again house those who come to our shores seeking safety in such an inappropriate and inhumane place.[19]

In July 2024, the incoming Labour Government confirmed that the *Bibby Stockholm* was to be shut down from January 2025.[20]

Austerity specifically impacting those at whom the hostile environment is aimed

Increase in inequality among minority ethnic communities

In Chapter 6, I discussed Cameron's proclamation of a new 'age of austerity' heralded by the unleashing by Chancellor George Osborne of extreme and callous fiscal austerity. I spelt out the general impact of the draconian measures that included widespread poverty and misery, and that had a severely negative effect on health and life expectancy for the working class in general, as did the dismantling of the broader social safety net.

Among the hardest hit were people seeking asylum and migrants. In June 2019, the United Nations Human Rights Office of the High Commission issued a press release confirming that the UK Government's policies 'exacerbate discrimination, stoke xenophobic sentiment and further entrench racial inequality.'[21] In the report presented to the Human Rights Council in July, E. Tendayi Achiume, Special Rapporteur for racism, cited persistent racial disparities in, among other areas, 'education, employment, housing, health, surveillance, interactions with police, prosecutions, and incarceration'.[22] 'The structural socio-economic exclusion of racial and ethnic minority communities in the United Kingdom is striking', she said in her report, based on a fact-finding visit to the UK in April and May 2018. Expanding her concerns to other inequality issues, Achiume stated: '[N]otwithstanding the existence of a legal framework devoted to combating racial discrimination, the harsh reality is that race, ethnicity, religion, gender, disability status and related categories all continue to determine the life chances and well-being of people in Britain in ways that are unacceptable and, in many cases, unlawful.'[23] 'Reliable reports have shown that the austerity measures', she went on, 'have been disproportionately detrimental to members of racial and ethnic minority communities, who are also the hardest hit by unemployment'.[24] Moreover, Achiume pointed out that, at the same time, 'racial and ethnic minorities are overrepresented in criminal justice enforcement and underrepresented within the institutions that adjudicate crime and punishment'.[25] Achiume also argued that public and private actors have played 'dangerous roles in fuelling intolerance'.[26] 'Among them', she concluded, 'politicians and media outlets deserve special attention given the significant influence they command in society'.[27]

Upsurge in racism: hate crime

In an exhaustive empirical microeconometric study, Kerry Bray, Nils Braakmann and John Wildman, writing in the *Journal of Urban Economics*, come to the conclusion that the UK's austerity programme initiated in 2010 'led to increases in the number of racially or religiously motivated (RRM) crimes recorded in England and Wales'.[28] They begin their analysis by stressing that the substantial welfare cuts that were part of Cameron's new 'age of austerity' occurred alongside increasing anti-immigrant rhetoric and at a time of rising unemployment and economic hardship. Bray et al cite a speech by May in 2015, when Home Secretary, as an example (see also Chapters 3 and 5 of this book):

> Now I know there are some people who say, yes there are costs of immigration, but the answer is to manage the consequences, not reduce the numbers. But not all of the consequences can be managed, and doing so for many of them comes at a high price. We need to build 210,000 new homes every year to deal with rising demand. We need to find 900,000 new school places by 2024. And there are thousands of people who have been forced out of the labour market, still unable to find a job.[29]

Certain tabloid newspapers also contributed to the racist rhetoric, to a perception that the UK is over-populated, linking this to migrants 'having lots of children' and 'jumping the queue' for housing.[30] The cuts were implemented largely beginning April 2013, meaning that Government welfare spending decreased by around 16 per cent per person in real terms.[31]

However, this varied widely in different local authorities, the largest being up to 46 per cent, often in the poorest areas.[32] Bray et al demonstrate that for each £100 loss per working-age adult, 'racially' or religiously motivated crimes went up in England and Wales by approximately 5–6 per cent in 2013/2014 and 2014/2015.[33] These effects are large given a mean loss of £450 per working-age adult and survive multiple robustness checks. Using individual data, they find no evidence that these crimes were driven by increased anger of the benefit recipients per se but find evidence for a decline in community cohesion.[34]

Antiracist and community organizing under threat

From 2010, the voluntary and community sector underwent major changes. Cuts to public spending were accompanied by a neoliberal rhetoric that stressed that an 'oversized and over-centralised' public sector was 'crowding out' the private sector, and stressed the need for a local governance system that relied on the community sector to engage with public services.[35] This, in turn, enforced an agenda that civil society needs to become more entrepreneurial in order to make up for those losses.[36] Describing these changes, Mike Aiken notes how the post-war idea that voluntary organizations would be funded through grants in order to provide 'additionality' gave way to a model based on individual contracts,[37] with the voluntary and community sector having to fill gaps in state provision also to become 'active citizens', increasingly self-reliant and market-oriented.[38] This market orientation is further evidenced by the move from grant funding to contracts for pre-defined projects and by the introduction of Community Interest Companies. These are expected to fund themselves from a range of contracts while remaining a 'benefit to the community'.[39]

At the same time, the Equality Act of 2010 replaced previous anti-discrimination legislation in the workplace legislation with a single Act. While this was said to simplify the legal complexities, it has resulted in a 'dilution' of protections and a loss of resources.[40] In practice, this means that challenging racism (or other forms of discrimination) is discouraged.[41]

For Black and minority ethnic (BME)-led organizing, these changes have major implications. The language and proposed practice of 'active citizenship' and mainstreaming prioritizes 'integration' and a politicized concept of what makes a good citizen.[42] Moreover, this relates very much to the Tory ideology of anti-multiculturalism and the superiority of so-called 'British values', and attempts to render superfluous the realities of institutional and structural racism: if 'they' are made 'socially and culturally British' at a local level, all will be well. This rests on a racialized conception of 'community' and mitigates against the right for people to define themselves in relation to different communities living in the same area.⁴³ Thus, this resonates with Tory ideology in that:

> [A]usterity can act as an alibi for what are a series of revived practices that manage and undermine the most marginalized, and, contributes to the further diminution of race as a policy concern. It highlights how organizations and activists are encouraged to act as entrepreneurs and confront each other as competitors, rather than allies in a political struggle. This leads to a very real sense that solidarities are being deliberately ruptured in order to 'divide and conquer' and thus diminish collective organizing capacity.⁴⁴

A specific example of the interrelationships between racism and social class: Grenfell Tower

In Chapter 3, I pointed out that the Grenfell Tower fire in 2017 needs to be understood in terms of both racism and social class and that, of the 72 who died, the majority were people of colour and working class. I also noted that local people had no confidence in Martin Moore-Beck, who May appointed to chair the public inquiry, and that the traumatized families had asked for more diverse panel members. The Grenfell Tower Inquiry's final report was published on 4 September 2024. Kathrin Lauber, Claudia Fernandez de Cordoba Farini and Adelle Mansour, writing for Croakey Health Media, a not-for-profit organization, have provided a useful analysis of how political and economic systems, rather than the health and wellbeing of communities, impacted the Grenfell Tower disaster. The Tory Government deregulation agenda formed part of a wider austerity politics, characterized primarily by the erosion of public spending in areas such as local government, key services and health in pursuit of reduced deficit and economic growth. The push for deregulation and broader austerity politics is echoed in Cameron's 2012 New Year's resolution to 'kill off the health and safety culture for good',⁴⁵ thus reflecting 'a wider ideological shift towards prioritising economic liberalism over protections for public welfare'.⁴⁶

As Lauber et al put it, while, seven years on, the inquiry has finally concluded, exposing a series of catastrophic failures and decisions that led to the tragedy, 'the deeper issue lies in a political and economic system that, through austerity, has systematically devalued the lives of working-class and marginalised communities'.⁴⁷ Residents of the tower, that largely consisted of social housing, had been raising concerns about safety since at least 2010, 'but were met with inaction and neglect'.⁴⁸ The report concluded that the deadly blaze was 'the culmination of decades of failure by central government and other bodies in positions of responsibility in the construction industry to look carefully into the danger of incorporating combustible materials into the external walls of high-rise residential buildings and to act on the information available to them'.⁴⁹ The report documents Government decisions not to act on warnings about the inadequacy of fire safety regulations, companies' deception about the safety of their cladding and insulation materials, and a cavalier attitude towards fire safety by the Tenant Management Organization and contractors involved in the tower's refurbishment.⁵⁰

Lauber et al conclude: 'Preventing another Grenfell will require not just regulatory reforms, but systemic action to challenge the institutions that prioritise cost-cutting and profit over people.'⁵¹

Some immediate solutions

Immediate solutions are, first, to stop all austerity measures and instead to increase public spending and investment, put up taxes on the wealthy and big businesses, and properly regulate business and financial institutions. Second, all hostile environment policies should be removed and replaced with the humane and viable alternative safe routes to claim asylum. At the same time, citizenship should be provided for and compensation given to the Windrush generation to end the scandal. I will consider each in turn.

Stop all austerity measures

As we saw in Chapter 2, there is an increasing consensus among economists, both journalists and academics, that austerity does not work in its professed objective of bringing down inflation, reducing debt and boosting economic growth. In that chapter, I referred to Richard Partington of the *Guardian* as typical of the former and Mark Blyth as representing the latter. Blyth argues, as noted in that chapter, that austerity neither lowers debt nor improves economic growth. I also looked at the work of Clara Mattei who views austerity as a deliberate act of capitalist crisis management and class warfare from above whose aim is to redistribute wealth upwards even more, at the expense of the working class. At this, it is successful and *does* work. I have made my position clear that I favour Mattei's analysis. All austerity measures, I would maintain therefore, need to be halted immediately. There is simply no justification for it whether you are a mainstream economist or see more logic in a Marxist analysis, although it becomes obvious why the Tories favoured and adopted it.

Here are the views of left social democrat, Grace Blakeley, who argues correctly that there is nothing inevitable about more austerity, it is 'a deliberate decision to avoid confronting the powerful'.⁵² She suggests what could replace austerity. First, the Government should issue new debt to cover expenditure.⁵³ As long as that debt is used for productive purposes, such as education, expanding physical and social infrastructure, and promoting decarbonization, it will be recouped over the medium- to long-term.⁵⁴ Second, since the British state controls the UK's monetary system, the Government could manage inflation in much more targeted and effective ways through, for example, taxing the big corporations that have been profiteering through the cost-of-living crisis.⁵⁵

Blakeley then busts the neoliberal myth that if a government tries to raise taxes or impose new regulation, wealthy individuals and corporations will simply leave the country. This argument, she notes, always goes out the window when capital finds itself in crisis. For example, as demonstrated in Chapter 6, when the banks needed a bailout after 2008, the state was there to provide it.⁵⁶ Moreover, when asset markets failed to recover in the wake of this crisis, the state once again stepped up and when big businesses needed rescuing during the pandemic, the state was there to provide support. In that period, the state was even powerful enough to shut down the entire economy (see Chapter 7).⁵⁷ As she argues:

> Whenever anyone has attempted to resist the exercise of its power, similarly, it has become very clear quite how powerful the state really is. Whether imprisoning peaceful protesters or imposing brutal anti-union legislation, the British state has had no problem exerting extreme force against any groups that pose a threat to the status quo.⁵⁸

As discussed in the Postscript, this can also be applied to far-right protesters, in this case justifiably, when deemed necessary. Blakeley concludes, despite Labour Chancellor Rachel Reeves claiming that her aim would be to significantly reduce the amount the Government was spending on private consultants, KPMG (Klynveld, Peat, Marwick, Goerdeler), an international artificial intelligence and technology conglomerate, recently won a £223 million Government contract, the second largest contract the firm has ever won:⁵⁹

> Starmer would never admit it, but he has the power to raise public spending and investment, increase taxes on the wealthy and big businesses, and properly regulate big businesses and financial institutions. Instead, he will impose renewed austerity on those least able to bear it. Not because he has to, but because he wants to.⁶⁰

Remove all hostile environment policies

The Joint Council for the Welfare of Immigrants (JCWI) has insisted that hostile environment policies be removed in their entirety and the UK made a welcoming environment for all those affected by the policies, including members of the Windrush generation and their descendants.⁶¹ They rightly point out that the policies 'are designed to make life in the

UK unliveable for people without formal immigration status'. These are the JCWI's recommendations:

- Repeal the Right to Rent scheme, which was found by both the High Court and the Court of Appeal to cause racial discrimination in the private rental market.
- End Right to Work checks, which render people vulnerable to exploitation and trafficking, and make it harder for labour inspectorates to do their jobs effectively.
- Scrap the 'No Recourse to Public Funds' condition, which discriminates against women, disabled people as well as Black and Brown people, and pushes thousands into poverty and insecure housing.
- Roll back NHS charging and data-sharing regimes, which deter people from seeking healthcare, undermine public health measures and make it harder for healthcare workers to do their jobs.[62]

Provide safe routes

Analysis by the Refugee Council has found that three-quarters of those people who cross the Channel in small boats would be expected to be granted refugee status if their asylum claims were processed in the UK.[63] People arrive having fled the Taliban in Afghanistan, the wars in Syria and Sudan, and persecution in Iran and Eritrea. There are many reasons why some refugees will want to find safety in the UK, but the options for travelling safely through a formal immigration route are extremely limited. There is no one policy that will significantly reduce the number of Channel crossings, but providing safe alternatives to dangerous journeys must be part of the strategy.[64] Yet since the increase in people travelling by small boats, the provision of safe routes for refugees has reduced. Three-quarters of the world's refugees are hosted by low- and middle-income countries, and 70 per cent of refugees live in the countries neighbouring the one they have fled.[65] The UK can and should be doing much more to support those seeking asylum, and expanding safe routes to protection in the UK is a vital component of that.[66]

On the day I write this, in October 2024, nearly 1,000 migrants in 17 boats crossed the English Channel. The day before, four people died attempting to cross, including a two-year-old child who was 'trampled to death'.[67] As always, politicians blame 'evil' and/or 'criminal' gangs, without a word about Government responsibility for providing safe routes. Rightly so, there is widespread consensus that people should not be forced to risk their lives taking dangerous journeys to reach the UK to apply for asylum. The Tory Government's response, as detailed in this book, focused on increasingly regressive measures to try and deter people from making those journeys, including by effectively banning asylum through the Illegal Migration Act of 2023 (see Chapter 5). There has been far less energy put into creating safe alternatives that would give people another option.[68] Even after many calls for new safe routes and extending existing ones, the Sunak Government did neither, and instead undertook a review of safe routes.[69] Published in January 2024, it contained no commitments to enact either.

Three safe routes

The UK operates two main safe routes for refugees and their families – resettlement and refugee family reunion. Both routes have shrunk in recent years. Resettlement numbers have not returned to their pre-COVID-19 levels, with only 766 refugees resettled to the UK in the year ending September 2023.[70] While refugee family reunion visa grants have started to return to previous levels, the process is beset with delays and continues to be restrictive.[71]

The Refugee Council makes the case for three key safe routes to form part of any government's future policy: first, an expansion of resettlement; second, refugee family reunion; and third, the piloting of a new refugee visa that would allow people with a high likelihood of success to travel to the UK to submit an asylum claim.[72]

Currently, the only way to apply for asylum in the UK is to be physically present in the country. There is no way to apply for asylum from outside the UK.[73] As a result, the only ways to apply for asylum in the UK are to have entered on another type of visa, be a national of a country that doesn't require a visa to travel to the UK or to enter the UK irregularly. For most refugees, only the last of those options is possible.[74]

A humanitarian or refugee visa

A humanitarian visa or refugee visa would have the potential to offer a safe route to the UK for refugees who do not qualify for either resettlement or refugee family reunion. Such a scheme could allow people to travel to the UK to apply for asylum after having applied for a visa from a country neighbouring the country they have fled.[75] People who are granted a visa would then have their asylum application processed once they are in the UK. The asylum process would not be 'offshored',[76] as was the intention of the failed and now abandoned (by the incoming Labour Government in 2024) Rwanda scheme (see Chapters 4 and 5).

Ensure citizenship and further compensation to end the Windrush scandal

None of the policies that caused the Windrush scandal, the JCWI remind us, have been rolled back.[77] With respect to citizenship and compensation, as of 2024:

- 17,000 people have received documentation confirming their status or British citizenship (up to the end of March).
- 8,800 claims have been made for compensation, of which 2,600 have received payments (up to the end of July).[78]

Six years since the scandal came to light, there is an urgent need to confirm citizenship to all immediately and to pay substantial compensation to all affected now.

And finally ...

Having looked at some immediate and viable solutions to end austerity and the hostile environment, I now turn to some very brief comments on my own views on a longer-term solution. During a lifetime of ongoing studying, reading, writing and teaching about and being active in politics and the trade union movement, I become more and more convinced daily, especially in the context of the critical state of the contemporary world, that there is only one solution to end racism, exacerbated by the rightward march of the Tory Party, in the context of the global rise of the far right, and austerity, whereby the excessive greed of the ruling class that tries, usually successfully, to redistribute wealth ever upward in a relentless class war from above. This solution, I believe, is socialism. I mean a socialism that distributes wealth fairly and puts the people, not a capitalist elite, in control, a socialism that is antiracist and fully inclusive for *all*, a socialism that deals with climate change emergency and halts planetary destruction. It is my contention that only socialism has the potential to liberate the working class and to end poverty, deprivation and despair for good. Given the fourth industrial revolution[79] and the growth of artificial intelligence, this is now more feasible than ever before in the history of the planet, as long as the profit motive is removed from the development of both. There are countless texts on socialism, but none, to my knowledge, on the *various* ways to achieve it. This is the subject of a forthcoming book.[80] In the meantime, it is crucial and essential to immediately and urgently address the needs of the working class as a whole who have most felt the brunt of more than 14 years of Tory austerity.

Suffice it to say here that, while capitalism is a resilient and adjustable world force that has been very successful at maintaining its hegemony, the biggest impediment to the creation of socialism is not capital's resistance but its success in heralding capitalism's continuation as being the only option. And, as argued in Chapter 2, when citing the work of Clara Mattei, austerity is particularly effective in solidifying class relations, thus safeguarding the capitalist system. Therefore, as Alex Callinicos argued a quarter of a century ago, we need to break through the 'bizarre ideological mechanism' that seeks to convince us that '*every* conceivable alternative to the market' has been discredited by the collapse of the Soviet Union,[81] whereby 'the market' has been regenerated as 'a natural force unresponsive to human wishes'.[82] In the words of John McMurtry, capitalism presents itself as 'determining the future as surely as the laws of nature make tides rise to lift boats'.[83] Or, as Peter McLaren put it, capitalism is promoted 'as if it has now replaced the natural environment. It announces itself through its business leaders and politicians as coterminous with freedom, and indispensable to democracy such that any attack on capitalism as exploitative or hypocritical becomes an attack on world freedom and democracy itself'.[84] Callinicos concludes on a note of optimism: despite the inevitable intense resistance from capital, the 'greatest obstacle to change is not ... the revolt it would evoke from the privileged, but the belief that it is impossible'.[85]

Postscript: Election 2024 – Labour Wins, Far-Right Riots and the Tories Elect a New Leader

The 2024 General Election

On 22 May, following weeks of speculation that the 2024 General Election would be held in the autumn, thus giving Rishi Sunak at least two complete years in office and allowing the economic outlook a greater opportunity to improve, he gave a speech outside Number 10.¹ A rain-drenched Prime Minister, beleaguered with the knowledge that most of the electorate had had enough of him and 14 years of Tory rule, called the election for 4 July. Writing on the day of the announcement, Chris Mason, Political Editor, BBC News, reported that two very senior Government figures had very recently confirmed autumn as the date.² Those favouring an earlier date, however, were worried if he did go for that, things could get even worse. In the event, Labour had a landslide victory, gaining 211 seats, giving them a total of 412; the Tories lost 251 seats, giving them just 121; Reform UK got five seats up from zero and Nigel Farage, who had become its leader the month before the election, won his first Westminster seat. Reform UK came third, with 14.3 per cent of the vote compared to the Tories' 23.7 per cent and Labour's 33.7 per cent.³

London rally

Just over three weeks after the election, on 27 July, thousands of supporters of far-right activist Tommy Robinson filled Trafalgar Square in central London after a march.⁴ In 2018, former Trump advisor Steve Bannon had described Robinson as 'not just a guy but a movement in and of himself [who] represents the working class and channels a lot of the frustration of everyday, blue-collar Britons. ... He is a force of nature ... not built to be managed'.⁵ At the time, Bannon was forming a Europe-wide far-right campaign group – and had been in touch with Boris Johnson.⁶ Addressing the rally, Robinson claimed it was the 'biggest patriotic rally' in the UK ever.⁷ He had organized it as part of his efforts to create a far-right street movement off the back of the large vote for Farage at the General Election. Robinson asked the crowd: 'How many people here voted for Labour?' and 'How many people here voted for the Conservative Party?', with both questions eliciting boos from the crowd, while a sea of hands and cheers followed the same question for Reform UK.⁸ He revealed he had asked Farage to speak at the protest, but the Reform UK leader told him he 'couldn't make it'.⁹

Nation-wide far-right riots

Three days after the rally, on 30 July, there began a week of far-right, anti-immigration protests and riots. A message, believed to have originated in Liverpool, told followers: 'THEY WON'T STOP COMING UNTIL YOU TELL THEM … NO MORE IMMIGRATION. MASK UP. SPREAD THIS AS FAR AND WIDE AS YOU CAN', along with a dozen fire emojis.¹⁰ Between 30 July and 7 August 2024, an estimated 29 anti-immigration demonstrations and riots took place across 27 towns and cities in the UK.¹¹ Many of these were extremely violent, with participants attacking mosques and hotels housing people seeking asylum.¹² Flash mobs tried to set buildings alight and cars were stopped to check if the occupants were 'white and English' before letting them pass.¹³ Others were pulled from their cars.¹⁴ Viral video footage showed far-right rioters blocking traffic in North Yorkshire.¹⁵ The area was described at the time as a 'no go zone' for Black and Asian people.¹⁶ *The Independent* has provided horrifying details that include a Black man beaten by a mob, an Asian man stabbed at a train station, mosques under siege and Muslim graves vandalised,¹⁷ while footage shared online appeared to show rioters dragging an Asian man, believed to be a taxi driver, out of his car in Hull, while hurling racist abuse by repeatedly yelling 'P★★I', and damaging the vehicle.¹⁸

In Liverpool, Father Peter Morgan, the priest of St Anne's Church, which hosts an immigration centre that featured on a far-right 'hitlist', said that people there who were seeking asylum had been 'terrified, absolutely terrified', and his church had to be boarded up, as police on horseback patrolled the nearby streets.¹⁹ Morgan described as 'nonsense' calls for the country to 'defend' its Christian values: 'It's actually crazy what they're saying and here we are having to defend our Christian church. It just doesn't make sense. All we're doing is actually helping to feed the hungry.'²⁰

In the midst of the riots, Farage condemned the violence, at the same time stoking it up by suggesting the escalation in violence came as a result of 'soft policing' during 'Black Lives Matter' protests in the summer of 2020 (see Chapter 4).²¹ He went on to claim that ever since then, the impression of two-tier policing has become widespread. As always, Farage proceeded to blame immigration for everything:

> The majority of our population can see the fracturing of our communities as a result of mass, uncontrolled immigration, whether legal or illegal. Yet to attempt to debate this in the public arena leads to immediate howls of condemnation. A population explosion without integration was always going to end badly. I have said this for many years. We must have a more honest debate about these vital issues and give people the confidence that there are political solutions that are relevant to them.[22]

Farage also stated wrongly, 'What you've seen on the streets of Hartlepool, London or Southport is nothing compared to what could happen over the course of the next few weeks.'[23] In May, he had said that Muslims do not share British values.[24]

Riots organized outside the UK

So, what was the spark for the anti-immigration far-right riots? On 29 July, there was a mass stabbing in Southport, a seaside town 17 miles north of Liverpool, in which three little girls (Bebe King, Elsie Dot Stancombe and Alice Dasilva Aguias) were killed. When the stabbings happened, the far-right conspiracy theorist Silvano Trotta, who lives in Strasbourg in France, posted false information to the messaging app Telegram that the attack was carried out by an immigrant who had arrived on a small boat and that his name was Ali Al Shakati (a fake name).[25] An investigation by *Sky News* shows that his post was one of the most influential of any of those making similar misleading claims on Telegram. When Tom Cheshire, Data and Forensics Correspondent for *Sky*, pointed out that this was 'entirely false', Trotta responded 'Who doesn't make mistakes? But whatever happened, he is still a migrant, even if he was born in Wales'.[26] Trotta had been banned from a number of social media sites, including Twitter, but became reinstated when Elon Musk rebranded it as X. Trotta posts mainly about immigration.

Working with the organization Prose,[27] which monitors more than 10,000 extremist and conspiracist groups on Telegram, every day collecting and archiving everything they post, *Sky News* found that the people flooding Telegram and other platforms of misinformation were 'largely based outside the UK': 'What it shows is the nature of the new far-right – not a tightly organised hierarchy based in a specific location, but an international network of influencers and followers, working together almost like a swarm to stir up trouble.'[28]

Rather than specific organizations, it is a 'crowd-sourced model'.[29] Inciting those on the ground was a specific goal of the online far-right, according to

Al Baker, at Prose: 'These are communities which are expressly specifically and in a very dedicated and organised fashion devoted to exploiting racial divisions internationally.'[30] Tellingly, he goes on:

> Any incident which could plausibly involve an immigrant, a Muslim, someone who isn't white, regardless of whether in fact they did it or not, these communities are going to kick into action and try and stoke up division and racial hatred ... [in this case] to incite a race war on the back of the Southport murders.[31]

Baker explains that they are 'fully paid-up neo-Nazis who want to see the extermination of non-white people'.[32] Ned Mendez, Director of Consultancy at Clash Digital, found that the most widely shared and retweeted content on Twitter/X during the initial three days of the riots was primarily authored by non-domestic accounts from the United States and mainland Europe.[33]

Back in the UK

Back in the UK, there were calls for protests at fixed times and places.[34] The events drew from a common wellspring of anger that often recycles the same slogans – in particular, 'Enough is Enough', 'Stop the Boats' and 'Save Our Children' (a common trope from conspiracy theorists, picked up by the far right is that 'elites' are somehow covering up 'the truth', including the abuse of British children by Muslims).[35] A video from an influencer on X, associated with Tommy Robinson, who posts as 'Lord Simon', and who also falsely claimed that the attacker had recently arrived by boat, was viewed over a million times.[36] As well as Muslims and migrants, some of the far-right rioters, as we have seen, targeted people thought not to be White and/or English.

Daniel De Simone, Investigations Correspondent for BBC In-Depth, says of this kind of extremism:

> Right-wing extremism itself can be thought of as a spectrum, rather than a coherent whole. It includes genocidal neo-Nazis treated as terrorists by the state, who hide behind online aliases, scorn campaigning, want to destroy society and venerate Adolf Hitler. But the term is also used to describe people who stand in democratic elections, engage in public campaigns and put forward policy platforms.[37]

De Simone concludes that the far-right is far more mainstream than most people would care to think. Putting further flesh on the bones of this comment, on 17 August 2024, the final two candidates in the Tory leadership contest (see the last main section of this Postscript) appeared on GB News.

However, while the far-right is clearly becoming more accepted as part of the political spectrum:

> The reaction of the public, police and courts to the riots has shown how most people do not share the violent hatreds and fantasies of the far and extreme right. But many others will feel a UK of far-right flash mobs is more scary, unpredictable and racist than they believed and wonder what the future holds. This remains a dangerous moment.[38]

On 23 August, the United Nations Committee on the Elimination of Racial Discrimination (CERD), the committee responsible for combating racism, slammed the UK over continuing hate crimes, hate speech and xenophobic incidents, following riots fuelled by hate and misinformation that gripped the country that summer, adding that it was concerned by the presence of racist speech on various platforms, particularly where perpetuated by politicians and public figures.[39]

Classic fascist mobilization

Appearing on Sky News' 'Politics Hub with Sophie Ridge' on 15 October 2024, left-wing MP John McDonnell described the events as classic fascist mobilization in that they entailed demagogues at the pinnacle of a pyramid, active fascists in the middle, and a mass of disgruntled and impoverished working-class people at the base. I will quote him at length:

> To understand why the riots have taken place and how to respond to them, you have to start by looking at who has been involved. Drawing on other historical examples, it looks like a classic fascist mobilisation. At the top are leading demagogues, the political provocateurs, willing to exploit any issue for their political advantage no matter what the consequences for the people or communities involved. Beneath them are a relatively small phalanx of hardline foot-soldiers, who have been trained and involved in fascist groups like the English Defence League over the years. These are the true-believing fascist muscle behind the riots. Then there is a larger group: the disgruntled, the dispossessed and the disillusioned. This is the combustible material that the fascists target to set alight: people who are so discontented with their lives – with so little hope, with so little understanding of the real forces that drive our society – that they are prey to the simple, beguiling message that someone else is to blame for how they feel.[40]

He goes on, 'All the leaders have to do is point the finger at whichever group is the scapegoat this time round and wait for a spark, an incident, to set the tinder alight. The truth of any incident doesn't matter. It's what they can convince people of.'[41] The General Election campaign provided the ideal environment for far-right politicians to bring the anger 'to boiling-over point'.[42]

The solutions must be to call and confront the demagogues and those in mainstream politics who are exacerbating the anger, along with those using social and conventional media to make things worse, and crucially to address and solve the issues of the neglected sections of the working class with 14 years of austerity having produced 14 million people living in poverty, including four million children, a housing crisis, collapsed and broken public services, McDonnell goes on, and a 'grotesque visible level of inequality generating a sense of unfairness overall'.[43]

Antiracists respond

Historically, the far-right has usually been outnumbered by the left on protests and demonstrations. On Wednesday, 7 August 2024, while England held its breath across the country and in Belfast police 'were braced for the most widespread night of violence' since the riots began,[44] contrary to expectations and fears, it was antiracist demonstrators who thronged the streets, and by the middle of the evening, there was nothing to counter. Instead of far-right terror, the atmosphere was 'almost carnival-like'.[45] There were banners proclaiming, 'Nans Against Nazis'; 'Immigrants welcome. Racists not'; and 'When the poor blame the poor only the rich win.'[46] In Brighton the antiracist demonstrators so outnumbered the far-right that the police surrounded the latter for their own protection and, by 9pm, only three far-right activists remained, surrounded by antiracists, 'so sound systems were set up. It became a party'.[47]

Starmer's response to the far-right riots

To his credit, Starmer responded robustly to the far-right riots:

> I utterly condemn the far-right thuggery we have seen this weekend. Be in no doubt: those who have participated in this violence will face the full force of the law. The police will be making arrests. Individuals will be held on remand. Charges will follow. And convictions will follow. I guarantee you will regret taking part in this disorder. Whether directly or those whipping up this action online, and then running away themselves. This is not protest. It is organised, violent thuggery. And it has no place on our street or online.[48]

Lengthy sentences immediately followed the riots, with terms in prison of three years or more commonplace.[49] Using information from the police and courts, BBC News collected data on 470 people in England and Wales charged in connection with the violent disorder.[50] Of 652 charges analysed, violent disorder was the most common, with 310 counts. There were 51 counts of harassment, alarm or distress, and 42 of assaulting an emergency worker.[51] As of 10 October 2024, 400 had been jailed.

Tories respond by choosing a new leader further to the right than Sunak

Tory MPs reacted to the Labour win and the far-right riots by narrowing down the leadership contenders to two, Robert Jenrick and Kemi Badenoch, both solidly identified with the hard right of the Tory Party. On 2 November 2024, Badenoch defeated Jenrick in a vote of party members by 53,806 votes to 41,388, after a months-long contest to replace Sunak as leader. The first Black woman to lead a major British political party, Olukemi Olufunto Adegoke was born in 1980 in Wimbledon, London, to comfortable upper-class British parents of Nigerian origin. Her mother was a professor of physiology and her father, a medical doctor. Badenoch grew up in Nigeria.[52] Her win represents a further lurch to the right for the Tories (see Part II of this book), as would have a win by Jenrick, who focused his campaign on cutting both 'legal' and 'illegal' immigration and withdrawing Britain from the European Convention on Human Rights to try to halt the latter.

A culture wars warrior accused of Islamophobia

Badenoch has railed against identity politics and 'wokeism'. A 'culture wars' warrior, she has called for a defence of 'British values' and a crackdown on immigration. She has also been accused of Islamophobia. In September 2024, she declared that she found the election of five progressive independent MPs in the 4 July General Election more worrying than the rise of Farage's Reform Party.[53] The MPs, four of them Muslims elected for the first time, and the fifth, non-Muslim Jeremy Corbyn, denounced her for 'an outrageous slur'.[54] Badenoch had said: 'I was far more worried about the five new MPs elected on the back of sectarian Islamist politics; alien ideas that have no place here. The sort of politics we need to defeat and defeat quickly.'[55] The five MPs, who have formed a new parliamentary group, the Independents Alliance, responded at length:

> Kemi Badenoch's outrageous slur is an attack on democracy. As democratically elected MPs, we are proud to speak up on the issues that matter to our constituents, including the two-child-benefits cap, the rights of refugees and the ongoing massacre of Palestinians. By describing these demands as 'sectarian Islamist politics,' Badenoch maligns thousands of voters and peace campaigners. Her smear should

be called out for what it is: Islamophobia. Last month, we witnessed horrific far-right violence across the country, fuelled by racist rhetoric from mainstream politicians. Kemi Badenoch's reckless comments add fuel to the fire – and she should retract them immediately. We are proud to represent diverse communities – and we were elected to serve our constituents in pursuit of a more hopeful, united and peaceful society. We would urge Kemi Badenoch to do the same.[56]

'Islamist' is a term for fundamentalist Muslims and is commonly used by Islamophobes, including the far right, to refer to *all* Muslims. Later in September, Badenoch proclaimed: 'We cannot be naive and assume immigrants will automatically abandon ancestral ethnic hostilities at the border, or that all cultures are equally valid. They are not.'[57] Forced by the BBC's Laura Kuenssberg to clarify these comments made in the *Sunday Telegraph*, she said, 'I actually think it extraordinary to think that's an unusual or controversial thing to say.'[58] After a discussion which focused on Badenoch stating that she was struck by the number of recent immigrants who hate Israel, she was asked by Kuenssberg which cultures she was referring to. Badenoch stated, 'I know what you're trying to do, Laura, you want me to say, "Muslims," but it isn't all Muslims, so I'm not going to do that. I'm not going to play this game.'[59]

Misunderstands Critical Race Theory, supports the Sewell Report that denied institutional racism and appoints Jenrick as Shadow Justice Secretary
During the aforementioned Black Lives Matter protests when many politicians were 'taking the knee' (see Chapter 4) to show support for the cause, Badenoch had viewed all this as a pernicious ideology that portrays 'blackness as victimhood and whiteness as oppression'.[60] Later in 2020, she declared war on Critical Race Theory (CRT), claiming in Parliament that the 'ideology' informing Black Lives Matter derives from CRT.[61] In fact, CRT is much more complicated than this. While Critical Race Theorists do see 'Whiteness' as a form of oppression, they do not view 'Blackness' as 'victimhood'.[62] On the contrary, Critical Race Theorists, of which there are many varieties,[63] are committed to fighting for social justice.[64] Badenoch also supported the Sewell Report of 2021, which denied the existence of institutional racism in Britain (also discussed in Chapter 4). Following her win over Jenrick, Badenoch chose this anti-immigration advocate of leaving the European Convention on Human Rights as Shadow Justice Secretary, an appointment many true believers in social justice would see as an Orwellian choice. Jenrick exhibited his ignorance of Islam, when, speaking to Sky News in August 2024, he stated that he thought 'it was quite wrong that somebody could shout "Allahu Akbar" on the streets of

London and not be immediately arrested'.⁶⁵ Naz Shah, the MP for Bradford West, commented:

> This is complete ignorance and textbook Islamophobia from Robert Jenrick. It literally equates every Muslim in the world with extremism. … It's a basic Islamic saying that every Muslim in the world says in prayer. Imagine in this climate, either being that ignorant or deliberately trying to stigmatise all Muslims. He should apologise and speak to Muslim communities and learn more about our faith.⁶⁶

Interestingly for future interactions between the two, his Labour Government opposite number, Justice Secretary Shabana Mahmood, is a devout Muslim.

In February 2025, Tell MAMA, the organization that monitors Islamophobia, recorded the highest number of anti-Muslim hate incidents between 2023 and 2024 since it was founded in 2011. This was as a result of the Southport murders, the Israel-Gaza War and 'grooming concerns' (see Chapter 5). Between 2012 when Cameron was Prime Minister and 2024, Tell MAMA saw a 2,253% increase in reported street-based hate crime.⁶⁷

On economics

Katy Balls, the *Spectator*'s Political Editor, informs us that Badenoch is a devotee of Thomas Sowell, the American economist, who she describes as 'the greatest black intellectual that has ever lived'.⁶⁸ Sowell started his academic life as a Marxist, but now identifies as a libertarian or a fiscal conservative. The following account of Sowell's theoretical views extracted from Robert Freeman and David Coates reveal their similarity with Tory austerity policies.

Fiscal conservatism is based on a fundamental belief in the superiority of free-market capitalism, prudence in government spending and debt, with limited government as its ideological foundation. Fiscal conservatives advocate the lowering of taxes and the reduction of government spending, but they will usually choose debt over tax increases.⁶⁹ Fiscal conservatives strongly believe in libertarianism, individualism and free enterprise and promote deregulation, privatization and free trade.⁷⁰

A former banker, and Secretary of State for the Department of Business and Trade in Rishi Sunak's Government that promoted fiscal and industrial austerity and went to war against the unions (see Chapter 8), Badenoch is opposed to state spending and has said she would reverse Labour's imposition of value added tax on private school fees.⁷¹ She has denounced 'excessive tax … excessive regulation and excessive government interference',⁷² citing minimum wage and maternity pay rules as among regulations 'overburdening businesses'.⁷³ After a media storm, she said she did not mean that maternity pay was 'excessive' and that it was a good thing. No such retraction was made on the minimum wage.[74]

Attends far-right conference

At a conference organised by the Alliance for Responsible Citizenship (ARC, whose backers include Paul Marshall, one of the owners of GB News) in London in February 2025, Badenoch pronounced that ' "our country and all of western civilisation will be lost" if efforts to renew the Tory Party and drive forward right wing ideas globally fail'.[75] She also likened her own leadership to Trump's, attacked Keir Starmer for once 'taking the knee' in support of 'Black Lives Matter', and described 'pronouns, diversity policies and climate activism' as a 'poison' (cited in Quinn, 2025).

Also attending the conference were Nigel Farage and Canadian right-winger, Jordan Peterson (co-founder of ARC and vocal supporter of Tommy Robinson) who has described climate activism as a 'totalitarian lie'[76] and supporters of far-right parties in Germany, Austria, Spain and Hungary, including its Prime Minister, Viktor Orbán.[77]

Turbulent times ahead

As I conclude the Postscript in early 2025, with the ongoing rightward movement of the Tories and the growing rise of Reform UK consistent with developments in other parts of Europe and, most significantly, in the United States, great challenges confront the left. The left needs first to acknowledge with the utmost soberness the gravity of our situation.[78] Second, it is equally important to avoid despair and especially not to forget that a real alternative to capitalism exists.[79] In the Introduction, I referred to the work of Judy Cox on why we need Marxist theory.[80] As she argues, the far right 'puts forward supposedly coherent explanations of social crisis which express people's anger against elites, but points them in entirely the wrong direction for solutions'.[81] However, Marxism can cut through these false explanations. What we see and experience only partially expose the truth about the hidden processes that drive those appearances.[82] Marx argued that capitalism is especially good at disguising its true nature. Our societies are shaped by hidden forces that need to be explored.[83] When Marx wrote *Capital*,[84] Cox continues, 'he did not tell people that their lives were hard and their wages low. They knew that from their experience'.[85] What Marx wanted to find out was why – and what could be done about it. So, he studied the inner workings of capitalism. His method enables us to look beneath the surface, underneath the dynamism of capitalism to see how wealth is created by labour,[86] and explains that capitalism inevitably create crises. Superficial explanations of society, Cox concludes, can work when workers are passive but right-wing ideas can gain purchase when workers are angry. Thus, from a socialist perspective, workers have an interest in understanding how society really works: the experience of previous struggles combines with theoretical insights in Marxism. 'The combination of struggle and politics reveals the oppressive logic of capitalism and how to transform it.'[87] To end on a note of optimism from Callinicos. Challenging the status quo 'requires courage, imagination and willpower inspired by the injustice that surrounds us. Beneath the surface ... these qualities are present in abundance. ... Once mobilized ... we ... can turn the world upside down'.[88]

Notes

Introduction

1   While 'Tory' and 'Conservative' today mean the same thing, albeit with the former more consistently used by the Tory Party's opponents, 'Tory' dates back hundreds of years before the Conservative Party was formed (Sanderson, 2022). As journalist Ginny Sanderson explains, writing for *The Scotsman*, its first use can be traced back to the Exclusion Crisis during the right of King Charles II of England, Scotland and Ireland from 1679 to 1681, when there were failed attempts to exclude Charles' brother and heir presumptive James from the throne because he was a Roman Catholic. That political faction in support of James becoming King became known as 'Tories'; those who were against it as 'Whigs'. Tory was derived from the Middle Irish word, '*tóraidhe*', which meant 'outlaw' or 'robber', while 'Whig' came from 'whiggamore' that was used to describe Scottish cattle drivers and was meant to imply the politicians were 'country bumpkins' (Sanderson, 2022). The Tory Party was dissolved in 1834 when Robert Peel became the first Conservative Prime Minister, but 'Tory' lives on as an alternative to 'Conservative'.
2   See Cole (2023a) for a lengthy discussion of racism in the Tory Party from Disraeli up to the end of premiership of Boris Johnson in 2022.
3   Engels (1890). For a brief but engaging analysis of why we *need* Marxist theory, see, for example, Cox (2024a; see also Cox, 2024b).
4   Engels (1880 [2003]).
5   Engels (1880 [2003]).
6   Engels (1880 [2003]).
7   See Cole (2023b: 265–269) for a discussion of the misunderstandings and manipulations, such as: it always leads to totalitarianism; it is contrary to human nature; those who have 'done well' in life deserve more benefits; someone will always want to be boss; and some people have to do the drudge jobs. This reference also includes rebuttals to these assertions from a Marxist point of view.
8   Lavery et al (2022). Writing in June 2022, at the onset of the contemporary trade union fightback against the industrial and fiscal austerity of the Tory Governments, Ian Lavery, Jon Trickett and Laura Smith refer to the outrage of the Tory press that the workers were taking action, 'a real fear drumming at the heart of the establishment' of a looming class war from below. They point out that Waren Buffett, as of April 2024, with a net worth of US$139 billion, the ninth richest person in the world (Bloomberg, 2024), once declared, 'There's class warfare, all right, but it's my class, the rich class, that's making war, and we're winning' (Lavery et al, 2022). Lavery et al conclude: 'Buffett's analysis is right. We agree with it. The rich elite have launched a class war against the rest of society, against the vast majority. We cannot allow ourselves to simply remain under attack. The fight back requires us to continue to act the way the RMT have taken action this week, and to continue to speak out in solidarity with all those working people whose standards

of living are under siege from the wealthy few. The pandemic made it clearer than ever which side we have to be on – the side of the key workers who kept the country running during those terrible years, and who are now having that vital contribution thrown back in their faces. It is an affront. It is time to stand up' (Lavery et al, 2022).

9   See Cole (2023a) for a comprehensive and thorough account of rampant racism in the Tory Party from Disraeli to Major. The contents are summarized briefly at the end of Chapter 1.
10 Marx actually used the term 'labour power' to denote capacity of workers to work. When employers hire workers in the labour market, they are buying their capacity to work, rather than their labour, or work itself.
11 Marx (1845).
12 Marxism, of course, is not just about theory, but about practice (praxis). For Marx, 'praxis' refers to the free, universal, creative and self-creative activity through which human beings construct and change their world and themselves. Praxis is an activity uniquely human and distinguishes humankind from all other beings (Petrovic, 1991: 435). From a Marxist perspective, 'changing the world' is moving towards the creation of socialism. See Cole (2023b) for an analysis of socialism; see also Cole (forthcoming) for a discussion of different roads to socialism and different perspectives on what should happen on arrival.
13 Finney et al (2023).
14 Blyth (2015: 114–115).
15 Blyth (2015: 115).

Chapter 1

1   Owolade (2023). Owolade's article focuses on the 2023 report, 'Racism and Ethnic Inequality in a Time of Crisis' discussed later in this chapter.
2   Abbott (2023). Abbott's letter is the second one on the page in this link: https://www.theguardian.com/theobserver/commentisfree/2023/apr/23/success-for-women-not-same-as-for-men-letters
3   Allegretti (2023).
4   Anonymous (2023).
5   Anonymous (2023).
6   Anonymous (2023).
7   Chakrabortty (2023a).
8   Malik (2023, cited in Chakrabortty, 2023a).
9   For a spirited defence of this position, see Gillborn (2008). See Farmer and Farmer (2020) for a comprehensive overview of Critical Race Theory; see also Delgado and Stefancic (2000). For a critical appraisal and Marxist critique of CRT, see Cole (2017).
10 Delgado and Stefancic (2001: 69). For contemporary examples of CRT literature that focus on the Black dimension and experience, see, for example, Bradley (2020) and James-Gallaway et al (2020).
11 See Cole (2017: 19–27).
12 I put 'race' in inverted commas because it is now almost universally acknowledged among the mainstream scientific and social scientific communities that 'race' is socially constructed rather than biological reality. In 1972 the evolutionary geneticist Richard Lewontin argued that 85 per cent of human genetic diversity occurred within, rather than between, populations, with the rest associated with the broadly defined 'races' (Lewontin, 1972). That 'race' is a social construct is explained succinctly by neuroscientist Steven Rose and sociologist Hilary Rose (Rose and Rose, 2005). They explain that most of the diversity between populations is accounted for by the readily visible genetic variation of skin colour, hair form and so on. The everyday business of seeing and acknowledging such

difference is not the same as the project of genetics. For genetics, and more importantly, for the prospect of treating genetic diseases, the difference is important, since humans differ in their susceptibility to certain diseases, and genetics can have something to say about this. However, beyond medicine, 'race' has no legitimate meaning.

13 Racialization is used in different ways by non-Marxists. See, for example, Barot and Bird (2001).
14 Miles (1993: 50–52).
15 Camara (2002: 88).
16 Lawrence (1982: 48).
17 Gramsci (1978: 419).
18 Coben (2002: 206).
19 Gramsci (1978: 330–331).
20 Gramsci (1978: 9).
21 See Cole (2021: 61–84) for a discussion of the case for an antiracist, all-inclusive ecosocialism; see also Cole (2023e).
22 Marx (1870 [1978]: 254).
23 My thanks to Alpesh Maisuria for suggesting this formulation to me.
24 Kovel (1970).
25 Dovidio and Gaertner (1986).
26 Kick It Out (2024).
27 Scientific racism is an ideology that appropriates the methods and legitimacy of science to argue the case for the superiority of White Europeans and the inferiority of non-White people whose social and economic status have been historically marginalized. Scientific racism grew out of: the misappropriation of revolutionary advances in medicine, anatomy and statistics during the 18th and 19th centuries; Charles Darwin's theory of evolution through natural selection; and Gregor Mendel's laws of inheritance from our parents. Eugenic theories and scientific racism drew support from racism, xeno-racism, antisemitism, sexism, colonialism and imperialism, as well as justifications of slavery, particularly in the United States (National Human Genome Research Institute, 2022).
28 See Cole (2023a: 11–13).
29 I include this form of racism under the heading of 'non-colour-coded racism' because my focus is the UK. Many European Roma people, of course, have darker skin and this will be a component of the racism directed at them.
30 Sivanandan (2009).
31 Jones and Goodwin (2021); Stevens (2021).
32 Fekete (2001).
33 For some manifestations of this xeno-racism, see Cole (2012a: 62–64).
34 Sivanandan (2009: ix). The arguments in the preceding paragraphs have been developed and applied in a number of publications, the most recent of which are Cole (2023b, 2023c).
35 Ball (1990: 18).
36 In other historical periods, there were other groups who were more prominently racialized and on the receiving end of discourses of derision (see Cole, 2023a, *passim*).
37 International Rescue Committee (2024).
38 UNHCR (2024).
39 UNHCR (2024).
40 Cited in UNHCR (2024).
41 House of Commons Library (Georgina Sturge) (2022).
42 TUC (2023a).
43 UN News (2023).
44 House of Commons Library (2023).

45 Race Equality Foundation (2023).
46 Independent Commission for Equity in Cricket (2023).
47 Finney et al (2023).
48 Finney et al (2023).
49 Finney et al (2023).
50 Finney et al (2023).
51 Finney et al (2023).
52 Butler (2023a).
53 Butler (2023a).
54 Butler (2023a).
55 Butler (2023a).
56 Butler (2023a).
57 For an extended analysis, see Cole (2023a).
58 Fraser (2015, cited in Cole, 2023a: 44).
59 Cited in Cole (2023a: 37).
60 Disraeli (1852: 496, cited in Cole, 2023a: 47).
61 Disraeli (1852: 496, cited in Cole, 2023a: 47).
62 Cole (2023a: chapter 1).
63 Cole (2023a: 77–79).
64 Rosenberg (2011: 22–23).
65 Holmes (1979: 27, cited in Spartacus Educational, 2020).
66 Cole (2023a: 79–80).
67 Balfour (1905).
68 Cole (2023a: 97).
69 Jones (2012).
70 Ohlinger (1966: 33).
71 Ohlinger (1966: 33).
72 Cole (2023a: 100).
73 O'Mally (2016).
74 Cole (2023a: 111–118).
75 Cole (2023a: chapter 3).
76 Powell (1968).
77 Cole (2023a: 138–178).
78 Thatcher (1978), emphasis added. Note her use of 'hostile' here in relation to the 'hostile environment', the subject matter of Part II of the book.
79 Cited in *BBC News* (2018a).
80 Cited in *BBC News* (2018a).
81 Donaghy (2018).
82 *The Irish Times* (2013).
83 Cole (2023a: 248–249).
84 Mr Major's speech to Conservative Group for Europe (1993).

Chapter 2

1 Blyth (2015). An account of the economic liberalism of Locke, whose vision was naturalizing income and wealth inequality, appears in his *Second Treatise of Government* that was published in 1690. Locke's liberalism is an economic liberalism that pits the individual against the state, with Locke's legacy being the minimalist nature of the state, with its only function to protect property. The last decade of the 17th century, in Blyth's view, heralds the start of austerity's intellectual history (2015: 104–105) with what Blyth refers to as 'The state: can't live with it, can't live without it, don't want to pay for it',

in other words, the liberal dilemma of the tension between not wanting a state and the *necessity* of a minimalist one, if only to pay for the protection of property (2015: 106).

For states to protect property, they need to raise money, which can put them in debt. For Hume, writing in the next century, the basic problem with debt is that it has no limit (that is until interest rates on it become overwhelming) (2015: 108). In Hume's words: 'It is very tempting to a minister to employ such an expedient, as it enables him to make a great figure during his administration, without overburdening the people with taxes. … The practice, therefore, of contracting debt will almost infallibly be abused, in every government' (Hume, 1777: 206).

When this debt hits a ceiling, governments will eventually need to sell it to foreigners, creating a dependency, and thereby threatening those governments' liberty. Accordingly, Hume promoted the image of 'the honourable merchant' who could advance the prosperity of the age, as well as freedom and peace, thus safeguarding modern commerce (Blyth, 2015: 111). Hume offers a guide for the improvement of the merchant's character, a catalogue of virtues that would bolster the fulfilment of contracts and diminish generational decline. Giving the example of the sale of cloth, Hume states: 'the merchant, who exports the cloth, cannot raise its price, being limited by the price which it yields in foreign markets. Every man, to be sure, is desirous of pushing off from himself the burden of any tax, which is imposed, and of laying it upon others: But as every man has the same inclination, and is upon the defensive; no set of men can be supposed to prevail altogether in this contest' (Hume, nd). There, therefore, Hume concludes, 'must be very heavy taxes, indeed, and very injudiciously levied' (Hume, nd).

Finally, Smith, also writing in the 18th century, believed that saving leads to investment, rather than hoarding. Thus, debt has no role to play, and saving is both good and natural to us (Blyth, 2015: 111). As Blyth puts it, 'Smith's capitalism rests upon a predisposition to save rather than spend' (Blyth, 2015: 111). Blyth quotes Smith's hopeful assertion that while 'some men may increase their expense very considerably though their revenue does not increase at all, we may be assured that no class or order of men ever does so … because the principles of common prudence … always influence … the majority of every class' (Smith, 1776, cited in Blyth, 2015: 110).

2 Blyth (2015: 114).
3 Blyth (2015: 115).
4 Blyth (2015: 114–115).
5 Blyth (2015: 115).
6 Ricardo (1817 [1996]: 66, cited in Blyth, 2015: 116).
7 Blyth (2015: 116).
8 Blyth (2015: 116).
9 Blyth (2015: 117).
10 Blyth (2015: 117).
11 Hemerijck (2012: 33).
12 These phases are adapted from Gamble (2024).
13 Gamble (2024).
14 Partington (2023a).
15 Partington (2023a).
16 Partington (2023a).
17 Partington (2023a).
18 Partington (2023a).
19 Partington (2023a).
20 The Resolution Foundation (2023).
21 Partington (2023a).

22 Partington (2023a).
23 Partington (2023a).
24 Blyth (2015).
25 Blyth (2015: 203).
26 Mattei (2022a).
27 Mattei (2022a: 3).
28 Blyth's reply appears in an endorsement of Mattei's book and is on its back page.
29 Mattei (2022a: 5).
30 Mattei (2022a: 5).
31 Mattei (2022a: 5–6).
32 Mattei (2022a: 6), emphasis added. Wage relations under capitalism are best explained by the concept of the capital–labour [labor in US spelling] relation. I return to this later in the book.
33 Mattei (2022a: 6).
34 Mattei (2022a: 6).
35 Some of the key features of the first workers' state and its demise are addressed in Cole (2018: 291–292).
36 Sewell (2013).
37 Woods (2017). Woods provides a full account of the history of and the aftermath of the Hungarian Soviet Republic.
38 Woods (2017).
39 Woods (2017).
40 Woods (2017).
41 Woods (2017).
42 Woods (2017).
43 Woods (2017).
44 Simkin (2023).
45 Simkin (2023).
46 Simkin (2023).
47 Simkin (2023).
48 Keller (2022). There is a detailed account in Keller.
49 Keller (2022).
50 Woods (2017).
51 Woods (2017). For a discussion of the Paris Commune of 1871, see Cole (2018: 288–290).
52 Cited in Sewell (2013).
53 Cited in Sewell (2013).
54 Cited in Sewell (2013).
55 Cited in Mattei (2022a: 5).
56 Undiscovered Scotland (2023). Gallacher was later to win West Fife for the Communist Party of Great Britain, keeping the seat from 1935 until 1950, making him the longest serving of the four Communist MPs elected to Parliament in the 20th century.
57 Mattei (2022a: 6–7).
58 Mattei (2022a: 7).
59 Mattei (2022a: 161).
60 Austen Chamberlain, HC Deb March 16, 1920, vol. 126, cc 2069, cited in Mattei (2022a: 162).
61 Mattei (2022a: 162).
62 Cited in Blyth (2015: 123).
63 Mattei (2022a: 162).
64 People's History Museum (2024).
65 Cited in Steinmetz-Jenkins (2023).

66 Mattei in Steinmetz-Jenkins (2023).
67 Mattei (2022a: 163). In Part III, I expand on these three forms of austerity, using contemporary examples under the Tory Party.
68 Marx argued that capitalism relies for its very existence on the extraction of surplus value from workers who have to sell their labour power to survive: capitalists pay them less than the value they produce, with the value added by workers' labour appropriated as profit by and for the capitalist when goods are sold. For an elucidation of Marx's value theory, see Marx (1887 [1965], especially chapter 1). For a brief summary and a numerical example of how this works, see Cole (2011: 42–44).
69 My own views on the Marxist alternative to capitalism, a form of ecosocialism that is ecofeminist, antiracism and all-inclusive, have been discussed elsewhere, most recently in Cole (2023b).
70 Steinmetz-Jenkins (2023).
71 Cited in Steinmetz-Jenkins (2023).
72 Mattei (2022a: 163). By workers 'need to be disciplined' into accepting 'private property' and 'wage relations', Mattei is referring to the role of the economic 'experts' in formulating, and of the capitalist state in enforcing, the notion that both private property and the capital–labour relation are 'natural', rather than political choices made by and in the interests of the ruling class and their allies under capitalism. As Friedrich Engels argues in *Socialism: Utopian and Scientific* (Engels, 1880 [2003]), the capital–labour relation explains the basis of the social antagonism between workers and capitalists and their allies, in Engels' terms, '*the germ of the whole of the social antagonisms of today*' (italics in original): this is further explained by the Marxist formulation, 'value theory' (see endnote 68). The capital–labour relation, the source of profit and class struggle in capitalist society, is maintained by the regulation of the labour market by capitalist states.
73 Mattei (2022b).
74 Mattei (2022b).
75 Martin (2023).
76 Cited in Martin (2023). COVID 19 is discussed in Chapter 7.
77 Cited in Martin (2023).
78 Cited in Martin (2023).
79 See endnote 68 for further explanation.
80 Cited in Martin (2023).
81 Cited in Martin (2023).
82 Martin (2023).
83 Martin (2023).

Chapter 3
1 Cited in Turnnidge (2022).
2 McCallig (2022).
3 Cited in McCallig (2022).
4 *Full Fact* is a team of independent fact checkers and campaigners who find, expose and counter the harm bad information does.
5 Turnnidge (2022).
6 Turnnidge (2022).
7 Turnnidge (2022).
8 Cited in Turnnidge (2022).
9 Gentleman (2019).
10 Gentleman (2023a).
11 Cited in Gentleman (2023a).

12 Cole (2023a).
13 Prince (2010).
14 Cited in White and Perkins (2002).
15 Cited in White and Perkins (2002). May also referred to the lack of women Tory MPs.
16 Whitehead (2009).
17 *BBC News* (2009).
18 Cited in Whitehead (2009).
19 Cited in Whitehead (2009).
20 *BBC News* (2009).
21 Prince (2010).
22 Cited in Prince (2010).
23 Cited in Prince (2010).
24 *BBC News* (2010a).
25 Cole (2012b: 5).
26 GOV.UK (2010).
27 GOV.UK (2010).
28 GOV.UK (2010).
29 GOV.UK (2010).
30 'David Cameron on immigration: full text of the speech' (2011).
31 'David Cameron on immigration: full text of the speech' (2011).
32 'David Cameron on immigration: full text of the speech' (2011).
33 'David Cameron on immigration: full text of the speech' (2011).
34 'David Cameron on immigration: full text of the speech' (2011).
35 Cited in Topping (2011).
36 Cited in Topping (2011).
37 The following bullet points were compiled by Richard Chambers Immigration Barristers (2012).
38 For the most recent updates, see GOV.UK (ongoing).
39 Osborn (2013).
40 Osborn (2013).
41 Helm (2012).
42 Cited in Helm (2012).
43 Helm (2012).
44 Cited in Helm (2012).
45 'David Cameron's immigration speech' (2013).
46 Cited in Helm (2012).
47 Cited in Helm (2012).
48 Aitkenhead and Wintour (2013).
49 Aitkenhead and Wintour (2013).
50 Cole (2023a: 282).
51 Hattenstone (2018).
52 Tomlinson (2019: 189).
53 Chorley et al (2013).
54 Chorley et al (2013).
55 Chorley et al (2013).
56 GOV.UK (2013); for updates on UK immigration legislation from 2015 to the present, see GOV.UK (ongoing).
57 EIN (2014).
58 Cole (2023a: 289–291).
59 Cited in Dearden (2015).

NOTES

60 Kirkup (2015).
61 Kirkup (2015).
62 Cited in Kirkup (2015).
63 Cited in Kirkup (2015).
64 Kirkup (2015).
65 Kirkup (2015).
66 Kirkup (2015).
67 Kirkup (2015).
68 Cited in Stone (2017).
69 Cited in Stone (2017).
70 Cited in Stone (2017).
71 Cited in Stone (2017).
72 See, for example, Fryer (1984), Visram (1986), Walvin (1973). For a brief summary, see Cole (2023d: 99–100).
73 Taylor (2024a).
74 Taylor (2024a).
75 Taylor (2024a).
76 Taylor (2024a).
77 Cited in Taylor (2024a).
78 Lea (2016).
79 JCWI (2016).
80 Moore and Ramsey (2017). Xeno-racism would have been central here.
81 Cited in Lindsay (2017).
82 Lindsay (2017).
83 Lindsay (2017). Farron's speech, though it makes some good antiracist points, was very much pro-capitalist and patriotic, arguing for capitalism and against socialism.
84 Cited in *BBC News* (2020b).
85 Justice4Grenfell (2019).
86 Justice4Grenfell (2019).
87 Justice4Grenfell (2019).
88 Justice4Grenfell (2019).
89 Hopkins (2017).
90 *BBC News* (2017).
91 Justice4Grenfell (2019).
92 Justice4Grenfell (2019).
93 Justice4Grenfell (2019).
94 Justice4Grenfell (2019).
95 Cole (2023a: 302–304).
96 Immigration Law Practitioners' Association (2018).
97 Global Justice Now (2018).
98 Cited in Global Justice Now (2018).
99 Global Justice Now (2018).
100 Global Justice Now (2018).
101 Global Justice Now (2018).
102 Global Justice Now (2018).
103 Global Justice Now (2018).
104 Usborne (2018).
105 Travis (2017a).
106 Cole (2023a: 312).
107 McIntyre and Taylor (2018).

108 McIntyre and Taylor (2018).
109 Cited on *BBC* 'Newsnight' (2019).
110 Batty (2011).
111 Batty (2011).
112 Kirkup (2011).
113 Cited in Kirkup (2011).
114 Cited in Kirkup (2011).
115 Travis (2017b).
116 Hasan (2017).
117 Hasan (2017).
118 Hasan (2017).
119 Hasan (2017).
120 GOV.UK (2015).
121 Hasan (2017).
122 Hasan (2017).
123 Hasan (2017).
124 Not to be confused with the other Tory, David Davis.
125 Craig (2016). Davies had said that it sent out the message that women are 'property'.
126 Cited in Hasan (2017).
127 Hasan (2017).
128 *The Independent* (2019).
129 *The Independent* (2019).
130 *The Independent* (2019).
131 *The Independent* (2019).
132 *The Independent* (2019).
133 *The Independent* (2019).
134 *The Independent* (2019).
135 Cited in Johnston (2019).
136 Wickham (2019).
137 Cited in Wickham (2019).
138 Wickham (2019).
139 Wickham (2019).
140 Wickham (2019).
141 Wickham (2019).
142 Cited in Wickham (2019).
143 Home Affairs Select Committee (2018: 5).
144 Home Affairs Select Committee (2018: 5).
145 Home Affairs Select Committee (2018: 5).
146 Home Affairs Select Committee (2018: 5).
147 Home Affairs Select Committee (2018: 23). In Cole (2023a: 327–329) and Cole (2020a: 78–81), I discuss the tragic cases of Paulette Wilson and Anthony Bryan, respectively. Wilson received a letter from the Home Office in 2015, informing her she was an 'illegal immigrant' and had six months before she would be sent back to Jamaica, the country which she had left when she was ten, and to which she had never returned. Bryan was held in removal centres for five weeks and booked on a flight to Jamaica that he had left in 1965 when he was eight. In 2018, Paulette Wilson finally got leave to remain. She died in 2020. Anthony Bryan's story, *Sitting in Limbo*, was turned into a BAFTA-winning film in 2020. It is on BBC iPlayer. While officials have acknowledged he was in the UK legally, in 2022, he appealed against the compensation offered by the Home Office: 'Their offer doesn't reflect what I went

through it felt like an insult. I don't think the Home Office has changed; when the spotlight is on them they make promises, but once the public attention moves away nothing happens' (cited in Gentleman, 2022a). In 2023, after five years of what he says were constant setbacks and delays, Bryan, who is on medication for a serious lung condition, accepted a compensation offer from the Home Office (Campbell and Lee, 2024).

[148] This final section of the chapter is based on the last section of chapter 9 of Cole (2023a: 330–331). At the end of that chapter, readers may be interested in an Appendix (2023a: 331–335), in which I provide details of my own experiences of the hostile environment in the form of a personal testimony, which started in 2011 and is ongoing. I cover such aspects as my being seriously ill in hospital in Bangkok, and the British Embassy in Phnom Penh saying they would only allow my future wife to visit me on condition that she started her visa application all over again; leaving our daughter (my stepdaughter) crying at the airport several times because she was not allowed to come with us; having to prove we were not a sham family; and the prohibitive costs and length of time for my wife and daughter to gain British citizenship.

[149] Helm (2019).
[150] Cited in Helm (2019).
[151] Helm (2019).
[152] Cited in Helm (2019).
[153] Helm (2019).

Chapter 4

[1] Stewart et al (2018).
[2] Stewart et al (2018).
[3] Poole (2018).
[4] Gentleman (2018).
[5] Gentleman (2018).
[6] Gentleman (2018).
[7] Gentleman (2018).
[8] Stewart (2019).
[9] Stewart (2019).
[10] Cited in Stewart (2019).
[11] See Chapter 1, note 27.
[12] Halliday and Goodman (2019).
[13] Johnson (2000).
[14] Stone (2019).
[15] Johnson (2000).
[16] Cited in Kuo (2016).
[17] Stone (2020).
[18] Powell was one of the most infamous racists in the Tory Party. For a discussion, see Cole (2023a: 161–164).
[19] Theodoracopulos (2003).
[20] *Evening Standard* (2008).
[21] JTA (2018). Apparently, the headline over his D-Day article changed during the day. The first read 'In praise of Wehrmacht: The real story of D-Day is the heroism of the German soldiers who were vastly outnumbered but fought nobly and to the death', while the second read 'The truth about D-Day: Don't believe the Hollywood version. The fact is the Wehrmacht were sitting ducks' (JTA, 2018).
[22] Cited in Booth (2017).

23 Cited in Booth (2017).
24 Booth (2017).
25 Booth (2017).
26 Cited in Booth (2017). Britain fought three wars there, then Burma, in the 19th century, suppressing widespread resistance (Booth, 2017). For a brief history of British colonial rule in Burma, see Cole (2023a: 125–126).
27 Booth (2017).
28 Booth (2017).
29 Cited in Booth (2017).
30 Cited in Booth (2017).
31 Cited in Booth (2017).
32 Booth (2017).
33 Cited in Bloom (2019).
34 Cited in Proctor (2020).
35 Cited in Mason (2020).
36 Mason (2020).
37 *BBC News* (2000).
38 *BBC News* (2020a).
39 Syal et al (2019).
40 Cited in Walker et al (2021).
41 Walker et al (2021).
42 Xinhua (2021).
43 Cited in Walker et al (2021).
44 Siddique (2021).
45 Cited in Siddique (2021).
46 *BBC News* (2019c).
47 *BBC News* (2019d).
48 Merrick (2019).
49 Helm et al (2019).
50 Prorogation is a formal mechanism to end a session of Parliament, normally for only a short time until proceedings begin again with a new King's speech. It means Parliament's sitting is suspended and it ends all current legislation under discussion (Elgot, 2019).
51 Meredith (2019).
52 O'Carroll (2019).
53 *BBC News* (2019a).
54 Kanagasooriam and Simon (2021). Kanagasooriam coined this term 'red wall' to refer to what he defined in a tweet as a huge edifice 'stretching from N Walesinto Merseyside, Warrington, Wigan, Manchester, Oldham, Barnsley, Nottingham and Doncaster' (Kanagasooriam, 2019). 'When you talk about cultural barriers to voting Tory', he concluded, 'this is where it is' (Kanagasooriam, 2019).
55 Hyland (2017).
56 Hyland (2017).
57 *BBC News* (2019b).
58 Clarke (2019).
59 UK Parliament (2022).
60 Cited in Kimber (2022).
61 Cited in Woodcock (2022).
62 Syal (2022a).
63 Mararike (2022).
64 Solomon (2022).

NOTES

65 Solomon (2022).
66 See Cole (2023a: 331–335) and for a very brief summary, see endnote 155 of Chapter 3 in this volume. There is also an account of my experiences in Cole (2019).
67 Syal (2022b).
68 Syal (2022b).
69 *BBC News* (2022c).
70 Kirby (2021).
71 Agnew-Pauley and Akintoye (2021).
72 Monbiot (2022).
73 Forrest (2021).
74 Forrest (2021).
75 Monbiot (2022).
76 Monbiot (2022).
77 Cited in Forrest (2021).
78 Cited in Forrest (2021).
79 Cited in Forrest (2021).
80 Cited in Forrest (2021).
81 Cited in Forrest (2021).
82 PA Mediapoint and Press Gazette (2019).
83 Cited in PA Mediapoint and Press Gazette (2019).
84 Cited in Murphy (2019); see also Cole (2023a: 357–359). Islamophobia is also discussed in various parts of this book.
85 Booth (2022).
86 Booth (2022).
87 Booth (2022).
88 Booth (2022).
89 Cited in Booth and Sinmaz (2024).
90 Macfarlane (2021).
91 Macfarlane (2021).
92 Cited in Macfarlane (2021).
93 Macfarlane (2021).
94 Cited in Macfarlane (2021).
95 Taylor (2022).
96 Taylor (2022).
97 Cited in Taylor (2022).
98 Cited in Taylor (2022).
99 Cited in Taylor (2022).
100 Gentleman (2022a).
101 Gentleman (2020).
102 Gentleman (2022a).
103 Cited in Gentleman (2022a).
104 Gentleman (2022a).
105 Cited in Gentleman (2022a).
106 Cited in Gentleman (2022a).
107 Cited in Gentleman (2022a).
108 Gentleman (2022a).

Chapter 5

1 Peck (2022).
2 Cited in Peck (2022).

3. Peck (2022). Cruella de Vil is a fictional character in the novel, *The Hundred and One Dalmations* by Dodie Smith. She has featured in a number of Disney productions.
4. Syal (2022c).
5. Syal (2022c).
6. Syal (2022c).
7. Cited in Syal (2022c).
8. Allegretti (2022).
9. Cited in Allegretti (2022).
10. Allegretti (2022).
11. Diwakar (nd).
12. Cited in Diwakar (nd).
13. Cited in Diwakar (nd).
14. Diwakar (nd).
15. Diwakar (nd).
16. One might raise the case of Sajid Javid, who first rose to prominence in the Tory Party under Cameron's first premiership, and has held seven different ministerial posts. In a bid for Tory Party leadership in 2019, Javid was eliminated from the contest after achieving fewer votes than his three remaining competitors in the fourth round of voting (Colson et al, 2019). Javid has said of religion, 'My own family's heritage is Muslim. Myself and my four brothers were brought up to believe in God, but I do not practise any religion. My wife is a practising Christian and the only religion practised in my house is Christianity' (Farley, 2018).
17. https://x.com/JamieBrysonCPNI/status/1546173430730571782?lang=en. This was, of course, before Twitter became 'X'.
18. Cited in Swinford (2022).
19. Matthews (2022).
20. Matthews (2022).
21. Swinford (2022). For an alternative viewpoint, see Cole (2023a: *passim*).
22. Cited in Matthews (2022).
23. Aljazeera (2022a).
24. Cited in Aljazeera (2022b).
25. Cited in Aljazeera (2022b).
26. Cited in Aljazeera (2022b).
27. Aljazeera (2022a).
28. Aljazeera (2022a).
29. GOV.UK (2022b).
30. GOV.UK (2022b).
31. Cited in GOV.UK (2022b).
32. Cited in GOV.UK (2022b).
33. Cited in GOV.UK (2022b).
34. GOV.UK (2022b).
35. GOV.UK (2022b).
36. In reality, I would maintain that only safe routes will stop small boats and people-smuggling gangs, not further restrictions.
37. GOV.UK (2022b).
38. Cited in GOV.UK (2022b).
39. GOV.UK (2022b).
40. Cited in GOV.UK (2022b).
41. Cited in GOV.UK (2022b).
42. Cited in GOV.UK (2022b).

NOTES

43 Cited in Crerar (2023).
44 Crerar (2023).
45 Crerar (2023).
46 PA Media (2023).
47 Cited in PA Media (2023). When she was in her seventies and studying for a master's degree, Salter went through some archives (Chakrabortty, 2023b). She read a parliamentary debate from 1943, about 2,000 Jewish children in France refused British visas and who were then deported to Nazi Germany (Oryszczuk, 2022). She read Foreign Secretary Anthony Eden claiming 'no knowledge' of the matter. Then she read the minutes and memos that proved he was lying: he was in the War Cabinet meeting where the issue was discussed. Still the children were abandoned, just as her family were left to their fate (Chakrabortty, 2023b) (Eden was later to become Prime Minister – his premiership is discussed in Cole [2023a: 138–143]).
48 Cited in PA Media (2023).
49 Cited in PA Media (2023).
50 Cited in PA Media (2023).
51 PA Media (2023).
52 Cited in Davies and Clinton (2023).
53 Sparrow (2023).
54 Stevens (2023).
55 Cited in Stevens (2023).
56 Stevens (2023).
57 Cited in Stevens (2023).
58 Cited in Stevens (2023).
59 Stevens (2023).
60 Stevens (2023).
61 Braverman (2023).
62 Braverman (2023).
63 Braverman (2023).
64 Cockbain (2023).
65 Waterson (2023).
66 Cited in Weaver (2023).
67 Cited in Weaver (2023).
68 Cited in Weaver (2023).
69 Cited in Weaver (2023).
70 Cited in Hajjaji (2023).
71 Cited in Hajjaji (2023).
72 Cited in Syal (2023a).
73 Syal (2023a).
74 Taylor (2023a).
75 Taylor (2023a).
76 Cited in Taylor (2023a).
77 Townsend and Nonyelum (2023).
78 Townsend and Nonyelum (2023).
79 Townsend and Nonyelum (2023).
80 Townsend and Nonyelum (2023).
81 Cited in Townsend and Nonyelum (2023).
82 Townsend and Nonyelum (2023).
83 Gentleman (2022b).
84 Gentleman (2022b).

85 Cited in Gentleman (2022b).
86 Cited in Gentleman (2022b).
87 Cited in Gentleman (2022b).
88 Cited in Gentleman (2022b).
89 Gentleman (2023b).
90 Gentleman (2023b).
91 Gentleman (2023b).
92 Cited in Gentleman (2023b).
93 Cited in Gentleman (2023b).
94 Cited in Gentleman (2023b).
95 Cited in Gentleman (2023b).
96 Cited in Gentleman (2023b).
97 Cited in Quinn (2023).
98 Cited in Quinn (2023).
99 Quinn (2023).
100 Syal (2021).
101 Quinn (2023).
102 Quinn (2023). The 'alt-right' (alternative right) movement is a far-right racist movement in the United States, originating in the late 2000s, that reached prominence in the August, 2017, Unite the Right rally in Charlottesville, Virginia. For an analysis of the alt-right, including Charlottesville, see Cole (2020b: *passim*).
103 Cited in Spirit (2023).
104 Cited in Spirit (2023).
105 Huskisson (2023).
106 Dearden and McHardy (2023).
107 Dearden and McHardy (2023).
108 Cited in Dearden and McHardy (2023).
109 Drax is a controversial figure. Under fire for his ancestors' role in slavery, multimillionaire Drax is due for a multimillion pay-out from the Barbados Government from the sale of his land, described as a 'killing field' (Smith and Lashmar, 2024).
110 Cited in Dearden and McHardy (2023).
111 Cited in Dearden and McHardy (2023).
112 Dearden and McHardy (2023).
113 Gentleman (2023c).
114 Gentleman (2023c).
115 Taylor (2023b).
116 Taylor (2023b). Charlotte Khan of the refugee charity Care4Calais commented: 'If Mickey Mouse is too "welcoming" for ministers, the question is what will they replace him with in order to inflict more fear on traumatised asylum seeking children – Maleficent? Ursula? Maybe even Cruella herself? The real villains in this sorry tale are Robert Jenrick and the rest of this heartless bunch that call themselves ministers' (cited in Taylor, 2023b).
117 Cited in Gentleman (2023c).
118 Gentleman (2023c).
119 Taylor (2024b).
120 Cited in Taylor (2024b).
121 Taylor (2024b).
122 Taylor and Syal (2023).
123 Taylor and Syal (2023).
124 Refugee Council (2023).

NOTES

125 Refugee Council (2023).
126 Refugee Council (2023).
127 Solomon (2023).
128 Solomon (2023).
129 Pang (2023).
130 Solomon (2023).
131 Cited in UN (2023).
132 UN (2023).
133 Solomon (2023).
134 Solomon (2023).
135 Walawalkar and Taylor (2023).
136 Walawalkar and Taylor (2023).
137 Refugee Council (2024a).
138 Refugee Council (2024a).
139 Refugee Council (2024a).
140 GOV.UK (2024).
141 Home Office (2023).
142 Mitchell (2023).
143 Mitchell (2023).
144 Mitchell (2023).
145 Cited in Mitchell (2023).
146 Cited in Mitchell (2023).
147 Cited in Mitchell (2023).
148 Cited in Mitchell (2023).
149 Cited in Mitchell (2023).
150 Cited in Mitchell (2023).
151 Cited in Mitchell (2023).
152 Hayhurst (2023).
153 Keynote Address by UK Home Secretary Suella Braverman (2023).
154 Keynote Address by UK Home Secretary Suella Braverman (2023).
155 Keynote Address by UK Home Secretary Suella Braverman (2023).
156 Syal and Quinn (2023).
157 Heffer (2023).
158 Cited in Syal (2023b).
159 Syal (2023b).
160 Smith (2023).
161 Syal (2023b).
162 Cited in Syal (2023b).
163 For a summary of the lack of basic human rights in Bahrain, see Bahrain Human Rights Watch (2023).
164 Cited in Badshah (2023).
165 Cited in Badshah (2023).
166 Cited in Badshah (2023).
167 Cited in Badshah (2023).
168 Aljazeera (2023).
169 Adu (2023).
170 Another reason might have been her (racist) remarks on homelessness: 'we cannot allow our streets to be taken over by rows of tents occupied by people, *many of them from abroad*, living on the streets as a lifestyle choice' (Otte, 2023; emphasis added).
171 Otte (2023).

172 Smout (2023).
173 Mason (2023a). Other GB News Tories include Jacob Rees-Mogg, Esther McVey (not at the time of writing [May 2024] since she is a Minister) and Philip Davies. Former Tories include Nigel Farage and Michael Portillo.
174 Adu (2023).

Chapter 6

1 Adapted from Kingsley (2012). Here is not the place to engage with the complex debates pertaining to the cause of the crisis. For opposing views within the Marxist tradition, see, for example, Kliman (2015) and Harvey (2015).
2 Giles et al (2008). Following the theories of Keynes, Keynesian economics refers to government borrowing to spend on labour-intensive infrastructure to projects to stimulate employment and stabilize wages. A fuller explanation may be found in Jahan et al (2014).
3 Mor (2018).
4 Wearden (2009).
5 Aljazeera (2024).
6 Mueller (2019).
7 Mueller (2019).
8 Mueller (2019).
9 Mueller (2019).
10 Kingsley (2012).
11 See Ryder (2014).
12 Bramble (2018).
13 Mueller (2019).
14 For the history of neoliberal capitalism, see Harvey (2005). See also Maisuria and Cole (2017).
15 See Kynaston (2010).
16 Brady (2009).
17 Krugman (2015).
18 Krugman (2015).
19 Tabb (2010).
20 Bramble (2018).
21 'David Cameron on immigration: full text of the speech' (2011).
22 'David Cameron on immigration: full text of the speech' (2011). For a Marxist interpretation of 'common sense', see Chapter 1.
23 'David Cameron on immigration: full text of the speech' (2011).
24 Pimlott et al (2010).
25 Pimlott et al (2010).
26 Pimlott et al (2010).
27 BBC News (2010b).
28 Dunn (2014: 417).
29 Schulmeister (2013, cited in Dunn, 2014: 417).
30 McKee et al (2012). The impact of austerity after the financial crisis discussed in Chapter 6 and after the tax cuts for the rich, in Chapter 7.
31 Dunn (2014: 418).
32 Marx and Engels (1848 [1975]: 35).
33 Dunn (2014: 419).
34 Mattei (2022a: 3). See Chapter 2 for a discussion of Mattei's work.
35 Cited in Kentish (2018).

NOTES

36 Elliott (2023).
37 Michell et al (2023).
38 Michell et al (2023).
39 Cited in Elliott (2023).
40 This means an extremely strong capacity to meet its financial commitments, the highest issuer credit rating (Hargreaves Lansdown, 2024).
41 Blyth (2015: 1).
42 Blyth (2015).
43 Reicher et al (2019).
44 Cited in Topping (2011).
45 'David Cameron's full statement on the UK riots' (2011).
46 Reicher et al (2019).
47 Southwark (2011).
48 Drury et al (2019).
49 Reicher et al (2019).
50 Chakrabortty (2018).
51 Alston (2018).
52 Chakrabortty (2018).
53 Alston (2018: 1).
54 Alston (2018).
55 *BBC News* (2018b).
56 Alston (2018: 1).
57 Toynbee and Walker (2020a).
58 Alston (2018: 1).
59 Toynbee and Walker (2020a).
60 Social Metrics Commission (2018: 97).
61 Fitzpatrick et al (2018: 2–3).
62 Mueller (2019).
63 Alston (2018: 3).
64 Alston (2018).
65 Alston (2018: 2).
66 Fitzpatrick et al (2018).
67 Alston (2018: 1).
68 Alston (2018).
69 Alston (2018: 4).
70 Alston (2018).
71 Alston (2018: 5).
72 Cheetham et al (2018).
73 Cheetham et al (2018).
74 UK Parliament (2018).
75 Alston (2018: 5).
76 Alston (2018).
77 Alston (2018: 6).
78 Alston (2018).
79 Alston (2018: 9).
80 Boseley (2020).
81 Marmot et al (2020).
82 This was, in fact, Michael Marmot cited in Boseley (2020).
83 Marmot cited in Boseley (2020).
84 Marmot cited in Boseley (2020).

85 Toynbee and Walker (2020a).
86 Cited in Boseley (2020).
87 Toynbee and Walker (2020a).
88 Toynbee and Walker (2020a).
89 Toynbee and Walker (2020a).
90 Cited in Toynbee and Walker (2020a).
91 Cited in Toynbee and Walker (2020a).
92 Toynbee and Walker (2020a).
93 Alston (2018: 12–15).
94 Toynbee and Walker (2020a).
95 Toynbee and Walker (2020a: 15).
96 Alston (2018: 19).
97 Alston (2018: 18–20).
98 National Audit Office (2017: 14).
99 Shelter (2018).
100 The Trussell Trust (2018).
101 Duffy and Gillberg (2018: 11–12).
102 Alston (2018: 16).
103 This and the following quotes were compiled by Booth and Butler (2018).
104 Toynbee and Walker (2020a). See also Toynbee and Walker (2020b).
105 Toynbee and Walker (2011).
106 The term 'New Labour' appeared in print in the 1996 Labour Party Manifesto, *New Labour, New Life for Britain*. New Labour entailed a final break with socialism and an embrace of market economics. Its ideology is encapsulated by Thatcher's 1992 answer to the question, what was her greatest achievement? She replied, 'Tony Blair and New Labour. We forced our opponents to change their minds' (cited in Burns, 2008).
107 Toynbee and Walker (2020a).
108 Cited in Toynbee and Walker (2020a).
109 Cited in Toynbee and Walker (2020a).
110 'Statement from the new Prime Minister Theresa May' (2016).
111 Toynbee and Walker (2020a).
112 Toynbee and Walker (2020a).
113 Toynbee and Walker (2020a).
114 Toynbee and Walker (2020a).
115 Portes and Reed (2018).
116 Portes (2018).
117 Portes (2018).
118 Jonathan Portes, personal email, 7 May 2024.
119 This means you can only get more Child Tax Credit or Universal Credit for your third (or more) child if they were born before 6 April 2017, they are disabled or you qualify for an exemption (Turn 2 Us, 2019).
120 Patrick and Reeves (2024).

Chapter 7

1 Stewart et al (2020). The struggles over Brexit are discussed in various parts of the book.
2 Four years on, only 32 per cent thought Brexit was the right decision, compared to 56 per cent who thought it was the wrong decision (Statista, 2024). The majority view is encapsulated, I would suggest, by the 'European Movement United Kingdom', the UK's largest pro-European movement – 'Poor planning, chaotic implementation, and huge sums of taxpayers' money being wasted. All for no discernible benefits' (Knaggs, 2024).

NOTES

3. Bléland et al (2021).
4. Bléland et al (2021).
5. Bléland et al (2021).
6. Wood et al (2022).
7. TUC (2023b).
8. Clark (2021).
9. The capital–labour relation, a key concept in Marxist theory, is discussed in Kotz (2007).
10. Sunak (2020).
11. Sunak (2020).
12. Sunak (2020).
13. Michell (2022).
14. Michell (2022).
15. Partington (2022).
16. Cooban (2022).
17. Thomas (2022).
18. High Pay Centre (2023).
19. High Pay Centre (2024).
20. Tax Justice UK (2021a).
21. Tax Justice UK (2021a). For the full report, see Tax Justice UK (2021b).
22. Tax Justice UK (2021b).
23. Tax Justice UK (2021b).
24. Good Law Project (2022).
25. Cited in Good Law Project (2022).
26. Good Law Project (2022).
27. Good Law Project (2022).
28. The Good Law Project is a not-for-profit campaign organization that uses the law for a better world.
29. 'Every doctor' is a campaigning organization, originally set up by doctors, but now with a broader membership, that fights for patients, staff and the future of the NHS.
30. Good Law Project (2022).
31. Forrest (2022).
32. Forrest (2022).
33. Forrest (2022).
34. Forrest (2022).
35. Forrest (2022).
36. Franks (2023).
37. Conn (2024).
38. Conn et al (2022).
39. Mason (2023b).
40. Mason (2023b).
41. Cited in Mason (2023b).
42. Lawrence (2023).
43. Cited in Lawrence (2023).
44. Lawrence (2023).
45. Mahase (2021).
46. Mahase (2021).
47. Cited in Mahase (2021).
48. Mahase (2021).
49. Mahase (2021).
50. Mahase (2021).

51 Mahase (2021).
52 Mahase (2021).
53 Cited in Mahase (2021).
54 For example, Townsley et al (2021), Falcão et al (2023).
55 Cited in McGuinness and Rayner (2022).
56 McGuinness and Rayner (2022).
57 McGuinness and Rayner (2022).
58 McGuinness and Rayner (2022).
59 Macaskill and James (2022).
60 Macaskill and James (2022).
61 McGuinness and Rayner (2022).
62 Cited in McGuinness and Rayner (2022).
63 McGuinness and Rayner (2022).
64 McGuinness and Rayner (2022).
65 McGuinness and Rayner (2022).
66 McGuinness and Rayner (2022).
67 Nathoo and Francis (2023).
68 McKie and Louis (2022).
69 Cited in McKie and Louis (2022).
70 Partington (2022).
71 Kwarteng was dismissed as Chancellor on 14 October, and subsequently moved to the back benches. On 6 February 2024, he announced he would not seek re-election in the 2024 General Election.
72 Partington (2022).
73 Partington (2022).
74 Inman and Partington (2022).
75 Cited in Inman and Partington (2022).
76 Walker et al (2022).
77 The following six bullet points are adapted from PKF Smith Cooper (2022).
78 This refers to anti-avoidance tax legislation, the intermediaries contained in chapter 8 of the Income Tax (Earnings and Pensions) Act 2003.
79 Simon (2023).
80 Cited in Simon (2023).
81 Cited in Simon (2023).
82 Simon (2023).
83 Simon (2023).
84 Cited in Simon (2023).
85 Cited in Simon (2023).
86 Cited in Simon (2023).
87 Moore and Scripps (2023).
88 Office for National Statistics (2023: 2).
89 Crisis (2023).
90 Crisis (2023).
91 Cited in Crisis (2023).
92 Moore and Scripps (2023).
93 Cited in Moore and Scripps (2023).
94 Cited in Moore and Scripps (2023).
95 Cited in Moore and Scripps (2023).
96 Cited in Moore and Scripps (2023).
97 Cited in Moore and Scripps (2023).

NOTES

98 Cited in Moore and Scripps (2023).
99 Moore and Scripps (2023).

Chapter 8
1   Cited in Partington (2023b).
2   Evelyn (2022).
3   Cited in Evelyn (2022).
4   Partington (2023b).
5   Emmett (2022).
6   Emmett (2022).
7   Woodcock et al (2022).
8   Cited in Emmett (2022).
9   Emmett (2022).
10 Cited in Woodcock et al (2022).
11 Cited in Woodcock et al (2022).
12 Woodcock et al (2022).
13 Cited in Woodcock et al (2022).
14 Cited in Woodcock et al (2022).
15 International Transport Workers' Federation (2022).
16 Cited in International Transport Workers' Federation (2022).
17 Cited in International Transport Workers' Federation (2022).
18 Cited in International Transport Workers' Federation (2022).
19 Cited in Emmett (2022).
20 Cited in Crerar (2022).
21 Crerar (2022).
22 Crerar (2022).
23 GOV.UK (2022a).
24 GOV.UK (2022a).
25 GOV.UK (2022a).
26 GOV.UK (2022a).
27 GOV.UK (2022a).
28 GOV.UK (2022a).
29 GOV.UK (2022a).
30 Cited in Bienkov (2023).
31 Cited in Bienkov (2023).
32 Smith (2022).
33 Smith (2022).
34 Winchester College (2024).
35 Thornhill and Howard (2024).
36 Smith (2022).
37 O'Neill (2022).
38 O'Neill (2022).
39 *BBC News* (2022b).
40 *BBC News* (2022b).
41 Jones (2024).
42 Lloyd (2023).
43 Chakrabortty (2022).
44 Chakrabortty (2022).
45 Chakrabortty (2022).
46 Crerar and Stacey (2023).

47 We saw in Chapter 3 how Theresa May, having railed against the Tory Party being labelled 'the nasty party', actually increased its 'nastiness'.
48 Chakrabortty (2022). Chakrabortty's use of the term 'authoritarian austerity' relates to the arguments in Mattei's book, *The Capital Order*, that I refer to in the chapters of this book. Authoritarian austerity, Chakrabortty argues, is an ideology with a long and terrible history. Mattei reminds us that the greatest austerity the UK ever faced was in the early 1920s, when Whitehall rapidly slashed spending by 20 per cent. Wages crashed, and the economy was incapacitated for most of the decade. The technocrats at the Bank of England acknowledged: 'The process of deflation of prices ... must necessarily be a painful one to some classes of the community' (cited in Chakrabortty, 2022), a more honest response than the Tory mantra, 'We're all in this together'. Mattei points to the fact that Mussolini posed as an austerity politician when he took power. 'Thrift, work, discipline ... the budget has to be balanced as soon as possible', he declared in his first speech in Parliament (cited in Chakrabortty, 2022). When austerity fails to do the trick, Chakrabortty concludes, dissenters can be silenced. 'A clampdown on public finances, a crackdown on public disorder: the two went together in the 80s, in the 2010s – and they are what lie ahead now' (Chakrabortty, 2022).
49 Chakrabortty (2022).
50 At the time, UK nurses were paid less than in most European Union countries, the United States and Australia (Stevens, 2022).
51 RCN (2022).
52 Cited in RCN (2022).
53 Stewart et al (2023).
54 Stewart et al (2023).
55 Cited in Stewart et al (2023).
56 Cited in Stewart et al (2023).
57 Stewart et al (2023).
58 Scripps (2023).
59 Nanji (2023a).
60 *BBC News* (2023).
61 *BBC News* (2023).
62 *BBC News* (2023).
63 Scripps (2023).
64 Ewing and Hendy (2023).
65 The 1980 Employment Act restricted the definition of lawful picketing 'strictly to those who were themselves party to the dispute and who were picketing at the premises of their own employer' (Thatcher, 1993: 99) and introduced ballots on the existence of closed shops (where only union members can work), whereby at least 80 per cent of the workers in a particular industry need to support them for their maintenance.
66 Ewing and Hendy (2023).
67 Ewing and Hendy (2023).
68 Ewing and Hendy (2023).
69 Ewing and Hendy (2023).
70 Ewing and Hendy (2023) provide a most thorough and interesting analysis of the complexities, anomalies and weaknesses of the Act.
71 Farhat and Ashton (2023).
72 Cited in Farhat and Ashton (2023).
73 Farhat and Ashton (2023).
74 Nanji (2023b). Introduced in 2014 when the UK was still part of the EU, the cap was designed to curb excessive risk-taking in the financial services industry in the wake of the 2008 financial crash.

75 Thompson (2023).
76 Cited in Thompson (2023).
77 Cited in Thompson (2023).
78 Cited in Thompson (2023).
79 Cited in Thompson (2023).
80 Booth (2023).
81 Fitzpatrick et al (2023).
82 Schmuecker and Wincup (2023).
83 Fitzpatrick et al (2023: 2).
84 Fitzpatrick et al (2023).
85 Thompson (2023).
86 Thompson (2023).
87 Cited in Thompson (2023).
88 Cited in Thompson (2023).
89 Thompson (2023).
90 Butler (2023b).
91 Butler (2023b).
92 Butler (2023b).
93 Cited in Butler (2023b).
94 Disability Rights UK (2023).
95 Butler (2023b).
96 Butler (2023c).
97 Butler (2023b).
98 Osborne (2023).
99 Partington and Crerar (2023).
100 Partington and Stacey (2023).
101 Jolly (2023).
102 Jolly (2023).
103 Partington et al (2023).
104 Partington et al (2023).
105 Cited in Partington et al (2023).
106 Partington et al (2023).
107 Cited in Partington et al (2023).

Conclusion

1 Cited in Gentleman (2023b).
2 Gentleman (2024).
3 Cited in Gentleman (2024).
4 Cited in Gentleman (2024).
5 Womack (2020).
6 Womack (2020).
7 Womack (2020).
8 Womack (2020).
9 Womack (2020).
10 Womack (2020).
11 Womack (2020).
12 Mason (2015).
13 Cited in Mason (2015).
14 Mason (2015).
15 Taylor and Syal (2023).
16 Taylor and Syal (2023).

[17] Dearden (2023).
[18] Taylor (2023c).
[19] Letters (2023).
[20] Nicholson (2024).
[21] United Nations Human Rights Office of the High Commission (2019).
[22] Cited in United Nations Human Rights Office of the High Commission (2019).
[23] Cited in United Nations Human Rights Office of the High Commission (2019).
[24] Cited in United Nations Human Rights Office of the High Commission (2019).
[25] Cited in United Nations Human Rights Office of the High Commission (2019).
[26] Cited in United Nations Human Rights Office of the High Commission (2019).
[27] Cited in United Nations Human Rights Office of the High Commission (2019).
[28] Bray et al (2024: 15).
[29] *The Independent* (2015).
[30] Gietel-Basten (2016, cited in Bray et al, 2024: 1).
[31] Bray et al (2024: 1).
[32] Bray et al (2024).
[33] Bray et al (2024).
[34] Bray et al (2024).
[35] Bray et al (2024).
[36] Harries et al (2020).
[37] Aiken (2014).
[38] Aiken (2014).
[39] Aiken (2014).
[40] Walby et al (2012).
[41] Harries et al (2020).
[42] Harries et al (2020).
[43] Harrison (2012).
[44] Harries et al (2020).
[45] Gentleman (2024).
[46] Lauber et al (2024).
[47] Lauber et al (2024).
[48] Lauber et al (2024).
[49] Moore-Bick et al (2024: 7).
[50] Lauber et al (2024).
[51] Lauber et al (2024).
[52] Blakeley (2024).
[53] Blakeley (2024). Government Debt Issue allows governments to raise funds by promising to repay the lender at a certain point in the future. It is considered a safe investment when it is backed by full faith in the credit of the government. Since investors are guaranteed a return of the debt, interest rates on Government Debt Issues tend to be lower than rates on corporate debt issues.
[54] Blakeley (2024).
[55] Unite (2024).
[56] Blakeley (2024).
[57] Blakeley (2024).
[58] Blakeley (2024).
[59] Foy (2024).
[60] Blakeley (2024).
[61] JCWI (2023).
[62] JCWI (2023).
[63] Refugee Council (2024c).

[64] Refugee Council (2024b).
[65] Refugee Council (2024b).
[66] UNHCR (2022).
[67] *Sky News* (2024).
[68] Refugee Council (2024b).
[69] Refugee Council (2024b).
[70] Refugee Council (2024b).
[71] Refugee Council (2024b).
[72] Refugee Council (2024b).
[73] Refugee Council (2024b).
[74] Refugee Council (2024b).
[75] Refugee Council (2024b).
[76] Refugee Council (2024b). The Refugee Council provides a thorough and detailed analysis of how all this could work.
[77] JCWI (2023).
[78] UK Parliament (2024).
[79] For example, Cole (2021).
[80] Cole (forthcoming). This is a work in progress, but will likely encompass a discussion of at least the following roads to socialism: Leninism/Trotskyism/Stalinism and the Bolshevik Revolution; Cuba and the Committees for the Defence of the Revolution; liberation theology; the parliamentary road; the long march through the institution; Eurocommunism; Bolivarian socialism; ecosocialism and the great transition; and One Belt One Road: Socialism with Chinese Characteristics.
[81] Callinicos (2000: 122), emphasis in original.
[82] Callinicos (2000: 125).
[83] McMurtry (2000: 2).
[84] McLaren (2000: 32).
[85] Callinicos (2000: 128).

Postscript

[1] Mason (2024).
[2] Mason (2024).
[3] *BBC News* (2024).
[4] Symonds (2024).
[5] Sabbagh (2018).
[6] Sabbagh (2018). In the same interview, Bannon said he admired Johnson, whom he said had 'nothing to apologise for' after his controversial descriptions of fully veiled Muslim women (see Chapter 4).
[7] Cited in Symonds (2024).
[8] Tiernan (2024).
[9] Cited in *BBC News* (2024).
[10] Cited in Brown et al (2024).
[11] Downs (2024).
[12] De Simone (2024).
[13] White (2024a).
[14] White (2024a).
[15] White (2024a).
[16] White (2024a).
[17] White (2024a).
[18] White (2024b).

19. White (2024b).
20. Cited in Brown et al (2024).
21. Cooke (2024).
22. Cited in Cooke (2024).
23. Cited in Cooke (2024).
24. Aljazeera (2024).
25. Cheshire (2024).
26. Cited in Cheshire (2024).
27. Prose (nd).
28. Cheshire (2024).
29. Ken McCallum, Head of MI5, cited in Cheshire (2024).
30. Cited in Cheshire (2024).
31. Cited in Cheshire (2024).
32. Cited in Cheshire (2024).
33. Cheshire (2024).
34. De Simone (2024).
35. Right Response Team (2024).
36. Casciani and *BBC Verify* (2024).
37. De Simone (2024).
38. De Simone (2024).
39. Aljazeera (2024).
40. McDonnell (2024).
41. McDonnell (2024).
42. McDonnell (2024).
43. McDonnell (2024).
44. Brown et al (2024).
45. Brown et al (2024).
46. Brown et al (2024).
47. Brown et al (2024).
48. GOV.UK (2024).
49. Visual Journalism Team et al (2024).
50. Visual Journalism Team et al (2024).
51. Visual Journalism Team et al (2024).
52. Stillwerise (2021).
53. *Morning Star* (2024).
54. Cited in *Morning Star* (2024).
55. Cited in *Morning Star* (2024).
56. Cited in *Morning Star* (2024).
57. Wheeler (2024).
58. Cited in Burch (2024).
59. YouTube (2024).
60. Nelson (2020).
61. Nelson (2020).
62. In Chapter 1, I briefly discuss CRT and in endnote 9 I refer readers to relevant readings. I will repeat them here: for a spirited defence of CRT, see Gillborn (2008) and see Farmer and Farmer (2020) for a comprehensive overview of CRT; see also Delgado and Stefancic (2000). For a critical appraisal and Marxist critique of CRT, see Cole (2017).
63. See, for example, Cole (2017: chapter 2).
64. See, for example, Cole (2017: chapter 9).
65. Cited in Elgot (2024).

NOTES

66 Cited in Elgot (2024).
67 Tell MAMA (2025):
- Between 2012 and 2024, over 51,000 British Muslims used the services of Tell MAMA.
- There has been a large rise in the categorisation of 'threatening behaviour' in street-based cases, amounting to a 715% increase between 2023 and 2024.
- Cases of anti-Muslim hatred are becoming more threatening towards victims, higher in volume and much more prone to significant peaks.

68 Balls (2024).
69 Freeman (1999: 109).
70 Coates (2012: 392).
71 Stevens (2024).
72 Cited in Stevens (2024).
73 Cited in Stevens (2024).
74 Stevens (2024).
75 Cited in Quinn (2025).
76 Cited in Quinn (2025).
77 Quinn (2025).
78 Anderson (2024).
79 Anderson (2024).
80 Engels (1890). For a brief but engaging analysis of why we *need* Marxist theory, see, for example, Cox (2024a; see also Cox, 2024b).
81 Cox (2024a).
82 Cox (2024a).
83 Cox (2024a).
84 Marx (1887 [1965], 1893 [1967], 1894 [1966]).
85 Cox (2024a).
86 Marx argued that capitalism relies for its very existence on the extraction of surplus value from workers who have to sell their labour power to survive: capitalists pay them less than the value they produce, with the value added by workers' labour appropriated as profit by and for the capitalist when goods are sold. For an elucidation of Marx's value theory, see Marx (1887 [1965]), especially chapter 1. For a brief summary and a numerical example of how this works, see Cole (2011: 42–44) and Mattei (2022a: 163).
87 Cox (2024a).
88 Callinicos (2000: 129).

References

Abbott, Diane. 2023. 'Letters'. *The Observer/Guardian*, 23 April. https://www.theguardian.com/theobserver/commentisfree/2023/apr/23/success-for-women-not-same-as-for-men-letters

Adu, Aletha. 2023. 'Sunak seeks to appease Tory right by giving Esther McVey ministerial role'. *The Guardian*, 13 November. https://www.theguardian.com/politics/2023/nov/13/sunak-seeks-to-appease-tory-right-by-giving-esther-mcvey-ministerial-role

Agnew-Pauley, Winifred and Akintoye, Bisola. 2021. 'Stop and search disproportionately affects black communities – yet police powers are being extended'. *The Conversation*, 3 August. https://theconversation.com/stop-and-search-disproportionately-affects-black-communities-yet-police-powers-are-being-extended-165477#:~:text=The%20UK%20government%20has%20extended,who%20they%20stop%20and%20search

Aiken, Mike. 2014. *The Changing Shape of Voluntary Services: How This Affects Volunteer-Based Community Groups*. London: National Coalition for Independent Action.

Aitkenhead, Decca and Wintour, Patrick. 2013. 'Lib Dem MP attacks coalition's plans for immigration reform'. *The Guardian*, 13 July. https://www.theguardian.com/global/2013/jul/12/sarah-teather-lib-dem-mp-immigration-reform

Aljazeera. 2022a. 'UK home secretary slammed for asylum seeker "invasion" remarks', 1 November. https://www.aljazeera.com/news/2022/11/1/uk-home-secretary-slammed-for-asylum-seeker-invasion-remarks

Aljazeera. 2022b. 'Attack on UK immigration centre "terrorist" incident, police say', 5 November. https://www.aljazeera.com/news/2022/11/5/attack-on-uk-immigration-centre-terrorist-incident-police

Aljazeera. 2023. 'UK minister Suella Braverman fired: here's what to know', 13 November. https://www.aljazeera.com/news/2023/11/13/uk-minister-suella-braverman-fired-heres-what-to-know

Aljazeera. 2024. 'UN committee slams UK over racism, incitement affecting minorities', 23 August. https://www.aljazeera.com/news/2024/8/23/un-committee-slams-uk-over-racism-incitement-affecting-minorities

Allegretti, Aubrey. 2022. 'Suella Braverman resignation letter: what she said and totally meant'. *The Guardian*, 19 October. https://www.theguardian.com/politics/2022/oct/19/suella-braverman-resignation-letter-what-she-said-and-totally-meant

Allegretti, Aubrey. 2023. 'Labour suspends Diane Abbott in attempt to stifle fresh antisemitism row'. *The Guardian*, 23 April. https://www.theguardian.com/politics/2023/apr/23/diane-abbott-suspended-by-labour-after-saying-jewish-people-not-subject-to-racism

Alston, Phillip. 2018. 'Statement on visit to the United Kingdom, by Professor Philip Alston, United Nations special rapporteur on extreme poverty and human rights', London, 16 November. https://www.ohchr.org/sites/default/files/Documents/Issues/Poverty/EOM_GB_16Nov2018.pdf

Anderson, Kevin B. 2024. 'The US election: how can we move forward while staring negativity in its face?' *The International Marxist-Humanist*, 8 November. https://imhojournal.org/articles/the-us-election-how-can-we-move-forward-while-staring-negativity-in-its-face/

Anonymous. 2023. 'Hurt and disappointed by Diane Abbott's letter'. *The Guardian*, 25 April. https://www.theguardian.com/politics/2023/apr/25/hurt-and-disappointed-by-diane-abbott-letter

Badshah, Nadeem. 2023. 'Tory MP Bob Stewart guilty of racially abusing activist'. *The Guardian*, 3 November. https://www.theguardian.com/uk-news/2023/nov/03/tory-mp-bob-stewart-racial-hostility-activist-court-told

Bahrain Human Rights Watch. 2023. *World Report 2023*. https://www.hrw.org/world-report/2023/country-chapters/bahrain

Balfour, Arthur. 1905. 'Speech in the House of Commons', 2 May. https://api.parliament.uk/historic-hansard/commons/1905/may/02/aliens-bill-1#S4V0145P0_19050502_HOC_228

Ball, Stephen J. 1990. *Politics and Policymaking in Education*. London: Routledge

Balls, Katy. 2024. '"High energy, high risk": Tories already wonder if Kemi Badenoch will last until the next election'. *The Guardian*, 4 November. https://www.theguardian.com/politics/commentisfree/2024/nov/04/tories-kemi-badenoch-election

Barot, Rohit and Bird, John. 2001. 'Racialization: the genealogy and critique of a concept'. *Ethnic and Racial Studies* 24(4): 601–618. https://www.tandfonline.com/doi/abs/10.1080/01419870120049806

Batty, David. 2011. 'Lady Warsi claims Islamophobia is now socially acceptable in Britain'. *The Guardian*, 20 January. https://www.theguardian.com/uk/2011/jan/20/lady-warsi-islamophobia-muslims-prejudice

BBC News. 2000. 'School gap blamed on black culture'. http://news.bbc.co.uk/1/hi/education/890214.stm

BBC News. 2009. 'European election 2009: UK results'. http://news.bbc.co.uk/1/shared/bsp/hi/elections/euro/09/html/ukregion_999999.stm

BBC News. 2010a. 'Gordon Brown resigns as UK prime minister', 11 May. http://news.bbc.co.uk/1/hi/uk_politics/election_2010/8675913.stm

BBC News. 2010b. 'Spending review: chancellor's speech in full'. https://www.bbc.co.uk/news/uk-politics-11585941

BBC News. 2017. 'Grenfell fire: MP calls for inquiry chairman to quit', 4 July. https://www.bbc.co.uk/news/uk-40491449

BBC News. 2018a. 'Margaret Thatcher was the "quintessential hate figure" says Mary Lou McDonald', 28 December. https://www.bbc.co.uk/news/uk-northern-ireland-46611049

BBC News. 2018b. 'World Mental Health Day: PM appoints suicide prevention minister'. https://www.bbc.co.uk/news/health-45804225

BBC News. 2019a. 'Election results 2019: Boris Johnson hails "new dawn" after historic victory', 13 December. https://www.bbc.co.uk/news/election-2019-50776671

BBC News. 2019b. 'Prime Minister Boris Johnson: does his cabinet reflect "modern Britain"', 25 July. https://www.bbc.co.uk/news/uk-politics-49034735

BBC News. 2019c. 'Brexit: Tory MP defects ahead of crucial no-deal vote', 3 September. http://www.bbc.co.uk/news/uk-politics-49570682

BBC News. 2019d. 'Brexit: Boris Johnson defeated as MPs take control', 4 September. http://www.bbc.co.uk/news/uk-politics-49573555

BBC News. 2020a. 'Charity boss Tony Sewell to head government race commission'. https://www.bbc.co.uk/news/uk-politics-53428248

BBC News. 2020b. 'Grenfell Tower inquiry: "fire inextricably linked with race"', 7 July. https://www.bbc.co.uk/news/uk-53320082

BBC News. 2022a. 'Gloucestershire's Muller dairy staff go on strike over rotas', 26 August. https://www.bbc.co.uk/news/uk-england-somerset-62673302

BBC News. 2022b. 'Stonehouse: Müller lorry drivers strike over rota changes', 20 October. https://www.bbc.co.uk/news/uk-england-somerset-63326988

BBC News. 2022c. 'What is the Police and Crime Bill and how will it change protests?', 28 April. https://www.bbc.co.uk/news/uk-56400751

BBC News. 2023. 'Budget summary: key points from Jeremy Hunt's 2023 budget', 16 March. https://www.bbc.co.uk/news/business-64789405

BBC News. 2024. 'UK general election 2024 results'. https://www.bbc.co.uk/news/election/2024/uk/results

BBC 'Newsnight'. 2019. 28 February.

Bienkov, Adam. 2023. 'Rishi Sunak is an "upper class" leader of an "elite" and "out of touch" party, say voters'. *Byline Times*, 13 October. https://bylinetimes.com/2023/10/13/rishi-sunak-is-an-upper-class-leader-of-an-elite-and-out-of-touch-party-say-voters/

Blakeley, Grace. 2024. 'Labour's austerity is a choice'. *Tribune*, 28 August. https://tribunemag.co.uk/2024/08/labours-austerity-is-a-choice-starmer-pain

Bléland, Daniel, Cantillon, Bea, Hick, Rod and Moreira, Amilcar. 2021. 'Social policy in the face of a global pandemic: policy responses to the COVID-19 crisis'. *Social Policy and Administration* 50(2). https://onlinelibrary.wiley.com/doi/abs/10.1111/spol.12718

Bloom, Dan. 2019. 'Boris Johnson said "bunch of black kids" made him "turn a hair" in old column'. *Daily Mirror*, 21 November. https://www.mirror.co.uk/news/politics/boris-johnson-said-bunch-black-20889302

Bloomberg. 2024. 'Bloomberg billionaires index # 9 Warren Buffett'. https://www.bloomberg.com/billionaires/profiles/warren-e-buffett/

Blyth, Mark. 2015. *Austerity: The History of a Dangerous Idea*. New York: Oxford University Press.

Booth, Robert. 2017. 'Boris Johnson caught on camera reciting Kipling in Myanmar temple'. *The Guardian*, 30 September. https://www.theguardian.com/politics/2017/sep/30/boris-johnson-caught-on-camera-reciting-kipling-in-myanmar-temple

Booth, Robert. 2022. 'Fire safety official admits tests showed cladding danger 15 years before Grenfell'. *The Guardian*, 28 February. https://www.theguardian.com/uk-news/2022/feb/28/cladding-danger-evidence-15-years-before-grenfell-tower-fire

Booth, Robert. 2023. 'UK "in violation of international law" over poverty levels, says UN envoy'. *The Guardian*, 5 November. https://www.theguardian.com/society/2023/nov/05/uk-poverty-levels-simply-not-acceptable-says-un-envoy-olivier-de-schutter

Booth, Robert and Butler, Patrick. 2018. 'UK austerity has inflicted "great misery" on citizens, UN says'. *The Guardian*, 16 November. https://www.theguardian.com/society/2018/nov/16/uk-austerity-has-inflicted-great-misery-on-citizens-un-says

Booth, Robert and Sinmaz, Emine. 2024. 'Grenfell Tower fire report: who was at fault and what was landlord's role?'. *The Guardian*, 4 September. https://www.theguardian.com/uk-news/article/2024/sep/04/grenfell-tower-fire-report-key-takeaways

Boseley, Sarah. 2020. 'Austerity blamed for life expectancy stalling for first time in century'. *The Guardian*, 25 February. https://www.theguardian.com/society/2020/feb/24/austerity-blamed-for-life-expectancy-stalling-for-first-time-in-century

Bradley, Anthony B. 2020. 'Black liberation theology, personalism, and black economic freedom in critical race perspective', in Vernon Lee Farmer and Evelyn Shepherd W. Farmer (eds) *Critical Race Theory in the Academy*. Charlotte: Information Age Publishing.

Brady, Brian. 2009. 'Cameron: this will be the new age of austerity'. *The Independent*, 26 April. https://www.independent.co.uk/news/uk/politics/cameron-this-will-be-the-new-age-of-austerity-1674374.html

Bramble, Tom. 2018. 'The crisis in neoliberalism and its ramifications'. *Marxist Left Review*, 12 July. https://marxistleftreview.org/articles/the-crisis-in-neoliberalism-and-its-ramifications/

Braverman, Suella. 2023. 'My mission to ensure there really is no hiding place for the evil gangs grooming our vulnerable young girls'. *Daily Mail*, 25 September. https://www.dailymail.co.uk/debate/article-11928629/SUELLA-BRAVERMAN-mission-ensure-really-no-hiding-place-gangs-grooming-young-girls.html

Bray, Kerry, Braakmann, Nils and Wildman, John. 2024. 'Austerity, welfare cuts and hate crime: evidence from the UK's age of austerity'. *Journal of Urban Economics* 141. https://www.sciencedirect.com/science/article/pii/S009411902200016X

Brown, Mark, Halliday, Josh, Murray, Jessica, Quinn, Ben, Vinter, Robert, van der Zee, Bibi, et al. 2024. 'United against hate: England's counter-protesters left with little to counter'. *The Guardian*, 8 August. https://www.theguardian.com/world/article/2024/aug/07/anti-racism-protesters-fill-streets-of-english-cities-as-far-right-threat-recedes

Burch, Druin. 2024. 'Badenoch is right: not all cultures are equally valid'. *The Spectator*, 2 October. https://www.spectator.co.uk/article/badenoch-is-right-not-all-cultures-are-equally-valid/

Burns, Connor. 2008. 'Margaret Thatcher's greatest achievement: New Labour'. *Conservative Home*, 11 April. https://conservativehome.blogs.com/centreright/2008/04/making-history.html

Butler, Patrick. 2023a. 'Most British people hold positive view of immigration, survey reveals'. *The Guardian*, 3 November. https://www.theguardian.com/uk-news/2023/nov/03/most-british-people-hold-positive-view-of-immigration-survey-reveals#:~:text=The%20latest%20poll%2C%20for%202022,place%20to%20live%20(56%25))

Butler, Patrick. 2023b. 'More than 1 million children in UK sleep on floor or share bed, study finds'. *The Guardian*, 29 September. https://www.theguardian.com/society/2023/sep/29/more-than-1-million-children-in-uk-sleep-on-floor-or-share-bed-study-finds#:~:text=More%20than%20a%20million%20children,to%20the%20children's%20charity%20Barnardo's

Butler, Patrick. 2023c. 'Two-child limit on UK welfare benefits "has failed to push parents into jobs"'. *The Guardian*, 1 June. https://www.theguardian.com/society/2023/jun/01/two-child-limit-on-uk-welfare-benefits-has-failed-to-push-parents-into-jobs

Callinicos, Alex. 2000. *Equality*. Oxford: Oxford University Press.

Camara, Babacar. 2002. 'Ideologies of race and racism', in Paul Zarembka (ed) *Confronting 9-11, Ideologies of Race, and Eminent Economists*. Oxford: Elsevier Science.

Campbell, Adina and Lee, Anthea. 2024. 'Home Office asks Windrush man's son for DNA test'. *BBC News*, 15 May. https://www.bbc.co.uk/news/articles/c97z6dgjey9o

Casciani, Dominic and *BBC Verify*. 2024. 'Violent Southport protests reveal organising tactics of the far-right'. *BBC*, 2 August. https://www.bbc.co.uk/news/articles/cl4y0453nv5o

Chakrabortty, Aditya. 2018. 'The epitaph for Tory austerity has been written, and it's damning'. *The Guardian*, 16 November. https://www.theguardian.com/commentisfree/2018/nov/16/epitaph-theresa-may-goverment-damning-un-report

Chakrabortty, Aditya. 2022. 'Discipline the poor, protect the rich – it's the same old Tories, same old class war'. *The Guardian*, 10 November. https://www.theguardian.com/commentisfree/2022/nov/10/poor-rich-tories-brexit-austerity-cameron-osborne-sunak

Chakrabortty, Aditya. 2023a. 'The lesson from the Diane Abbott row: if we fight racism in silos, we just can't win'. *The Guardian*, 27 April. https://www.theguardian.com/commentisfree/2023/apr/27/diane-abbott-racism-letter-racial-politics

Chakrabortty, Aditya. 2023b. 'Suella Braverman proved it again: racism is a fire the Tories love to play with'. *The Guardian*, 19 January. https://www.theguardian.com/commentisfree/2023/jan/19/suella-braverman-racism-tories-holocaust

Cheetham, Mandy, Moffatt, Suzanne and Addison, Michelle. 2018. '"It's hitting people that can least afford it the hardest" the impact of the roll out of Universal Credit in two North East England localities: a qualitative study'. Final Report. November. Middlesbrough: Teesside University. https://www.gateshead.gov.uk/media/10665/The-impact-of-the-roll-out-of-Universal-Credit-in-two-North-East-England-localities-a-qualitative-study-November-2018/pdf/Universal_Credit_Report_2018pdf.pdf?m=636778831081630000

Cheshire, Tom. 2024. 'Riots and the far right: the global network behind the violence'. *Sky News*, 15 October. https://news.sky.com/story/riots-and-the-far-right-the-global-network-behind-the-violence-13232023

Chorley, Matt, Slack, James and Chapman, James. 2013. '"Immigration system is like a never-ending game of snakes and ladders": Theresa May vows to kick out illegal migrants BEFORE they get chance to appeal'. *MailOnline*, 30 September. https://www.dailymail.co.uk/news/article-2438130/Theresa-May-Ill-kick-illegal-migrants-BEFORE-chance-appeal.html

Clark, Harriet. 2021. 'Examining the end of the furlough scheme'. UK Parliament. https://commonslibrary.parliament.uk/examining-the-end-of-the-furlough-scheme/#:~:text=Risk%20of%20redundancies%20and%20unemployment&text=In%20late%20October%2C%20it%20was,were%20classified%20as%20%E2%80%9Cother%E2%80%9D

Clarke, Seán. 2019. 'How representative is Boris Johnson's new cabinet?'. *The Guardian*, 25 July. https://www.theguardian.com/politics/ng-interactive/2019/jul/25/how-representative-is-boris-johnsons-new-cabinet

Coates, David. 2012. *The Oxford Companion to American Politics*. Vol 2. Oxford: Oxford University Press.

Coben, Diana. 2002. 'Metaphors for an educative politics "common sense", "good sense" and educating adults', in Carmel Borg, Joseph Buttigieg and Peter Mayo (eds) *Gramsci and Education*. Lanham and Oxford: Rowman & Littlefield.

Cockbain, Ella. 2023. 'Not even Suella Braverman's own department agrees with her about "grooming gangs"'. *The Guardian*, 4 April. https://www.theguardian.com/commentisfree/2023/apr/04/suella-braverman-grooming-gangs-child-seual-abuse-home-secretary-prejudice

Cole, Mike. 2011. *Racism in the UK and the US: Towards a Socialist Alternative*. New York: Palgrave Macmillan.

Cole, Mike. 2012a. 'Racism in the UK: change and continuity', in Mike Cole (ed) *Education, Equality and Human Rights: Issues of Gender, 'Race', Sexuality, Disability and Social Class*, 3rd edition. London: Routledge.

Cole, Mike. 2012b. 'Introduction: human rights, equality and education', in Mike Cole (ed) *Education, Equality and Human Rights: Issues of Gender, 'Race,' Sexuality, Disability and Social Class*. London: Routledge.

Cole, Mike. 2017. *Critical Race Theory and Education: A Marxist Response*, revised 2nd edition. New York: Palgrave Macmillan.

Cole, Mike. 2018. 'Social class, Marxism and socialism', in Mike Cole (ed) *Education, Equality and Human Rights: Issues of Gender, 'Race', Sexuality, Disability and Social Class*, 4th edition. London: Routledge.

Cole, Mike. 2019. 'We must never forget Theresa May's full frontal assault on families like mine'. *HuffPost*, 7 June. https://www.huffingtonpost.co.uk/entry/theresa-may-minimum-income-requirement_uk_5cfa1db5e4b06af8b506823e

Cole, Mike. 2020a. *Theresa May, the Hostile Environment and Public Pedagogies of Hate and Threat*. London: Routledge.

Cole, Mike. 2020b. *Trump, the Alt-Right and Public Pedagogies of Hate and for Fascism: What is to be Done?* New York: Routledge.

Cole, Mike. 2021. *Climate Change, the Fourth Industrial Revolution and Public Pedagogies: The Case for Ecosocialism*. London: Routledge.

Cole, Mike. 2023a. *Racism and the Tory Party: From Disraeli to Johnson*. New York and London: Routledge.

Cole, Mike. 2023b. 'Social class, neoliberal capitalism and the Marxist alternative', in Mike Cole (ed) *Education, Equality and Human Rights: Issues of Gender, 'Race', Sexuality, Disability and Social Class*, 5th edition. London: Routledge.

Cole, Mike. 2023c. '"Race" and racism in the UK: through history and today', in Mike Cole (ed) *Education, Equality and Human Rights: Issues of Gender, 'Race', Sexuality, Disability and Social Class*, 5th edition. London: Routledge.

Cole, Mike. 2023d. 'Racism and education: from empire to Johnson', in Mike Cole (ed) *Education, Equality and Human Rights: Issus of Gender, 'Race', Sexuality, Disability and Social Class*, 5th edition. London: Routledge.

Cole, Mike. 2023e. 'Marx and the Marxist alternative to neoliberal capitalism: the case for a fully inclusive ecosocialism for today', in Mike Cole (ed) *Equality, Education, and Human Rights in the United States: Issues of Gender, Race, Sexuality, Disability, and Social Class*. New York: Routledge.

Cole, Mike. Forthcoming. 'The roads to Socialism: what are they, where should they lead and what should happen on arrival?'.

Colson, Thomas, Payne, Adam and Blenkov, Adam. 2019. 'Sajid Javid knocked out of the Conservative Party leadership contest'. *Business Insider*, 20 June. https://www.businessinsider.com/sajid-javid-eliminated-from-the-conservative-party-leadership-contest-2019-6?r=US&IR=T

Conn, David. 2024. 'Cameron broke convention when he made Michelle Mone a peer, says Tory MP'. *The Guardian*, 25 January. https://www.theguardian.com/politics/2024/jan/25/david-cameron-broke-convention-when-he-made-michelle-mone-a-peer-says-tory-mp#:~:text=David%20Cameron%20breached%20%E2%80%9Cproper%20process,at%20the%20time%2C%20has%20said

Conn, David, Lewis, Paul and Evans, Rob. 2022. 'Private emails reveal Gove's role in Tory-linked firm's PPE deals'. *The Guardian*, 24 March. https://www.theguardian.com/politics/2022/mar/24/michael-gove-private-emails-ppe-deals-tory-linked-firms

Cooban, Anna. 2022. 'UK workers suffer biggest hit to their wages since records began'. *CNN Business*, 16 August. https://www.cnn.com/2022/08/16/economy/uk-real-wages-biggest-drop-on-record/index.html

Cooke, Millie. 2024. 'Farage joins calls for Parliament to be recalled and claims "soft policing" at BLM protests to blame for riots'. *The Independent*, 5 August. https://www.independent.co.uk/news/uk/politics/uk-riots-nigel-farage-recall-parliament-b2591246.html

Cox, Judy. 2024a. 'What is Marxist theory and why do we need it?'. *Socialist Worker* 2943, 30 November. https://socialistworker.co.uk/teach-yourself-marxism/what-is-marxist-theory-and-why-do-we-need-it/

Cox, Judy. 2024b. 'The combination of ideas and action made Karl Marx'. *Socialist Worker* 2933, 23 November. https://socialistworker.co.uk/teach-yourself-marxism/the-combination-of-ideas-and-action-made-karl-marx/

Craig, Ian. 2016. 'MP's claims that Islamic headwear is "an excuse for sexual violence against women" are branded "ridiculous"'. *South Wales Argus*, 29 April. https://www.southwalesargus.co.uk/news/14462308.mps-claims-that-islamic-headwear-is-an-excuse-for-sexual-violence-against-women-are-branded-ridiculous/

Crerar, Pippa. 2022. 'Striking union members should "get back to work", says Liz Truss'. *The Guardian*, 21 September. https://www.theguardian.com/politics/2022/sep/21/unions-workers-strikes-industrial-action-liz-truss

Crerar, Pippa. 2023. 'Sunak strives to be reassuring but is five-point plan all sleight of hand?' *The Guardian*, 4 January. https://www.theguardian.com/politics/2023/jan/04/sunak-vows-to-be-steady-hand-on-tiller-but-are-his-pledges-all-sleight-of-hand

Crerar, Pippa and Stacey, Kiran. 2023. 'Union fury as Rishi Sunak unveils anti-strike laws for "minimum service levels"'. *The Guardian*, 4 January. https://www.theguardian.com/uk-news/2023/jan/05/uk-ministers-announce-anti-strike-legislation

Crisis. nd. 'About us'. https://www.crisis.org.uk/about-us/

Crisis. 2023. 'Record number of households stuck in temporary accommodation in England – Crisis responds', 27 July. https://www.crisis.org.uk/about-us/media-centre/record-number-of-households-stuck-in-temporary-accommodation-in-england-crisis-responds/

'David Cameron on immigration: full text of the speech'. 2011. https://www.theguardian.com/politics/2011/apr/14/david-cameron-immigration-speech-full-text

'David Cameron's full statement on the UK riots'. 2011. https://www.theguardian.com/uk/2011/aug/09/david-cameron-full-statement-uk-riots#:~:text=These%20are%20sickening%20scenes%20%E2%80%93%20scenes,to%20be%20confronted%20and%20defeated

'David Cameron's immigration speech'. 2013. 25 March. https://www.gov.uk/government/speeches/david-camerons-immigration-speech

Davies, Caroline and Clinton, Jane. 2023. 'Gary Lineker responds to critics of his immigration policy comments'. *The Guardian*, 8 March. https://www.theguardian.com/football/2023/mar/08/gary-lineker-bbc-uk-asylum-policy-nazi-germany-match-of-the-day-presenter

Dearden, Lizzie. 2015. 'Tory conference 2015: Theresa May says she will overhaul asylum seeker process – as it happened'. *The Independent*, 6 October. https://www.independent.co.uk/news/uk/politics/tory-conference-2015-theresa-may-to-tell-conservative-party-mass-immigration-is-bad-for-britain-live-a6681231.html

Dearden, Lizzie. 2023. 'Bibby Stockholm: what life aboard "quasi-prison" barge will look like for asylum seekers'. *The Independent*, 7 August. https://www.independent.co.uk/news/uk/home-news/bibby-stockholm-barge-inside-portland-migrant-b2388754.html

Dearden, Lizzie and McHardy, Martha. 2023. 'Bibby Stockholm: migrant barge with less living space than an average parking bay arrives in Dorset'. *The Independent*, 18 July. https://www.independent.co.uk/news/uk/politics/inside-bibby-stockholm-migrant-barge-dorset-b2377231.html

Delgado, Richard and Stefancic, Jean (eds). 2000. *Critical Race Theory: The Cutting Edge*. Philadelphia: Temple University Press.

Delgado, Richard and Stefancic, Jean. 2001. *Critical Race Theory: An Introduction*. New York: New York University Press.

De Simone, Daniel. 2024. 'Riots show how the UK's far right has changed'. *BBC INDEPTH*, 21 August. https://www.bbc.co.uk/news/articles/c74lwnxxxzjo

Disability Rights UK. 2023. 'Bedroom tax', 12 April. https://www.disabilityrightsuk.org/resources/bedroom-tax#NumberBedroomsAllowed

Disraeli, Benjamin. 1852. *Lord George Bentinck: A Political Biography*. Ithaca, NY: Cornell University Library Press.

Diwakar, Amar. nd. 'Brown skin, Tory masks'. *TRT World News*. https://www.trtworld.com/magazine/brown-skin-tory-masks-37638

Donaghy, Gerard. 2018. 'Thatcher "wished the Irish wouldn't come to Britain", state papers reveal'. *Irish Post*. https://www.irishpost.com/news/thatcher-wishedirish-wouldnt-come-britain-state-papers-reveal-162970

Dovidio, John F. and Gaertner, Samuel L. 1986. 'The aversive form of racism', in John F. Dovidio and Samuel L. Gaertner (eds) *Prejudice, Discrimination and Racism*. Cambridge, MA: Academic Press. https://research.pomona.edu/sci/files/2017/08/dovidio-et-al-2017-cambridge-proof.pdf

Downs, William. 2024. 'Policing response to the 2024 summer riots'. *Insight*, House of Commons Library, 9 September. https://commonslibrary.parliament.uk/policing-response-to-the-2024-summer-riots/#:~:text=What%20was%20the%20scale%20of,and%20hotels%20housing%20asylum%20seekers

Duffy, Simon and Gillberg, Claudia. 2018. 'Extreme poverty in a time of austerity'. Centre for Welfare Reform, September. https://www.centreforwelfarereform.org/uploads/attachment/620/extreme-poverty-in-a-time-of-austerity.pdf

Dunn, Bill. 2014. 'Making sense of austerity: the irrationality in an irrational system'. *The Economic and Labour Relations Review* 25(3).

Drury, John, Ball, Roger, Neville, Fergus and Reicher, Stephen. 2019. 'Re-reading the 2011 English riots ESRC "Beyond Contagion" interim report'. ESRC, January. https://www.sussex.ac.uk/webteam/gateway/file.php?name=beyond-contagion-report-for-the-guardian-january-2019.pdf&site=557

EIN (Electronic Immigration Network). 2014. '"Movement Against Xenophobia" meeting: Immigration Act codifies racism into British law and will become Untenable'. www.ein.org.uk/news/movement-against-xenophobia-meeting-immigration-act-codifies-racism-british-law-and-will-become

Elgot, Jessica. 2019. 'As government announces it will prorogue parliament, we answer the key questions'. *The Guardian*, 28 August. https://www.theguardian.com/politics/2019/aug/28/what-is-prorogation-prorogue-parliament-boris-johnson-brexit

Elgot, Jessica. 2024. 'Robert Jenrick criticised for saying people shouting "Allahu Akbar" should be arrested'. *The Guardian*, 7 August. https://www.theguardian.com/politics/article/2024/aug/07/robert-jenrick-criticised-for-saying-people-shouting-allahu-akbar-should-be-arrested

Elliott, Larry. 2023. 'Tory austerity "has cost UK half a trillion pounds of public spending since 2010"'. *The Guardian*, 3 March. https://www.theguardian.com/business/2023/mar/03/tory-austerity-has-cost-uk-half-a-trillion-pounds-of-public-spending-since-2010

Emmett, Conrad. 2022. 'A day of national strike action'. *Rail Business Daily*, 21 June. https://news.railbusinessdaily.com/strike-action-underway/

Engels, Friedrich. 1880 [2003]. *Socialism: Utopian and Scientific*. In *Marx/Engels Selected Works*. Vol 3. Moscow: Progress Publishers, 1970. Translated from the French by Edward Aveling. Online Version: https://www.marxists.org/archive/marx/works/download/Engels_Socialism_Utopian_and_Scientific.pdf

Engels, Friedrich. 1890. Engels to J. Bloch, in Königsberg Marx-Engels Correspondence 1890. https://www.marxists.org/archive/marx/works/1890/letters/90_09_21.htm

Evelyn, Rupert. 2022. 'Rail strike: your questions answered as RMT workers vote for biggest strike action in decades'. *ITV News*, 24 May. https://www.itv.com/news/2022-05-24/railway-workers-vote-overwhelmingly-to-strike

Evening Standard. 2008. 'Boris says sorry over "blacks have lower IQs"'. 14 July. https://www.standard.co.uk/news/mayor/boris-says-sorry-over-blacks-have-lower-iqs-article-in-the-spectator-6630340.html

Ewing, Keith and Hendy, John. 2023. 'Strikes (Minimum Service Levels) Act 2023'. Institute of Employment Rights (IER), 6 December. https://www.ier.org.uk/comments/strikes-minimum-service-levels-act-2023/

Falcão, Filipe, Sousa, Bárbara, Pereira, Daniela S.M., Andrade, Renato, Moreira, Pedro, Quialheiro, Anna, et al. 2023. 'We vote for the person, not the policies: a systematic review on how personality traits influence voting behaviour'. *Discover Psychology* 3(1). https://link.springer.com/article/10.1007/s44202-022-00057-z

Farhat, Eamon and Ashton, Emily. 2023. 'UK trade unions vow to fight Rishi Sunak over anti-strike law'. *Bloomberg*, 11 September. https://www.bloomberg.com/news/articles/2023-09-11/uk-trade-unions-vow-to-fight-rishi-sunak-over-anti-strike-law

Farley, Harry. 2018. 'Sajid Javid: what has the new home secretary said about faith?' *Christian Today*, 30 April. https://www.christiantoday.com/article/sajid-javid-what-has-the-new-home-secretary-said-about-faith/128840.htm

Farmer, Vernon Lee and Farmer, Evelyn Shepherd W. (eds). 2020. *Critical Race Theory in the Academy*. Charlotte: Information Age Publishing.

Fekete, Liz. 2001. 'The emergence of xeno-racism'. *Race and Class* 43(2).

Finney, Nissa, Nazroo, James, Bécares, Laia, Kapadia, Dharmi and Shlomo, Natalie (eds). 2023. *Racism and Ethnic Inequality in a Time of Crisis*. Bristol: Policy Press.

Fitzpatrick, Suzanne, Bramley, Glen, Sosenko, Filip, Blenkinsopp, Janice, Wood, Jenny, Johnsen, Sarah, et al. 2018. *Destitution in the UK 2018*. Joseph Rowntree Foundation, 7 June. https://www.jrf.org.uk/cost-of-living/destitution-in-the-uk-2018

Fitzpatrick, Suzanne, Bramley, Glen, Treanor, Morag, Blenkinsopp, Janice, McIntyre, Jill, Johnsen, Sarah, et al. 2023. *Destitution in the UK 2023*. Joseph Rowntree Foundation, October. destitution_in_the_uk_2023_0.pdf

Forrest, Adam. 2021. 'Charities call on Tory MP to resign over "extremist" remarks about Travellers'. *The Independent*, 11 June. https://www.independent.co.uk/news/uk/politics/lee-anderson-tory-gypsy-travellers-b1864000.html

Forrest, Adam. 2022. 'Government condemned for "wasting" £8.7bn on PPE written off last year'. *The Independent*, 1 February. https://www.independent.co.uk/news/uk/politics/ppe-waste-nhs-spending-report-b2005093.html

Foy, Simon. 2024. 'KPMG wins £223mn UK government contract amid plans to cut consultant spending'. *Financial Times*, 26 August. https://www.ft.com/content/d6da606d-76c7-44cd-a6ca-b6cdd5ba2ea5

Franks, Josephine. 2023. 'Michelle Mone: who is she and what is the PPE controversy swirling around the Tory peer?' *Sky News*, 18 December. https://news.sky.com/story/michelle-mone-who-is-she-and-what-is-the-ppe-controversy-swirling-around-the-tory-peer-12762756

Fraser, Giles. 2015. 'The Lutfur Rahman verdict and the spectre of undue spiritual influence'. *The Guardian*, 29 April. https://www.theguardian.com/commentisfree/2015/apr/29/lutfur-rahman-tower-hamlets-mayor-verdict-undue-spiritual-influence

Freeman, Robert M. 1999. *Correctional Organization and Management: Public Policy Challenges, Behavior, and Structure*. Philadelphia: Elsevier.

Fryer, Peter. 1984. *Staying Power: The History of Black People in Britain*. London: Pluto Press.

Gamble, Andrew. 2024. 'The welfare state and the politics of austerity'. *BBVE Open Mind*. https://www.bbvaopenmind.com/en/articles/the-welfare-state-and-the-politics-of-austerity/#:~:text=The%20new%20politics%20of%20austerity,deserving%20and%20the%20undeserving%20poor

Gentleman, Amelia. 2018. 'UK government pauses hostile immigration policies after Windrush'. *The Guardian*, 11 July. https://www.theguardian.com/uk-news/2018/jul/11/windrush-uk-government-pauses-hostile-immigration-policies

Gentleman, Amelia. 2019. *The Windrush Betrayal: Exposing the Hostile Environment*. London: Guardian Faber Publishing.

Gentleman, Amelia. 2020. 'UK government to act on all 30 Windrush recommendations'. *The Guardian*, 23 June. https://www.theguardian.com/uk-news/2020/jun/23/uk-government-to-act-on-all-30-windrush-recommendations

Gentleman, Amelia. 2022a. 'Windrush: Home Office has failed to transform its culture, report says'. *The Guardian*, 31 March. https://www.theguardian.com/uk-news/2022/mar/31/windrush-home-office-has-failed-to-transform-its-culture-report-says

Gentleman, Amelia. 2022b. 'Windrush scandal caused by "30 years of racist immigration laws" – report'. *The Guardian*, 29 May. https://www.theguardian.com/uk-news/2022/may/29/windrush-scandal-caused-by-30-years-of-racist-immigration-laws-report

Gentleman, Amelia. 2023a. 'Theresa May says she regrets using term "hostile environment"'. *The Guardian*, 31 August. https://www.theguardian.com/politics/2023/aug/31/theresa-may-says-she-regrets-using-term-hostile-environment

Gentleman, Amelia. 2023b. 'Home Office minister heckled by victims of Windrush scandal'. *The Guardian*, 16 May. https://www.theguardian.com/uk-news/2023/may/16/home-office-minister-heckled-by-victims-of-windrush-scandal

Gentleman, Amelia. 2023c. '"Cabins slightly larger than a prison cell": life aboard the UK's barge for asylum seekers'. *The Guardian*, 21 July. https://www.theguardian.com/uk-news/2023/jul/21/life-aboard-bibby-stockholm-asylum-seeker-barge-home-office-tour

Gentleman, Amelia. 2024. 'Home Office forced to release critical report on origins of Windrush scandal'. *The Guardian*, 26 September. https://www.theguardian.com/uk-news/2024/sep/26/home-office-forced-to-publish-critical-report-on-origins-of-windrush-scandal

Gietel-Basten, Stuart. 2016. 'Why Brexit: the toxic mix of immigration and austerity'. *Population Development Review* 42(4).

Giles, Chris, Atkins, Ralph and Guha, Krishna. 2008. 'The undeniable shift to Keynes'. *The Financial Times*, 29 December.

Gillborn, David. 2008. *Racism and Education: Coincidence or Conspiracy?* London: Routledge.

Global Justice Now. 2018. 'Campaigners call immigration white paper "biggest attack on rights in Britain in a generation"', 19 December. https://www.globaljustice.org.uk/news/campaigners-call-immigration-white-paper-biggest-attack-rights-britain-generation/#:~:text=%E2%80%9CThe%20white%20paper%20is%20the,migrants%20have%20enjoyed%20to%20date

Good Law Project. 2022. 'Breaking: High Court finds government PPE "VIP" lane for politically connected suppliers "unlawful"', 12 January. https://goodlawproject.org/update/high-court-vip-lane-ppe-unlawful/

REFERENCES

GOV.UK. 2010. 'Immigration: Home Secretary's speech of 5 November 2010'. https://www.gov.uk/government/speeches/immigration-home-secretarys-speech-of-5-november-2010

GOV.UK. 2013. 'Speech by Home Secretary on second reading of Immigration Bill', 22 October. https://www.gov.uk/government/speeches/speech-by-home-secretary-on-second-reading-of-immigration-bill

GOV.UK. 2015. 'Theresa May: "a stronger Britain, built on our values"', 23 March. https://www.gov.uk/government/speeches/a-stronger-britain-built-on-our-values

GOV.UK. 2022a. 'Rishi Sunak's first speech as Prime Minister', 25 October. https://www.gov.uk/government/speeches/prime-minister-rishi-sunaks-statement-25-october-2022#:~:text=The%20government%20I%20lead%20will,out%20to%20deliver%20for%20you

GOV.UK. 2022b. 'PM statement on illegal migration', 13 December. https://www.gov.uk/government/speeches/pm-statement-on-illegal-migration-13-december-2022#:~:text=So%20early%20next%20year%20we,for%20asylum%20will%20be%20considered

GOV.UK. 2024. 'Starmer on far-right riots PM statement', 4 August. https://www.gov.uk/government/speeches/pm-statement-4-august-2024

GOV.UK. Ongoing. 'Updates: immigration rules'. https://www.gov.uk/guidance/immigration-rules/updates

Gramsci, Antonio. 1978. *Selections from Prison Notebooks*. London: Lawrence & Wishart.

Hajjaji, Danya. 2023. 'Essex pub that displayed golly dolls seized by police is vandalised'. *The Guardian*, 16 April. https://www.theguardian.com/uk-news/2023/apr/16/essex-pub-that-displayed-golly-dolls-seized-by-police-is-vandalised

Halliday, Josh and Goodman, Joe. 2019. 'Johnson accused of racial stereotyping with view on Nigerians'. *The Guardian*, 28 November. https://www.theguardian.com/politics/2019/nov/28/johnson-accused-of-racial-stereotyping-with-view-on-nigerians

Hargreaves Lansdown. 2024. 'What do the credit ratings mean?' https://www.hl.co.uk/help/funds-shares-and-other-investments/corporate-bonds-and-gilts/credit-ratings/what-do-the-credit-ratings-mean

Harries, Bethan, Byrne, Bridget, Garratt, Lindsey and Smith, Andy. 2020. '"Divide and conquer": anti-racist and community organizing under austerity'. *Ethnic and Racial Studies* 43(16). https://www.tandfonline.com/doi/full/10.1080/01419870.2019.1682176

Harrison, Elizabeth. 2012. 'Bouncing back? Recession, resilience and everyday lives'. *Critical Social Policy* 33(1).

Harvey, David. 2005. *A Brief History of Neoliberalism*. Oxford: Oxford University Press.

Harvey, David. 2015. 'Capitals' nature – a response to Andrew Kliman', *The New Left Project*, 30 March. http://gesd.free.fr/harvey2k.pdf

Hasan, Mehdi. 2017. 'Theresa May wants to fight Islamophobia in the U.K.? You must be joking'. *The Intercept*, 20 June. https://theintercept.com/2017/06/20/theresa-may-wants-to-fight-islamophobia-in-the-uk-you-must-be-joking/

Hattenstone, Simon. 2018. 'Why was the scheme behind May's "Go Home" vans called Operation Vaken?'. *The Guardian*, 26 April. https://www.theguardian.com/commentisfree/2018/apr/26/theresa-may-go-home-vans-operation-vaken-ukip.

Hayhurst, Claire. 2023. 'Police will take no further action regarding MP's leaflet on Traveller sites'. *The Independent*, 8 August. https://www.independent.co.uk/news/uk/police-gypsy-secretary-of-state-wales-conservative-b2389629.html

Heffer, Greg. 2023. 'Downing Street "backs Suella Braverman's threat to leave the European Convention on Human Rights" as court battle looms over Rwanda deportations'. *MailOnline*, 30 September. https://www.dailymail.co.uk/news/article-12570293/Downing-Street-backs-Suella-Bravermans-threat-leave-European-Convention-Human-Rights-court-battle-looms-Rwanda-deportations.html

Helm, Toby. 2012. 'UKIP on 14% as Labour restores double digit lead over the Tories – poll'. *The Guardian*, 15 December. https://www.theguardian.com/politics/2012/dec/15/ukip-labour-tories-poll

Helm, Toby. 2019. 'End game: the fall of Theresa May'. *The Guardian*, 26 May. https://www.theguardian.com/politics/2019/may/26/end-game-fall-of-theresa-may

Helm, Toby, Savage, Michael, Rawnsley, Andrew and Boffey, Daniel. 2019. 'Amber Rudd quits cabinet and attacks PM for "political vandalism"'. *The Guardian*, 7 September. https://www.theguardian.com/politics/2019/sep/07/amber-rudd-resignsfrom-cabinet-and-surrenders-conservative-whip

Hemerijck, Anton. 2012. 'Two or three waves of welfare state transformation?', in Nathalie Morel, Bruno Palier and Joakim Palme (eds) Towards a Social Investment Welfare State?: Ideas, Policies and Challenges, Bristol: Bristol University Press.

High Pay Centre. 2023. 'Pay inequalities at UK's largest companies remain constant, despite "cost of living" crisis', 18 December. https://highpaycentre.org/high-pay-centre-analysis-of-ftse-350-pay-ratios-2/

High Pay Centre. 2024. 'Post-pandemic, pay inequality is back in business', 21 February. https://highpaycentre.org/post-pandemic-pay-inequality-is-back-in-business/

Holmes, Colin. 1979. *Anti-Semitism in British Society 1876–1939*. London: Edward Arnold.

Home Affairs Select Committee. 2018. 'House of Commons Home Affairs Committee: The Windrush generation: Sixth Report of Session 2017–19: Report, together with formal minutes relating to the report: Ordered by the House of Commons to be printed 27 June 2018'. https://publications.parliament.uk/pa/cm201719/cmselect/cmhaff/990/990.pdf

Home Office. 2023. 'Irregular migration to the UK, year ending September 2023'. https://www.gov.uk/government/statistics/irregular-migration-to-the-uk-year-ending-september-2023/irregular-migration-to-the-uk-year-ending-september-2023#data-tablesOpens in a new window

Hopkins, Steven. 2017. 'Sir Martin Moore-Bick's appointment as Grenfell Tower investigation head sparks "alarm"'. *HuffPost*, 29 June. https://www.huffingtonpost.co.uk/entry/sir-martin-moore-bicks-appointment_uk_5954a6a9e4b05c37bb7bf1a4

House of Commons Library (Georgina Sturge). 2022. 'Asylum statistics', 5 December. https://researchbriefings.files.parliament.uk/documents/SN01403/SN01403.pdf

House of Commons Library. 2023. 'Racial discrimination in schools', 28 February. https://researchbriefings.files.parliament.uk/documents/CDP-2023-0049/CDP-2023-0049.pdf

Hume, David. nd. *Essay VII, 'Of Taxes'*. https://davidhume.org/texts/pld/ta

Hume, David. 1777. *Essays Moral, Political, Literary*. https://oll-resources.s3.us-east-2.amazonaws.com/oll3/store/titles/704/Hume_0059_EBk_v6.0.pdf

Huskisson, Sophie. 2023 'Tories go to war over unflattering photograph of London mayoral candidate'. *The Mirror*, 19 July. https://www.mirror.co.uk/news/politics/tories-go-war-over-unflattering-30506273

Hyland, Julie. 2017. 'Boris Johnson and the Grenfell Tower inferno'. *World Socialist Web Site*, 24 June. https://www.wsws.org/en/articles/2017/06/24/john-j24.html

Immigration Law Practitioners' Association. 2018. 'ILPA response to the Government White Paper: the UK's future skills-based immigration system', 19 December. https://ilpa.org.uk/wp-content/uploads/resources/34996/18.12.19-ILPA-Response-to-White-Paper.pdf

Income Tax (Earnings and Pensions) Act. 2003. https://www.legislation.gov.uk/ukpga/2003/1/contents

The Independent. 2015. 'Theresa May's speech to the Conservative Party Conference in full', 6 October. https://www.independent.co.uk/news/uk/politics/theresa-may-s-speech-to-the-conservative-party-conference-in-full-a6681901.html

The Independent. 2019. 'Tory councillor suspended over Islamophobic comments about bombing mosques made in Facebook group he moderates', 2 March. https://www.independent.co.uk/news/uk/politics/tory-islamophobia-councillor-mosque-facebook-martyn-york-a8804486.html

Independent Commission for Equity in Cricket. 2023. 'Holding up a mirror to cricket', June. https://theicec.com/wp-content/uploads/2023/06/HOLDING-UP-A-MIRROR-TO-CRICKET-REPORT-ICEC.pdf

Inman, Phillip and Partington, Richard. 2022. 'IMF urges UK government to reconsider tax-cutting plans'. *The Guardian*, 28 September. https://www.theguardian.com/politics/2022/sep/27/kwasi-kwartengs-tax-cuts-likely-to-increase-inequality-imf-says

International Rescue Committee. 2024. 'United Kingdom'. https://www.rescue.org/uk/country/united-kingdom

International Transport Workers' Federation. 2022. 'Trade unions across the world tell Grant Shapps: "UK's reputation is at risk"'. https://www.itfglobal.org/en/news/trade-unions-across-world-tell-grant-shapps-uks-reputation-risk

The Irish Times. 2013. 'Thatcher believed the Irish were "all liars"', 18 April. htttp://www.irishtimes.com/news/thatcher-believed-the-irish-were-all-liars-1.1363098

Jahan, Sarwat, Mahmud, Ahmed Saber and Papageorgiou, Chris. 2014. 'What is Keynesian economics?', *Finance and Development* 51(3). https://www.imf.org/external/pubs/ft/fandd/2014/09/basics.htm

James-Gallaway, Chaddrick, Minnett, Jari and Dixson, Adrienne. 2020. 'Scratching and surviving: critical race theory and being a "blackademic" in the academy', in Vernon Lee Farmer and Evelyn Shepherd W. Farmer (eds) *Critical Race Theory in the Academy*. Charlotte: Information Age Publishing.

JCWI (Joint Council for the Welfare of Immigrants). 2016. 'What's next for the Hostile Environment: the Immigration Act 2016 and the Queen's Speech', 23 May. https://jcwi.org.uk/blog/2016/05/23/what%E2%80%99s-next-hostile-environment-immigration-act-2016-and-queen%E2%80%99s-speech

JCWI (Joint Council for the Welfare of Immigrants). 2023. 'Making the UK a welcoming environment for all migrants', May. https://jcwi.org.uk/wp-content/uploads/2024/06/makingtheukawelcomingplaceformigrants-april2023.pdf

Johnson, Boris. 2000. 'Am I guilty of racial prejudice? We all are'. *The Guardian*, 28 November. https://www.theguardian.com/uk/2000/feb/21/lawrence.ukcrime3

Johnston, John. 2019. 'EXCL Tories slammed after activist suspended for Islamophobia allowed to stand as council candidate'. *PoliticsHome*, 4 March. https://www.politicshome.com/news/article/excl-tories-slammed-after-activist-suspended-for-islamophobia-allowed-to-stand-as-council-candidate

Jolly, Jasper. 2023. '"A vote of confidence": UK businesses welcome Jeremy Hunt's tax breaks'. *The Guardian*, 22 November. https://www.theguardian.com/uk-news/2023/nov/22/uk-businesses-jeremy-hunt-tax-breaks-full-expensing

Jones, Ian. 2024. 'More than five million working days lost since current period of strikes began'. *The Independent*, February 13. https://www.independent.co.uk/business/more-than-five-million-working-days-lost-since-current-period-of-strikes-began-b2495322.html#:~:text=Some%205.05%20million%20days%20are,July%201989%20to%20January%201991.

Jones, Nigel. 2012. 'Cameron, Churchill, race … and a historical howler', *Daily Mail*, 15 March. https://www.dailymail.co.uk/debate/article-2114950/amp/CameronChurchill-Race–historical-howler.html

Jones, Sara and Goodwin, Kinga. 2021. 'Lost in the storm: arts venues re-open too late for some migrant artists', *Byline Times*, 17 May. https://bylinetimes.com/2021/05/17/lost-in-the-storm-arts-venues-re-open-too-late-for-some-migrant-artists/

JTA. 2018. 'Respected British magazine publishes defense of Nazi German troops'. *Times of Israel*, 18 May. https://www.timesofisrael.com/respected-british-magazine-publishes-defense-of-nazi-german-troops/

Justice4Grenfell. 2019. 'Theresa May, your response to Grenfell is nothing to be proud of', 25 May. https://justice4grenfell.org/1849/

Kanagasooriam, James. 2019. ' "When you talk about cultural barriers to voting Tory", he concluded, "this is where it is"'. Twitter. https://twitter.com/jameskanag/status/1161639307536457730?lang=en-GB

Kanagasooriam, James and Simon, Elizabeth. 2021. 'Red wall: the definitive description'. *Political Insight* 12(3). https://journals.sagepub.com/doi/10.1177/20419058211045127

Keller, Florian. 2022. 'When the communists ruled in Bavaria'. *In Defence of Marxism*, 4 February. https://www.marxist.com/when-the-communists-ruled-in-bavaria.htm

Kentish, Benjamin. 2018. 'Theresa May declares "austerity is over" after eight years of cuts and tax increases'. *The Independent*, 3 October. https://www.independent.co.uk/news/uk/politics/theresa-may-austerity-end-over-speech-conservative-conference-tory-labour-a8566526.html

Keynote Address by UK Home Secretary Suella Braverman. 2023. 'UK-US security priorities for the 21st century'. https://www.aei.org/wp-content/uploads/2023/09/230926-Keynote-Address-by-UK-Home-Secretary-Suella-Braverman-Transcript.final_-1.pdf?x91208

Kick It Out. 2024. 'Kick It Out reports continue to rise', 24 July. https://www.kickitout.org/news-media/kick-it-out-reports-continue-rise

Kimber, Charlie. 2022. 'Use your right to protest – it's the best response to the Tory police bill', *Socialist Worker*, 2803, 28 April. https://socialistworker.co.uk/news/use-your-right-to-protest-its-the-best-response-to-tory-police-bill/

Kingsley, Patrick. 2012. 'Financial crisis: timeline'. *The Guardian*, 7 August. https://www.theguardian.com/business/2012/aug/07/credit-crunch-boom-bust-timeline

Kirby, Dean. 2021. 'Black Lives Matter: Patel says the 2020 protests were "dreadful"'. *The Independent*, 12 February. https://inews.co.uk/news/uk/black-lives-matter-priti-patel-2020-protests-dreadful-opposes-taking-knee-870528

Kirkup, James. 2011. 'Baroness Warsi: David Cameron won't back "Islamophobia" claims'. *Telegraph*, 20 January. https://www.telegraph.co.uk/news/religion/8272273/Baroness-Warsi-David-Cameron-wont-back-Islamophobia-claims.html

Kirkup, James. 2015. 'Theresa May's immigration speech is dangerous and factually wrong'. *Telegraph*, 6 October. https://www.telegraph.co.uk/news/uknews/immigration/11913927/Theresa-Mays-immigration-speech-is-dangerous-and-factually-wrong.html

Kliman, A. 2015. 'The great recession and Marx's crisis theory'. *American Journal of Economics and Sociology* 74. https://doi.org/10.1111/ajes.12094

Knaggs, Emma. 2024. Personal email, 27 March.

Kotz, David M. 2007. 'The capital-labor relation: contemporary character and prospects for change'. Paper written for the Second Forum of the World Association for Political Economy (WAPE), on 'The Political Economy of the Contemporary Relationship between Labor and Capital in the World,' University of Shimane, Japan, 27–28 October 2007. https://people.umass.edu/dmkotz/Cap_Labor_Reln_07_07.pdf

Kovel, Joel. 1970. *White Racism: A Psychohistory*. New York: Pantheon.

Krugman, Paul. 2015. 'The austerity delusion'. *The Guardian*, 29 April. https://www.theguardian.com/business/ng-interactive/2015/apr/29/the-austerity-delusion

Kuo, Lily. 2016. 'Britain's new foreign secretary once referred to Africa's "watermelon smiles" and "picaninnies"'. *Quartz Africa*, 1 July. https://qz.com/africa/731695/britains-new-foreign-secretary-once-referred-to-africas-watermelon-smiles-and-piccanninies/

Kynaston, David. 2010. *Austerity Britain, 1945–1951*. London: Bloomsbury Publishing.

Lauber, Kathrin, Fernandez de Cordoba Farini, Claudia and Mansour, Adelle. 2024. 'Deregulation and austerity policies undermine health and safety: lessons for the global community from Grenfell Tower Inquiry'. *Croakey Health Media*, 19 September. https://www.croakey.org/deregulation-and-austerity-policies-undermine-health-and-safety-lessons-for-the-global-community-from-grenfell-tower-inquiry/

Lavery, Ian, Trickett, Jon and Smith, Laura. 2022. 'The real class war is being waged from above'. *Tribune*, 27 June. https://tribunemag.co.uk/2022/06/rail-strike-media-city-pay-boris-johnson

Lawrence, Errol. 1982. 'Just plain common sense: the "roots" of racism', in Centre for Contemporary Cultural Studies, *The Empire Strikes Back: Race and Racism in 70's Britain*. London: Hutchinson.

REFERENCES

Lawrence, Felicity. 2023. 'Covid contracts: messages reveal extent of Tory donor access to Matt Hancock'. *The Guardian*, 18 May. https://www.theguardian.com/politics/2023/may/18/covid-contracts-messages-reveal-extent-of-tory-donor-access-to-matt-hancock

Lea, Sian. 2016. 'The Immigration Act 2016 In Plain English'. https://eachother.org.uk/immigration-act-2016-plain-english/

Letters. 2023. *The Guardian*, 15 December. https://www.theguardian.com/uk-news/2023/dec/15/bibby-stockholm-barge-must-be-closed-immediately

Lewontin, Richard. 1972. 'The apportionment of human diversity', in Theodosius Dobzhansky, Max K. Hecht and William C. Steere (eds) *Evolutionary Biology*. Vol 6. Berlin: Springer Nature.

Lindsay, Caron. 2017. 'In full: Tim Farron's speech: I love my country and I want it back from the nationalists'. *Liberal Democratic Voice*, 19 March. www.libdemvoice.org/in-full-tim-farrons-speech-i-love-my-country-and-i-want-it-back-from-thenationalists-53681.htm

Lloyd, Nina. 2023. 'Timeline: Rishi Sunak's first year in office'. *The Independent*, 25 October. https://www.independent.co.uk/news/uk/rishi-sunak-dominic-raab-volodymyr-zelensky-gavin-williamson-prime-minister-b2435458.html

Macaskill, Andrew and James, William. 2022. 'Drunkenness, vomiting and a scuff at UK government lockdown parties'. *Reuters*, 25 May. https://www.reuters.com/world/uk/drunkenness-sickness-fighting-during-lockdown-party-uk-government-report-2022-05-25/

Macfarlane, Jenna. 2021. 'Windrush scandal: who is the Windrush generation in the UK and the Windrush history explained', adapted from *The Scotsman*, 24 November. https://blogpeda.ac-poitiers.fr/help-yourself/files/2022/10/11.Windrush-Scandal.pdf

Mahase, Elisabeth. 2021. 'Covid-19: NHS Test and Trace failed despite "eye watering" budget, MPs conclude'. *BMJ* 375(2606). https://www.bmj.com/content/375/bmj.n2606#:~:text=Meg%20Hillier%2C%20chair%20of%20the,vast%20sums%20thrown%20at%20it

Maisuria, Alpesh and Cole, Mike. 2017. 'The neoliberalisation of higher education in England: an alternative is possible'. *Policy Futures in Education* 15(5). https://journals.sagepub.com/doi/full/10.1177/1478210317719792

Malik, Keenan. 2023. *Not So Black and White*. London: C Hurst & Co Publishers Ltd.

Mararike, Shingi. 2022. 'Rwanda: first glimpse inside the centre that will house Channel migrants'. *Sky News*, 14 April. https://news.sky.com/story/rwanda-first-glimpse-inside-the-centre-which-will-house-channel-migrants-12589911

Marmot, Michael, Allen, Jessica, Boyce, Tammy, Goldblatt, Peter and Morrison, Joanna. 2020. *Health Equity in England: The Marmot Review Ten Years On Executive Summary*. London: Institute of Health Equity UCL. https://www.health.org.uk/sites/default/files/2020-03/Health%20Equity%20in%20England_The%20Marmot%20Review%2010%20Years%20On_executive%20summary_web.pdf

Martin, Patrick. 2023. 'Millionaire speculator blurts out ruling class strategy of mass unemployment and wage-slashing', 14 September. https://www.wsws.org/en/articles/2023/09/15/uogh-s15.html

Marx, Karl. 1845. *The German Ideology*. https://www.marxists.org/archive/marx/works/1845/german-ideology/ch01b.htm

Marx, Karl. 1870 [1978]. 'Marx to Sigfrid Meyer and August Vogt in New York', in Karl Marx and Friedrich Engels. 1975. *Selected Correspondence*. Moscow: Progress Publishers.

Marx, Karl. 1887 [1965]. *Capital Vol. 1*. Moscow: Progress Publishers. https://www.marxists.org/archive/marx/works/download/pdf/Capital-Volume-I.pdf

Marx, Karl. 1893 [1967]. *Capital Vol. 2*. Moscow: Progress Publishers. https://www.marxists.org/archive/marx/works/1885-c2/

Marx, Karl. 1894 [1966]. *Capital Vol. 3*. Moscow: Progress Publishers. https://www.marxists.org/archive/marx/works/download/pdf/Capital-Volume-III.pdf

Marx, Karl and Engels, Friedrich. 1848 [1975]. *Manifesto of the Communist Party*. Peking Foreign Languages Press.

Mason, Chis. 2024. 'Chris Mason: why did Sunak decide to call summer election?' *BBC News*, 22 May. https://www.bbc.co.uk/news/uk-politics-69050402

Mason, Rowena. 2015. 'Theresa May "allowed state-sanctioned abuse of women" at Yarl's Wood'. *The Guardian*, 3 March. https://www.theguardian.com/uk-news/2015/mar/03/yarls-wood-may-state-sanctioned-abuse-women

Mason, Rowena. 2020. 'No 10 refuses to comment on PM's views of racial IQ'. *The Guardian*, 17 February. https://www.theguardian.com/politics/2020/feb/17/no-10-refuses-to-comment-on-pms-views-of-racial-iq

Mason, Rowena. 2023a. 'Boris Johnson to join GB News as presenter'. *The Guardian*, 27 October. https://www.theguardian.com/politics/2023/oct/27/boris-johnson-join-gb-news-presenter#:~:text=Boris%20Johnson%20is%20taking%20a,the%20US%20elections%20next%20year

Mason, Rowena. 2023b. 'PPE bought via "VIP lane" was on average 80% more expensive, documents reveal'. *The Guardian*, 10 December. https://www.theguardian.com/world/2023/dec/10/ppe-via-vip-lane-average-80-percent-more-expensive-documents-reveal

Mattei, Clara E. 2022a. *The Capital Order: How Economists Invented Austerity and Paved the Way for Fascism*. Chicago and London: University of Chicago Press.

Mattei, Clara. 2022b. 'Don't be fooled: policymakers are quietly invoking austerity by other names'. *The Guardian*, 8 October. https://www.theguardian.com/commentisfree/2022/oct/08/us-policymakers-austerity-by-other-names

Matthews, Chris. 2022. 'I'm proud of the British Empire, Suella Braverman proclaims: Attorney General praises the "ingenuity and the genius of the British people" as she blasts the Left for being "ashamed of our history"'. *MailOnline*, 17 June. https://www.dailymail.co.uk/news/article-10928237/Im-proud-British-Empire-Suella-Braverman-proclaims.html

McCallig, Elaine. 2022. 'Michael Gove lost his temper about the "hostile environment" policy and everyone made the same point'. *Indy100*, 15 March. https://www.indy100.com/politics/michael-gove-commons

McDonnell, John. 2024. 'John McDonnell: far-right riots have all the hallmarks of a fascist mobilisation'. *Labour Outlook*, 21 August. https://labouroutlook.org/2024/08/21/john-mcdonnell-far-right-riots-have-all-the-hallmarks-of-a-fascist-mobilisation/

McGuinness, Alan and Rayner, Tom. 2022. 'The rise and fall of Boris Johnson: the political magician who won power but lost control'. *Sky News*, 7 July. https://news.sky.com/story/the-rise-and-fall-of-boris-johnson-the-political-magician-who-won-power-but-lost-control-12519849

McIntyre, Niamh and Taylor, Diane. 2018. 'Britain's immigration detention: how many people are locked up'. *The Guardian*, 11 October. https://www.theguardian.com/uk-news/2018/oct/11/britains-immigration-detention-how-many-people-are-locked-up

McKee, Martin, Karanikolos, Marina and Stuckler, David. 2012. 'Austerity: a failed experiment on the people of Europe'. *Clinical Medicine* 12(4).

McKie, Robin and Louis, Yameen. 2022 'From "best" budget to a dead parrot: how Tory press turned against Liz Truss'. *The Guardian*, 16 October. https://www.theguardian.com/media/2022/oct/16/from-best-budget-to-a-dead-parrot-how-tory-press-turned-against-liz-truss

McLaren, Peter. 2000. *Che Guevara, Paulo Freire and the Pedagogy of Revolution*. Lanham: Rowman & Littlefield.

McMurtry, John. 2000. 'Education, struggle and the Left today'. *International Journal of Educational Reform* 10(2).

Meredith, Sam. 2019. 'What is the Irish backstop? All you need to know about the border dispute blocking an orderly Brexit'. *CNBC*, 16 October. https://www.cnbc.com/2019/09/11/brexit-what-is-the-irish-backstop-and-why-is-it-so-controversial.html

Merrick, Rob. 2019. 'Boris Johnson's brother quits government in protest at PM's leadership'. *The Independent*, 5 September. https://www.independent.co.uk/news/uk/politics/jo-johnson-resigns-boris-mp-conservative-party-protest-brexit-no-deal-parliament-family-latest-a9092751.html

Michell, Jo. 2022. 'The Johnson legacy: the economy'. *UK in a Changing Europe*, 2 September. https://ukandeu.ac.uk/the-johnson-legacy-the-economy/

Michell, Jo, Calvert Jump, Rob, Meadway, James and Nasciemento, Natassia. 2023. 'The macroeconomics of austerity'. *Progessive Economy Forum*, 3 March. https://progressiveeconomyforum.com/publications/the-macroeconomics-of-austerity/

Miles, Robert. 1993. *Racism after 'Race Relations'*. London: Routledge.

Mitchell, Archie. 2023. 'Police probe minister's "racist" campaign leaflet on Traveller sites'. *The Independent*, 3 August. https://www.independent.co.uk/news/uk/politics/david-davies-leaflet-racist-monmouth-b2386849.html

Monbiot, George. 2022. 'The UK is heading towards authoritarianism: just look at this attack on a minority'. *The Guardian*, 12 January. https://www.theguardian.com/commentisfree/2022/jan/12/uk-authoritarianism-minority-policing-billromagypsy-traveller

Moore-Bick, Martin, Akbor, Ali and Istephan, Thouria. 2024. *Grenfell Tower Inquiry: Phase 2 Report Overview Report of the Public Inquiry into the Fire at Grenfell Tower on 14 June*. https://www.grenfelltowerinquiry.org.uk/sites/default/files/CCS0923434692-004_GTI%20Phase%202_Report%20Overview_E-Laying_0.pdf

Moore, Dennis and Scripps, Thomas. 2023. 'Homelessness rises in the UK as rents skyrocket'. *World Socialist Web Site*, 28 September. https://www.wsws.org/en/articles/2023/09/28/jrih-s28.html

Moore, Martin and Ramsey, Gordon. (2017). 'UK media\ coverage of the 2016 EU Referendum campaign'. Centre for the Study of Media, Communication and Power, May. https://www.kcl.ac.uk/policy-institute/assets/cmcp/uk-media-coverage-of-the-2016-eu-referendum-campaign.pdf

Mor, Frederico. 2018. 'Bank rescues of 2007–09: outcomes and cost'. Briefing Paper Number 5748, 8 October. House of Commons Library. https://researchbriefings.files.parliament.uk/documents/SN05748/SN05748.pdf

Morning Star. 2024. 'Badenoch branded an "Islamophobe" after her attack on progressive independent MPs', 3 September. https://morningstaronline.co.uk/article/badenoch-branded-islamophobe-after-attack-progressive-independent-mps

Mr Major's speech to Conservative Group for Europe. 1993. 22 April. https://johnmajorarchive.org.uk/1993/04/22/mr-majors-speech-to-conservative-groupfor-europe-22-april-1993/

REFERENCES

Mueller, Benjamin. 2019. 'What is austerity and how has it affected British society?' *The New York Times*, 24 February. https://www.nytimes.com/2019/02/24/world/europe/britain-austerity-may-budget.html

Murphy, Simon. 2019. 'Sayeeda Warsi on Tory Islamophobia: "It feels like I'm in an abusive relationship"'. *The Guardian*, 27 November. https://www.theguardian.com/politics/2019/nov/27/sayeeda-warsi-tory-islamophobia-muslim-prejudice-investigation

Nanji, Noor. 2023a. 'People face biggest fall in spending power for 70 years'. *BBC News*, 15 March. https://www.bbc.co.uk/news/business-64963869

Nanji, Noor. 2023b. 'Cap on bankers' bonuses to be scrapped'. *BBC News*, 24 October. https://www.bbc.co.uk/news/business-67206997

Nathoo, Leila and Francis, Sam. 2023. Why did Boris Johnson resign? *BBC News*, 9 June. https://www.bbc.co.uk/news/uk-politics-65863730

National Audit Office. 2017. 'Homelessness', 13 September. https://www.nao.org.uk/wp-content/uploads/2017/09/Homelessness.pdf

National Human Genome Research Institute. 2022. 'Eugenics and scientific racism', 18 May. https://www.genome.gov/about-genomics/fact-sheets/Eugenics-and-Scientific-Racism

Nelson, Fraser. 2020. 'Kemi Badenoch: the problem with critical race theory'. *The Spectator*, 24 October. https://www.spectator.co.uk/article/kemi-badenoch-the-problem-with-critical-race-theory/

Nicholson, Kate. 2024. 'Controversial Bibby Stockholm barge meant to house asylum seekers to be closed down'. *The Huffington Post*, 23 July. https://www.huffingtonpost.co.uk/entry/controversial-bibby-stockholm-barge-to-be-closed-down_uk_669fba73e4b04ed80d39470d

O'Carroll, Lisa. 2019. 'Boris Johnson's Brexit alternative to the Irish backstop: what's new?'. *The Guardian*, 2 October. https://www.theguardian.com/politics/2019/oct/02/boris-johnsons-brexit-alternative-to-the-irish-backstop-whats-new

Office for National Statistics. 2023. 'Index of private housing rental prices, UK: August 2023', 20 September. file:///C:/Users/mccol/Downloads/Index%20of%20Private%20Housing%20Rental%20Prices,%20UK%20August%202023%20(2).pdf

Ohlinger, Gustavus A. 1966 (2015). 'WSC: a midnight interview, 1902', *International Churchill Society*, 15 March. https://winstonchurchill.org/publications/finest-hour/finest-hour-159/wsc-amidnight-interview-1902/

O'Mally, J.P. 2016. 'Churchill and his uneasy Irish legacy'. *Irish Independent*, 9 May. https://www.independent.ie/entertainment/books/churchill-and-his-uneasy-irish-legacy/34691865.html

O'Neill, Brendan. 2022. 'Of course Rishi Sunak doesn't have any working-class friends'. *The Spectator*, 11 July. https://www.spectator.co.uk/article/of-course-rishi-sunak-doesn-t-have-any-working-class-friends/

Oryszczuk, Stephen. 2022. 'Britain failed French Jews when we needed her most'. *Jewish News*, 13 July. https://www.jewishnews.co.uk/britain-failed-french-jews-when-we-needed-her-most/

Osborn, Andrew. 2013. 'Britain's PM Cameron unveils immigration crackdown'. *Reuters*, 25 March. https://www.reuters.com/article/us-britain-immigration-cameron-idUSBRE92O0ME20130325/

Osborne, Hilary. 2023. 'What is national insurance and who will benefit from Jeremy Hunt's cuts?' *The Guardian*, 23 November. https://www.theguardian.com/money/2023/nov/23/what-is-national-insurance-and-who-will-benefit-from-jeremy-hunts-cuts

Otte, Jedidajah. 2023. 'Suella Braverman says rough sleeping is "lifestyle choice"'. *The Guardian*, 4 November. https://www.theguardian.com/society/2023/nov/04/suella-braverman-says-rough-sleeping-is-lifestyle-choice

Owolade, Tomiwa. 2023. 'Racism in Britain is not a black and white issue. It's far more complicated'. *The Observer*, 15 April. https://www.theguardian.com/commentisfree/2023/apr/15/racism-in-britain-is-not-a-black-and-white-issue-it-is-far-more-complicated

PA Media. 2023. 'Suella Braverman tells Holocaust survivor she will not apologise for "invasion" rhetoric'. *The Guardian*, 14 January. https://www.theguardian.com/world/2023/jan/14/suella-braverman-wont-apologise-to-holocaust-survivor-for-calling-migrants-invasion

PA Mediapoint and Press Gazette. 2019. 'Boris Johnson's Telegraph column comparing Muslim women with "letterboxes" led to Islamophobia "spike"'. *Press Gazette*, 2 September. https://pressgazette.co.uk/news/boris-johnson-telegraph-column-muslim-women-letterboxes-bank-robbers-spike-islamophobic-incidents/

Pang, Jun. 2023. Liberty, 29 June (email correspondence).

Partington, Richard. 2022. 'The mini-budget that broke Britain – and Liz Truss'. *The Guardian*, 20 October. https://www.theguardian.com/business/2022/oct/20/the-mini-budget-that-broke-britain-and-liz-truss

Partington, Richard. 2023a. 'Using austerity economics to crush UK inflation would be a cure worse than the disease'. *The Guardian*, 2 July. https://www.theguardian.com/business/2023/jul/02/using-austerity-economics-to-crush-uk-inflation-would-be-a-cure-worse-than-the-disease#:~:text=The%20big%20concern%20is%20that,the%20alarm%20over%20this%20risk

Partington, Richard. 2023b. 'Number of days lost to strikes is highest since the Thatcher era'. *The Guardian*, 14 February. https://www.theguardian.com/uk-news/2023/feb/14/nearly-million-days-lost-strikes-december-uk-pay-growth#:~:text=With%20widespread%20disputes%20across%20the,end%20of%20Margaret%20Thatcher's%20government

Partington, Richard and Crerar, Pippa. 2023. 'Pressure grows on Hunt to cut income tax as millions more face paying it'. *The Guardian*, 21 November. https://www.theguardian.com/uk-news/2023/nov/21/pressure-grows-on-hunt-to-cut-income-tax-as-millions-more-face-paying-it

Partington, Richard and Stacey, Kiran. 2023. 'Autumn statement: Jeremy Hunt announces tax cuts for firms and workers'. *The Guardian*, 22 November. https://www.theguardian.com/uk-news/2023/nov/22/autumn-statement-jeremy-hunt-announces-sweeping-tax-cuts-for-firms-and-workers

Partington, Richard, Stacey, Kiran and Inman, Phillip. 2023. 'Hunt's tax cuts mean austerity "more painful" than under Osborne, warns IFS'. *The Guardian*, 23 November. https://www.theguardian.com/uk-news/2023/nov/23/jeremy-hunt-tax-cuts-austerity-more-painful-george-osborne-ifs-public-spending

Patrick, Ruth and Reeves, Arron. 2024. 'How UK welfare reform affects larger families'. Nuffield Foundation. https://www.nuffieldfoundation.org/project/how-uk-welfare-reform-affects-larger-families

Peck, Tom. 2022. 'Cruella de Vil had a "dream" and "obsession" about cruelty to dogs. Suella de Vil goes much further than that'. *The Independent*, 5 October. https://www.independent.co.uk/voices/suella-braverman-illegal-immigrants-rwanda-speech-b2195788.html

People's History Museum. 2024. 'General Strike 1926'. https://phm.org.uk/collection/labour-history-archive-study-centre/general-strike-1926/

Petrovic, Gajo. 1991. 'Praxis', in Tom Bottomore, Laurence Harris, Victor Kiernan and Ralph Miliband (eds) *The Dictionary of Marxist Thought*, 2nd edition. Oxford: Blackwell.

Pimlott, Daniel, Giles, Chris and Harding, Robin. 2010. 'UK unveils dramatic austerity measures'. *Financial Times*, 20 October. https://www.ft.com/content/53fe06e2-dc98-11df-84f5-00144feabdc0

PKF Smith Cooper. 2022. 'Mini-budget reversal – what is changing and remaining?', 17 October. https://www.pkfsmithcooper.com/news-insights/mini-budget-reversal/

Poole, Steven. 2018. '"Compliant environment": is this really what the Windrush generation needs?'. *The Guardian*, 3 May. https://www.theguardian.com/books/2018/may/03/compliant-environment-is-this-really-what-the-windrush-generation-needs

Portes, Jonathan. 2018. 'Austerity really has hit poor people hardest – the figures prove it'. *The Guardian*, 14 March. https://www.theguardian.com/commentisfree/2018/mar/14/austerity-poor-disability-george-osborne-tories

Portes, Jonathan and Reed, Howard. 2018. *The Cumulative Impact of Tax and Welfare Reforms: Executive Summary*. London: Equality and Human Rights Commission. https://www.equalityhumanrights.com/sites/default/files/cumulative-impact-assessment-report-large-print.pdf

Powell, Enoch. 1968. 'Rivers of Blood speech', delivered to a Conservative Association Meeting in Birmingham, 20 April. https://anth1001.files.wordpress.com/2014/04/enoch-powell_speech.pdf

Prince, Rosa. 2010. 'David Cameron: net immigration will be capped at tens of thousands'. *Telegraph*, 10 January.

Proctor, Kate. 2020. 'Calls for Tory aide to be sacked over "enforced contraception" remarks'. *The Guardian*, 16 February. https://www.theguardian.com/politics/2020/feb/16/tory-aide-wants-enforced-contraception-to-curb-pregnancies

Prose. nd. 'About us'. https://www.prose.ltd/about-us#:~:text=Prose%20Intelligence%20is%20a%20boutique,analyst%20and%20programmer%20Jordan%20Wildon

Quinn, Ben. 2023. 'Tory turmoil blamed for delays in tackling Islamophobia within party'. *The Guardian*, 24 July. https://www.theguardian.com/politics/2023/jul/24/tory-turmoil-blamed-for-delays-in-tackling-islamophobia-within-party

Quinn, Ben. 2025. 'Kemi Badenoch says "western civilisation will be lost" if Tory party fails. *The Guardian*, February 17. https://www.theguardian.com/politics/2025/feb/17/kemi-badenoch-western-civilisation-will-be-lost-tory-party-fails

RCN (Royal College of Nursing). 2022. 'We strike for the future of the NHS', 15 December. https://www.rcn.org.uk/news-and-events/news/uk-rcn-nhs-nursing-strikes-2022-first-day-151222#:~:text=Today%20(15%20December)%2C%20up,planned%20for%20Tuesday%2020%20December

Refugee Council. 2023. 'What is the Illegal Migration Act?', 3 October. https://www.refugeecouncil.org.uk/information/what-is-the-illegal-migration-act/#:~:text=The%20Illegal%20Migration%20Bill%20became,by%20those%20using%20unsafe%20routes

Refugee Council. 2024a. 'Refugee Council statement on Channel crossings in 2023', 2 January. https://www.refugeecouncil.org.uk/latest/news/refugee-council-statement-on-channel-crossings-in-2023/

Refugee Council. 2024b. 'Safe routes: the need for an ambitious approach', January. https://www.refugeecouncil.org.uk/wp-content/uploads/2024/01/Safe-routes-the-need-for-an-ambitious-approach-Refugee-Council-January-2024.pdf

Refugee Council. 2024c. 'The truth about Channel crossings and the impact of the Illegal Migration Act'. https://www.refugeecouncil.org.uk/information/resources/the-truth-about-channel-crossings-and-the-impact-of-the-illegal-migration-act/

Reicher, Stephen, Stott, Clifford and Drury, John. 2019. 'London's 2011 riots: report blames deprivation and poor policing – not mad, bad, dangerous people'. *The Conversation*, 14 February. https://theconversation.com/londons-2011-riots-report-blames-deprivation-and-poor-policing-not-mad-bad-dangerous-people-111770

The Resolution Foundation. 2023. 'Our work'. https://www.resolutionfoundation.org/our-work/

Ricardo. David. 1817 [1996]. *Principles of Political Economy and Taxation*. New York: Prometheus Books.

Richard Chambers Immigration Barristers. 2012. 'Summary of key changes in family immigration rules on 9 July 2012'. https://immigrationbarrister.co.uk/summary-of-key-changes-to-immigration-rules-on-9-july-2012/

Right Response Team. 2024. 'A weekend of unrest: dozens of protests planned in the wake of Southport'. *Hope Not Hate*, 2 August. https://hopenothate.org.uk/2024/08/02/a-weekend-of-unrest-dozens-of-protests-planned-in-the-wake-of-southport/

Rose, Steven and Rose, Hilary. 2005. 'Why we should give up on race'. *The Guardian*, 9 April. https://www.theguardian.com/world/2005/apr/09/race.science

Rosenberg, David. 2011. *Battle for the East End: Jewish Responses to Fascism in the 1930s*. Nottingham: Five Leaves Publications.

Ryder, Nicholas. 2014. *The Financial Crisis and White Collar Crime the Perfect Storm?*, Cheltenham: Edward Elgar. https://www.e-elgar.com/shop/gbp/the-financial-crisis-and-white-collar-crime-9781781000991.html#:~:text='In%20this%20well%2Dresearched%20and

Sabbagh, Dan. 2018. 'Steve Bannon praises Boris Johnson and Tommy Robinson'. *The Guardian*, 12 August. https://www.theguardian.com/us-news/2018/aug/12/steve-bannon-praises-boris-johnson-and-tommy-robinson

Sanderson, Ginny. 2022. 'Why are Conservatives called Tories'. *The Scotsman*, 6 July. https://www.scotsman.com/news/politics/why-are-conservatives-called-tories-is-it-an-insult-history-and-meaning-of-the-term-explained-3758439

Schmuecker, Katie and Wincup, Emma. 2023. 'Foreword'. *Destitution in the UK*. destitution_in_the_uk_2023_0.pdf

Schulmeister, Stephan. 2013. 'The European Monetary Fund: a systemic problem needs a systemic solution'. *Revue de'OFCE* 127.

Scripps, Thomas. 2023. 'UK budget deepens social catastrophe for workers'. *World Socialist Web Site*, 16 March. https://www.wsws.org/en/articles/2023/03/16/wgde-m16.html

Sewell, Rob. 2013. '1919: Britain on the brink of revolution'. *In Defence of Marxism*, 16 May. https://www.marxist.com/1919-britain-on-the-brink-of-revolution.htm

Shelter. 2018. 'Building more affordable homes', October. http://england.shelter.org.uk/__data/assets/pdf_file/0011/1597709/2018_10_19_Shelter_briefing_-_Building_more_affordable_homes_.pdf

Siddique, Haroon. 2021. 'UK's strictist headteacher Katharine Birbalsingh made social mobility chief'. *The Guardian*, 10 October. https://www.theguardian.com/society/2021/oct/10/uks-strictest-headteacher-katharine-birbalsingh-made-social-mobility-chief

Simkin, John. 2023. 'Kurt Eisner'. *Spartacus Educational.* https://spartacus-educational.com/GEReisner.htm

Simon, Emma. 2023. 'Reflecting on the infamous mini-budget, one year on'. *Mortgage Strategy*, 19 October. https://www.mortgagestrategy.co.uk/features/feature-reflecting-on-the-infamous-mini-budget-one-year-on/#:~:text=It%20is%20one%20year%20since,across%20stock%20and%20currency%20makets

Sivanandan, Ambalavaner. 2009. 'Foreword', in Liz Fekete, *A Suitable Enemy: Racism, Migration and Islamophobia in Europe.* London: Pluto Press.

Sky News. 2024. 'More than 970 migrants cross Channel – the highest daily number this year', 6 October. https://news.sky.com/story/more-than-970-migrants-cross-channel-the-highest-daily-number-this-year-13228992

Smith, Adam. 1776. *An Inquiry into the Nature and Causes of the Wealth of Nations*. Stansted: Wordsworth Editions.

Smith, Reanna. 2022. 'Rishi Sunak's privileged childhood with "no working class friends" and wealthy parents'. *The Mirror*, 25 July. https://www.mirror.co.uk/news/politics/rishi-sunaks-privileged-childhood-no-27567616

Smith, Jonathan and Lashmar, Paul. 2024. 'Tory MP from slave-owning family set to gain £3m from sale of former plantation'. *The Guardian*, 20 April. https://www.theguardian.com/world/2024/apr/20/tory-mp-from-slave-owning-family-set-to-gain-3m-from-sale-of-former-plantation#:~:text=The%20Observer-,Tory%20MP%20from%20slave%2Downing%20family%20set%20to%20gain%20%C2%A3,from%20sale%20of%20former%20plantation&text=The%20Conservative%20MP%20under%20fire,payout%20from%20the%20Barbados%20government

Smith, Liz. 2023. 'Thousands of asylum seekers face destitution due to UK's "Illegal Migration" legislation', *World Socialist Web Site*, 9 October. https://www.wsws.org/en/articles/2023/10/09/ihmi-o09.html

Smout, Alistair. 2023. 'Sacked minister Braverman attacks UK's Sunak as failing and weak'. *Reuters*, 14 November. https://www.reuters.com/world/uk/former-uk-interior-minister-braverman-says-pm-sunaks-plan-not-working-2023-11-14/

Social Metrics Commission. 2018. 'A new measure of poverty for the UK', September. https://socialmetricscommission.org.uk/MEASURING-POVERTY-FULL_REPORT.pdf

Solomon, Enver. 2022. 'UK asylum seekers sent to Rwanda? That takes punishment of fellow humans to a new level'. *The Guardian*, 14 April. https://www.theguardian.com/commentisfree/2022/apr/14/uk-asylum-seekers-rwanda-government

Solomon, Enver. 2023. 'The illegal migration bill has passed, and here's what will happen: children lost, abused and exploited'. *The Guardian*, 18 July. https://www.theguardian.com/commentisfree/2023/jul/18/illegal-migration-bill-children-abused-exploited-law

Southwark, Andy. 2011. 'Tottenham riots: a community on the edge'. *Socialist Appeal*, 8 August. https://www.socialist.net/tottenham-riots-a-community-on-the-edge.htm

Sparrow, Andrew. 2023. 'UN refugee agency "profoundly concerned" by UK's illegal migration bill saying it amounts to an asylum ban – as it happened'. *The Guardian*, 7 March. https://www.theguardian.com/politics/live/2023/mar/07/small-boat-crossings-immigration-rishi-sunak-suella-braverman-mps-details-uk-politics-latest?page=with:block-64073efd8f085cc80327c6d1

Spartacus Educational. 2020. 'Anti-Semitism in Britain'. https://spartacus-educational.com/U3Ahistory45.htm

The Spectator@spectator. 2023. 'Fraser Nelson in conversation with Kemi Badenoch at Tory conference'. Post on X, 17 October. https://x.com/spectator/status/1714303175925047406

Spirit, Lara. 2023. 'Susan Hall: Tory mayoral candidate liked tweet praising Enoch Powell'. *The Sunday Times*, 15 September. https://www.thetimes.co.uk/article/susan-hall-tory-mayoral-candidate-liked-tweet-praising-enoch-powell-zqsr6lvfk

'Statement from the new Prime Minister Theresa May'. 2016. 13 July. https://www.gov.uk/government/speeches/statement-from-the-new-prime-minister-theresa-may

Statista. 2024. 'In hindsight, do you think Britain was right or wrong to vote to leave the European Union? (January 2020 to February 2024)'. https://www.statista.com/statistics/987347/brexit-opinion-poll/

Steinmetz-Jenkins, Daniel. 2023. 'Common sense fiscal policy or austerity by another name?' *The Nation*, 18 July. https://www.thenation.com/article/economy/clara-mattei-austerity/#:~:text=Mattei%20argues%20that%20what%20is,to%20stabilize%20a%20faltering%20economy

Stevens, Robert. 2021. 'UK government crisis deepens as lorry driver shortage leaves fuel stations empty'. *World Socialist Web Site*, 28 September. https://www.wsws.org/en/articles/2021/09/29/ukfu-s29.html

Stevens, Robert. 2022. 'Tens of thousands of UK National Health Service nurses strike for first time'. *World Socialist Web Site*, 15 December. https://www.wsws.org/en/articles/2022/12/15/nust-d15.html

Stevens, Robert. 2023. 'UK Home Secretary Braverman pushes forward policy of mass deportations of asylum seekers'. *World Socialist Web Site*, 20 March. https://www.wsws.org/en/articles/2023/03/20/zajv-m20.html

Stevens, Robert. 2024. 'UK Tories elect Kemi Badenoch as leader in rightward lurch'. *World Socialist Web Site*, 3 November. https://www.wsws.org/en/articles/2024/11/03/vkdc-n03.html

Stewart, Heather. 2019. 'Boris Johnson elected new Tory leader'. *The Guardian*, 23 July. https://www.theguardian.com/politics/2019/jul/23/boris-johnson-elected-new-tory-leader-prime-minister

Stewart, Heather, Gentleman, Amelia and Hopkins, Nick. 2018. 'Amber Rudd resigns hours after Guardian publishes deportation targets letter'. *The Guardian*, 30 April. https://www.theguardian.com/politics/2018/apr/29/amber-rudd-resigns-as-home-secretary-after-windrush-scandal

Stewart, Heather, Elgot, Jessica and O'Carroll, Lisa. 2020. 'Boris Johnson: no-deal Brexit now a "strong possibility"'. *The Guardian*, 10 December. https://www.theguardian.com/politics/2020/dec/10/boris-johnson-tells-cabinet-to-prepare-for-no-deal-brexit#:~:text=He%20added%20on%20Thursday%3A%20%E2%80%9CI,Canadian%20relationship%20with%20the%20EU.%E2%80%9D

Stewart, Heather, Adams, Richard and Walker, Peter. 2023. 'Ministers and unions dig in amid widespread strike action across UK'. *The Guardian*, 1 February. https://www.theguardian.com/uk-news/2023/feb/01/ministers-and-unions-dig-in-amid-widespread-strike-action-across-uk

Stillwerise. 2021. 'Kemi Badenoch', 3 April. https://stillwerise.uk/2021/04/03/kemi-badenoch/

Stone, Jon. 2017. 'What Theresa May said in her infamous speech to Tory conference'. *The Independent*, 4 October. https://www.independent.co.uk/news/uk/politics/theresa-may-immigration-policies-speech-conference-2015-tory-conservative-party-views-a7209931.html

Stone, Jon. 2019. 'Boris Johnson said that seeing "bunch of black kids" makes alarm bells go off in his head, in old column'. *The Independent*, 22 November. https://www.independent.co.uk/news/uk/politics/boris-johnson-bunch-black-kids-racist-column-guardian-a9213356.html

Stone, Jon. 2020. 'Boris Johnson said colonialism in Africa should never have ended and dismissed Britain's role in slavery'. *The Independent*, 23 June. https://www.independent.co.uk/news/uk/politics/boris-johnson-colonialism-africa-british-empire-slavery-a9564541.html

Sunak, Rishi. 2020. 'The Chancellor Rishi Sunak provides an updated statement on coronavirus'. UK Government, 20 March. https://www.gov.uk/government/speeches/the-chancellor-rishi-sunak-provides-an-updated-statement-on-coronavirus

Swinford, Steven. 2022. 'Teachers should not pander to trans pupils, says Suella Braverman'. *The Times*, 27 May.

Syal, Rajeev. 2021. 'Tory Islamophobia report a "whitewash," say Muslims in party'. *The Guardian*, 25 May. https://www.theguardian.com/news/2021/may/25/tory-islamophobia-report-criticises-boris-johnson-over-burqa-remarks

Syal, Rajeev. 2022a. 'Rwanda plan for asylum seekers decried as inhumane, expensive and deadly'. *The Guardian*, 14 April. https://www.theguardian.com/uk-news/2022/apr/14/uk-rwanda-plan-for-asylum-seekers-decried-as-inhumane-deadly-and-expensive

Syal, Rajeev. 2022b. 'Theresa May questions "legality and practicality" of Rwanda asylum plan'. *The Guardian*, 19 April. https://www.theguardian.com/politics/2022/apr/19/theresa-may-questions-legality-and-practicality-of-rwanda-asylum-plan

Syal, Rajeev. 2022c. 'Liz Truss pushed on immigration plans after Suella Braverman exit'. *The Guardian*, 20 October. https://www.theguardian.com/politics/2022/oct/20/liz-truss-pushed-on-immigration-plans-after-suella-braverman-exit

Syal, Rajeev. 2023a. 'Does Suella Braverman have evidence to link boat arrivals to crime?' *The Guardian*, 26 April. https://www.theguardian.com/politics/2023/apr/26/does-suella-braverman-have-evidence-to-link-boat-arrivals-crime

Syal, Rajeev. 2023b. 'Suella Braverman claims "hurricane" of mass migration coming to UK'. *The Guardian*, 3 October. https://www.theguardian.com/politics/2023/oct/03/suella-braverman-claims-hurricane-of-mass-migration-coming-to-uk#:~:text=Braverman%20began%20her%20address%20with,is%20coming%2C%E2%80%9D%20she%20said

Syal, Rajeev and Quinn, Ben. 2023. 'UN rebukes Suella Braverman over her attack on refugee convention'. *The Guardian*, 26 September. https://www.theguardian.com/politics/2023/sep/26/un-suella-braverman-refugee-convention-unhcr-migration

Syal, Rajeev, Mason, Rowena and O'Carroll, Lisa. 2019. 'Sky executive among Johnson's first appointments'. *The Guardian*, 23 July. https://www.theguardian.com/politics/2019/jul/23/sky-executive-among-johnson-first-appointments-andrew-griffith-munira-mirza

Symonds, Tom. 2024. 'Thousands join Tommy Robinson march in London'. *BBC News*, 27 July. https://www.bbc.co.uk/news/articles/ce4qd4e4e1vo

Tabb, William K. 2010. 'Marxism, crisis theory and the crisis of the early 21st century'. *Science and Society* 74(3).

Tax Justice UK. 2021a. 'Six companies made £16 billion in excess profits during the pandemic', 19 September. https://www.taxjustice.uk/blog/six-companies-made-16-billion-in-excess-profits-during-the-pandemic

Tax Justice UK. 2021b. 'Pandemic profits', September. https://www.taxjustice.uk/uploads/1/0/0/3/100363766/pandemic_profits_-_final.pdf

Taylor, Diane. 2022. 'Windrush descendants lose high court fight to expand scheme'. *The Guardian*, 14 January. https://www.theguardian.cruom/uk-news/2022/jan/14/windrush-descendants-lose-fight-to-expand-compensation-scheme

Taylor, Diane. 2023a. 'Suella Braverman accused of breaching barristers' code over "racist" language'. *The Guardian*, 14 May. https://www.theguardian.com/politics/2023/may/14/suella-braverman-accused-of-breaching-barristers-code-over-racist-language#:~:text=The%20letter%20cites%20three%20specific,of%20the%20instruction%20not%20to

Taylor, Diane. 2023b. 'Robert Jenrick has cartoon murals painted over at children's asylum centre'. *The Guardian*, 7 July. https://www.theguardian.com/uk-news/2023/jul/07/robert-jenrick-has-cartoon-murals-painted-over-at-childrens-asylum-centre

Taylor, Diane. 2023c. 'More than 60 charities demand closure of Bibby Stockholm barge'. *The Guardian*, 15 December. https://www.theguardian.com/uk-news/2023/dec/15/bibby-stockholm-asylum-barge-50-charities-demand-closure

Taylor, Diane. 2024a. 'Refugee who left UK for holiday in 2008 stranded in east Africa for 16 years'. *The Guardian*, 22 April. https://www.theguardian.com/uk-news/2024/apr/22/refugee-left-uk-holiday-2008-stranded-east-africa-16-years#:~:text=A%20refugee%20who%20left%20the,two%20younger%20siblings%20from%20Somalia.

Taylor, Diane. 2024b. 'Family of man found dead on Bibby Stockholm turn to crowdfunding to repatriate his body'. *The Guardian*, 2 January. https://www.theguardian.com/uk-news/2024/jan/02/leonard-farruku-family-bibby-stockholm-crowdfunding

Taylor, Diane and Syal, Rajeev. 2023. 'Growing despair of asylum seekers on Bibby Stockholm over living conditions'. *The Guardian*, 13 December. https://www.theguardian.com/uk-news/2023/dec/13/growing-despair-of-asylum-seekers-on-bibby-stockholm-over-living-conditions

Tell MAMA. 2025. 'Tell MAMA records the highest number of anti-Muslim hate cases in 2024 since its founding'. https://tellmamauk.org/tell-mama-records-the-highest-number-of-anti-muslim-hate-cases-in-2024-since-its-founding/

Thatcher, Margaret. 1978. 'TV interview for Granada World in Action ("rather swamped")'. Margaret Thatcher Foundation, 27 January. https://www.margaretthatcher.org/document/103485

Thatcher, Margaret. 1993. *The Downing Street Years*. London: HarperCollins.

Theodoracopoulos, Taki. 2003.'Thoughts on thuggery'. *The Spectator*, 11 January. https://archive.spectator.co.uk/article/11th-january-2003/47/thoughts-on-thuggery

Thomas, Daniel. 2022. 'UK faces biggest fall in living standards on record'. *BBC News*, 17 November. https://www.bbc.co.uk/news/business-63659936

Thompson, Harvey. 2023. 'UN special rapporteur denounces extreme poverty in UK for second time'. *World Socialist Web Site*, 20 December. https://www.wsws.org/en/articles/2023/12/20/fpzn-d20.html

Thornhill, Jo and Howard, Laura. 2024. 'Average UK salary by age in 2024'. Forbes, 14 May. https://www.forbes.com/uk/advisor/business/average-uk-salary-by-age/#:~:text=The%20latest%20government%20data%20(published,salary%20of%20around%20%C2%A334%2C900

Tiernan, Laura. 2024. 'Tommy Robinson holds far-right rally in London weeks after UK election'. *World Socialist Web Site*, 29 July. https://www.wsws.org/en/articles/2024/07/29/axso-j29.html

Tomlinson, Sally. 2019. *Education and Race from Empire to Brexit*. Bristol: Policy Press.

Topping, Alexandra. 2011. 'Rioters were "unruly mob" claims Theresa May'. *The Guardian*, 18 December. https://www.theguardian.com/uk/2011/dec/18/london-riots-theresamay

Townsend, Mark and Nonyelum, Anigbo. 2023. 'Suella Braverman refusing to roll out asylum-support scheme deemed "more humane"'. *The Guardian*, 20 August. https://www.theguardian.com/world/2023/aug/20/suella-braverman-refusing-to-roll-out-asylum-support-scheme-deemed-more-humane#:~:text=The%20UN%20has%20backed%20a,described%20as%20%E2%80%9Cmore%20humane%E2%80%9D

Townsley Joshua, Trumm, Siim and Milazzo, Caitlin. 2021. '"The personal touch": campaign personalisation in Britain'. *The British Journal of Politics and International Relations* 24(4). https://doi.org/10.1177/13691481211044646

Toynbee, Polly and Walker, David. 2011. *The Verdict: Did Labour Change Britain?* London: Granta Books.

Toynbee, Polly and Walker, David. 2020a. 'The lost decade: the hidden story of how austerity broke Britain'. *The Guardian*, 3 March. https://www.theguardian.com/society/2020/mar/03/lost-decade-hidden-story-how-austerity-*broke*-britain

Toynbee, Polly and Walker, David. 2020b. *The Lost Decade 2010–2020 and What Lies Ahead for Britain*. London: Faber.

Travis, Alan. 2017a. 'UK asylum seekers' housing branded "disgraceful" by MPs'. *The Guardian*. https://www.theguardian.com/uk-news/2017/jan/31/uk-asylum-seekers-housingbranded-disgraceful-by-mps-yvette-cooper

Travis, Alan. 2017b. 'May says Islamophobia is a form of extremism, marking shift in rhetoric'. *The Guardian*, 19 June. https://www.theguardian.com/politics/2017/jun/19/may-says-islamophobia-form-extremism-marking-shift-rhetoric

The Trussell Trust. 2018. 'End of year stats'. https://www.trusselltrust.org/news-and-blog/latest-stats/end-year-stats/

TUC. 2023a. 'Institutional racism still remains a challenge at work and in wider society', 20 April. https://www.tuc.org.uk/blogs/institutional-racism-still-remains-challenge-work-and-wider-society

TUC. 2023b. 'Austerity and the pandemic', 23 June. https://www.tuc.org.uk/research-analysis/reports/austerity-and-pandemic

Turnnidge, Sarah. 2022. 'Did Labour invent the "hostile environment?"'. *Full Fact*, 17 March. https://fullfact.org/immigration/michael-gove-hostile-environment-labour/

UK Parliament. 2018. 'Hardship caused by Universal Credit', 26 October. https://publications.parliament.uk/pa/cm201719/cmselect/cmpubacc/1183/118307.htm

UK Parliament. 2022. 'Nationality and Borders Bill returns to the Lords', 5 April. https://www.parliament.uk/business/news/2021/december-2021/lords-debatesnationality-and-borders-bill/#:~:text=The%20Nationality%20and%20Borders%20Bill%20seeks%20to%3A,lives%20of%20those%20they%20endanger

UK Parliament. 2024. 'The government's response to the Windrush scandal: research briefing', 4 September. https://commonslibrary.parliament.uk/research-briefings/cbp-8779/

UN. 2023. 'UK Illegal Migration Bill: UN Refugee Agency and UN Human Rights Office warn of profound impact on human rights and international refugee protection system', 18 July. https://www.ohchr.org/en/press-releases/2023/07/uk-illegal-migration-bill-un-refugee-agency-and-un-human-rights-office-warn#:~:text=The%20Bill%20extinguishes%20access%20to,matter%20how%20compelling%20their%20circumstances

Undiscovered Scotland. 2023. 'Willie Gallacher'. https://www.undiscoveredscotland.co.uk/usbiography/g/williegallacher.html

UNHCR (United Nations High Commission for Refugees). 2022. 'Global trends report'. https://www.unhcr.org/global-trends-report-2022

UNHCR (United Nations High Commission for Refugees). 2024. 'Asylum in the UK'. https://www.unhcr.org/uk/asylum-in-the-uk.html

Unite. 2024. 'Profiteering is breaking the economy', 16 May. https://www.unitetheunion.org/news-events/news/2024/may/corporate-profiteering-unite-study-of-17-000-companies-shows-margins-jumped-30-since-the-pandemic

United Nations Human Rights Office of the High Commission. 2019. 'United Kingdom: UN expert condemns entrenched racial discrimination and inequality', 14 June. https://www.ohchr.org/en/press-releases/2019/06/united-kingdom-un-expert-condemns-entrenched-racial-discrimination-and

UN News. 2023. 'Systemic racism within UK criminal justice system a serious concern: UN human rights experts', 27 January. https://news.un.org/en/story/2023/01/1132912

Usborne, Simon. 2018. 'How the hostile environment crept into UK schools, hospitals and homes'. *The Guardian*, 1 August. https://www.theguardian.com/uk-news/2018/aug/01/hostile-environment-immigrants-crept-into-schools-hospitals-homes-border-guards

Visram, Rozina. 1986. *Ayahs, Lascars and Princes: The Story of Indians in Britain 1700–1947*. London: Routledge.

Visual Journalism Team, *BBC Verify* and England Data Unit. 2024. 'Who are the rioters and what jail sentences have they received?'. *BBC News*, 8 August. https://www.bbc.co.uk/news/articles/cm23y7l01v8o

Walawalkar, Aaron and Taylor, Diane. 2023. 'Suicides of asylum seekers in Home Office accommodation double in last four years'. *The Guardian*, 21 December. https://www.theguardian.com/uk-news/2023/dec/21/suicides-of-asylum-seekers-in-home-office-accommodation-double-in-last-four-years?utm_source=ground.news&utm_medium=referral

Walby, Sylivia, J., Armstrong, Jo and Strid, Sofia. 2012. 'Intersectionality and the quality of the gender equality architecture'. *Social Politics* 19(4).

Walker, Peter, Crerar, Pippa and Mason, Rowena. 2022. 'Liz Truss sacks Kwasi Kwarteng before corporation tax UY-turn'. *The Guardian*, 14 October. https://www.theguardian.com/politics/2022/oct/14/liz-truss-press-conference-u-turn-corporation-tax-kwasi-kwarteng

Walker, Peter, Mohdin, Aamna and Topping, Alexandra. 2021. 'Downing Street suggests UK should be seen as model of racial equality'. *The Guardian*, 31 March. https://www.theguardian.com/world/2021/mar/31/uk-an-exemplar-of-racial-equality-no-10s-race-commission-concludes

Walvin, James. 1973. *Black and White: Negro and English Society, 1555–1945*. London: Allen Lane.

Waterson, Jim. 2023. 'Braverman's claim about ethnicity of grooming gangs was false, regulator rules'. *The Guardian*, 28 September. https://www.theguardian.com/politics/2023/sep/28/braverman-ethnicity-child-grooming-gangs-false-mail-on-sunday#:~:text=The%20regulator%20said%20Braverman's%20decision,were%20mainly%20from%20white%20backgrounds

Wearden, Graeme. 2009. 'Timeline: UK recession'. *The Guardian*, 23 October. https://www.theguardian.com/business/2009/oct/23/uk-recession-timeline

Weaver, Matthew. 2023. 'Essex police deny Braverman rebuked them over pub seizure of golliwog dolls'. *The Guardian*, 10 April. https://www.theguardian.com/uk-news/2023/apr/10/essex-police-deny-braverman-rebuked-them-over-pub-seizure-of-golliwog-dolls

Wheeler, Brian. 2024. 'Not all cultures equally valid, says Kemi Badenoch'. *BBC News*, 28 September. https://www.bbc.co.uk/news/articles/cg56zlge8g5o

White, Michael and Perkins, Anne. 2002. '"Nasty party" warning to Tories'. *The Guardian*, 8 October. https://www.theguardian.com/politics/2002/oct/08/uk.conservatives2002

White, Nadine. 2024a. 'Far right thugs stop cars to check if drivers are white before letting them pass'. *The Independent*, 7 August. https://www.independent.co.uk/news/uk/home-news/far-right-race-riot-uk-b2591803.html

White, Nadine. 2024b. 'Street beatings, stabbing and mosques under siege: the horrifying racist attacks carried out by far-right mobs'. *The Independent*, 5 August. https://www.independent.co.uk/news/uk/crime/riots-uk-muslim-asians-rotherham-manvers-hotel-b2591159.html

Whitehead, Tom. 2009. 'European elections 2009: UKIP claims political breakthrough'. *Telegraph*, 8 June. https://www.telegraph.co.uk/news/worldnews/europe/eu/5478468/European-elections-2009-Ukip-claims-political-breakthrough.html

Wickham, Alex. 2019. 'The Tory Party has suspended 14 members over a series of anti-Muslim Facebook posts'. *Buzzfeed*, 5 March. https://www.buzzfeed.com/alexwickham/the-tory-party-suspended-14-members-over-islamophobia

Winchester College. 2024. 'Fees and deposits: what is involved?'. https://www.winchestercollege.org/admissions/fees

Womack, Amelia. 2020. 'Theresa may meet with Yarl's Wood hunger strikers before it's too late'. *The Independent*, 17 July. https://inews.co.uk/opinion/comment/yarls-wood-amelia-womack-hunger-strike-130863?srsltid=AfmBOoqJRFJAtkOX2-amHwpYzCyRGAd3NSAMx4Z4S6nFaAt7RaupK8NZ

Wood, James, Ausserladscheider, Valentina and Sparkes, Matthew. 2022. '"COVID-Keynesianism" was a short-term crisis management tactic: neoliberal policymaking is back'. LSE, 28 September. https://blogs.lse.ac.uk/politicsandpolicy/covid-keynesianism-was-a-short-term-crisis-management-tactic-neoliberal-policymaking-is-back/

Woodcock, Andrew. 2022. 'Priti Patel's controversial immigration plans pass through parliament despite warnings of harm to refugees'. *The Independent*, 27 April. https://www.independent.co.uk/news/uk/politics/priti-patel-refugees-immigration-unhcr-b2067028.html

Woodcock, Andrew, Cowburn, Ashley and Isaac, Anna. 2022. 'Boris Johnson warned against "race to bottom on pay" as rail strikes hit millions of travellers'. *The Independent*, 21 June. https://www.independent.co.uk/news/uk/politics/rail-strikes-johnson-tuc-ogrady-b2106257.html

Woods, Alan. 2017. 'The Hungarian Soviet Republic of 1919: the forgotten revolution'. *In Defence of Marxism*, 21 March. https://www.marxist.com/hungarian-soviet-republic-1919.htm

Xinhua. 2021. 'UK government's race report accused of trying to downplay structural racism'. *People's Daily Online*, 1 April. http://en.people.cn/n3/2021/0401/c90000-9834915.html

YouTube. 2024. 'Sunday with Laura Kuenssberg 29th September 2024'. https://www.youtube.com/watch?v=LHJGHIOva-8

Index

References to endnotes show the page number and the note number (185n3).

A

Abbott, Diane 13–14, 47, 136
Achiume, E. Tendayi 138–139
acts
  Aliens Act 1905 22
  Employment Act 1980 32, 130, 182n65
  Equality Act 2010 89, 140
  Illegal Migration Act 2023 6, 7, 83, 87–88, 144–145
  Immigration Act 1971 23
  Immigration Act 2014 5, 46–47
  Immigration Act 2016 5, 49
  Nationality and Borders Act (2022) 6, 65–67, 79
  Police, Crime, Sentencing and Courts Act (2022) 6, 67–70, 127–128
  Strikes (Minimum Service Levels) Act 2023 8, 32, 128, 130–131
  Trades Disputes Act 1927 32
Adegoke, Olukemi Olufunto 154
Aiken, Mike 140
Albania/Albanians 19, 50, 78, 79, 87, 88
Ali, Saleh Ahmed Handule 48–49
Aliens Act 1905 22
Alston, Philip 101, 102–103, 105–106, 131
alt-right movement 174n102
Alwadaei, Sayed Ahmed 91
Amersi, Mohamed 113, 114
Amnesty International 66
Anderson, Lee 68–70
Annan, Kofi 19
anti-asylum-seeker racism 17, 19
anti-Black racism 13, 14, 56, 61–62, 68
anti-capitalism 28–30
anti-discrimination legislation 140
anti-Gypsy, Roma and Traveller (GRT) racism 17, 68, 89
anti-Irish racism 16, 17, 22, 23
antiracism 68, 140–141, 153
antisemitism 13–14, 17, 22, 79–80
Aspinwall, Trudy 89

asylum seekers
  austerity on, impacts of 105–106, 138–139
  Bibby Stockholm barge 6–7, 85–87, 136, 137–138
  Channel crossings 18, 65–66, 77, 79, 87, 88–89, 144
  criminality claims of 82
  definitions for 18–19
  detention centres 6–7, 77, 85–87, 136–138
  hostile environment 48, 52–54, 77–79
  humane support for 83
  offshore processing 6, 66–67, 74, 80–81, 88–89, 145
  safer routes for 144–145
  see also Illegal Migration Act 2023; immigrants; refugees
Attlee, Clement 38
austerity
  arguments for 27, 32, 33
  authoritarian austerity 128, 182n48
  author's overview of 1–2, 4–5
  author's suggestions to address 142–146
  budget cuts under 98–99, 127–128
  capitalism and 5, 30–32
  COVID-19 response, impact of on 109–110
  economists on 26–27, 99, 108
  financial crisis (2007–2008) 95–96
  fiscal 7–8, 32, 98–99, 122, 123, 128, 138
  history of 25–26
  hostility and 135
  impacts of 7, 100–102, 105–107, 108, 131–133, 139–140
  industrial 7–8, 32, 122–125
  interpretations of 32, 99
  life expectancy under 103–105
  responses to 99–100
  social class and 7, 126
  taxes as alternative to 5, 34
authoritarian austerity 128, 182n48

225

B

Badenoch, Kemi 9, 154–155, 156, 157
Bailey, Dorinda 56
Baker, Al 151
Baker, Norman 54
Baldwin, Stanley 32
Balfour, Arthur 22
Balls, Katy 156
Bannon, Steve 148, 185n6
Barclay, Steve 128
Barnardo's 132–133
Basran, Jasmine 120
Batty, David 54
Bavaria 29–30
Bavarian Soviet Republic 29–30
Beadle, Ben 121
bed poverty 132–133
bedroom tax 133
Bethell, James 113, 114
Beveridge, Aneisha 120
Beveridge, William 26, 101
Bibby Stockholm migrant barge 6–7, 85–87, 136, 137–138
biological racism 14, 17, 20, 60
Birbalsingh, Katharine 64
Black and minority ethnic (BME)-led organizations 140
Black Caribbean people 14, 20, 57, 60, 132
Black Lives Matter 63, 68, 69, 149, 155, 157
Blair, Tony 107
Blakeley, Grace 142, 143, 184n53
Blyth, Mark 25, 26, 27–28, 31–32, 142, 162n1
BME *see* Black and minority ethnic (BME)-led organizations
BNP *see* British National Party (BNP)
Bolshevik Revolution 30
Booth, Robert 62, 70
Braakmann, Nils 139–140
Brady, Graham 116
Bramble, Tom 97
Braverman, Suella
　asylum seekers 6
　complaints against 82–83
　dismissal of 91–92
　European Convention on Human Rights 76, 87, 90–91
　hostile environment 76–77
　Human Rights Act 91
　on Labour Party 126
　offshore processing 80–81
　resignation of 74–75
　rhetoric/cruelty of 7, 74, 79–80, 81–82, 83, 89
Bray, Kerry 139–140
Brexit
　on immigration, impact of 52–54
　Johnson, Boris 58, 64–65
　resignation of Theresa May 58
　withdrawal from EU 65, 178n2
Brexit Party 58, 60
British Asian people 6, 72, 75–76, 149
British culture/values 23, 24, 81, 140–141, 150, 154
British Indian people 76
British National Party (BNP) 39, 85
British Pakistani people 81, 83
Brown, Gordon 8, 39, 40, 97, 107
Browne, Jeni 119
Bryan, Anthony 57, 168n147
budgets
　March 2020 budget (Sunak's) 7, 110–111
　mini budget 2022 (Truss's) 7, 75, 117–121
　autumn 2022 budget (Hunt's) 8, 127–128
　March 2023 budget (Hunt's) 8, 129–130
　autumn statement 2023 (Hunt's) 133–134
Buffett, Waren 159n8
Butler, Dawn 84, 136

C

Callinicos, Alex 146–147, 158
Calvert, Rob 99
Cameron, David
　austerity 7, 97–98, 139
　ConDem Coalition Government 40, 45, 98, 99
　European Union referendum 49–50
　hate crime under 156
　hostile environment 5, 45, 46, 141
　image of Tory Party 60
　on immigration 39–40, 41–42, 44–45, 75
　Islamophobia and 54
　on London uprisings 100
Capital (Marx) 157
capitalism
　anti-capitalism 28–30
　austerity and 5, 30–32
　capitalist crisis management 4, 5, 27–28, 34, 109, 142
　divide-and-rule tactics 4, 16
　Marxist theory and 2, 3, 15–16, 32–33, 34, 98–99, 157–158
　socialism and 146–147
The Capital Order (Mattei) 27, 182n48
CERD (UN Committee on the Elimination of Racial Discrimination) 152
Chakrabortty, Aditya 8, 14, 100–101, 127–128, 182n48
Chamberlain, Austen 31
Channel crossings 18, 65–66, 77, 79, 87, 88–89, 144–145
Cheshire, Tom 150
child refugees *see* refugees
Churchill, Winston 22–23, 32
Clarke-Smith, Brendan 75
class compromise 26

INDEX

class warfare from above 2–3, 4, 5, 34, 99, 125, 126, 142
Coalition Government *see* ConDem Coalition Government
Coben, Diana 15
Cockbain, Ella 81
Cole, Mike 169n148
colour-coded racism 6, 17, 22, 60–62, 63, 68, 69
Commission on Race and Ethnic Disparities (CRED) report *see* Sewell Report
common sense 3–4, 15–16, 98
communities *see* working class communities
ConDem Coalition Government 40, 45, 98, 99
Conservative Party 159n1 *see also* Tory Party
Cooper, Yvette 60, 137
Corbyn, Jeremy 58, 65, 80, 154
COVID-19 pandemic
  Johnson Government response to 7, 109–110, 110–111
  Partygate 115–116
  personal protective equipment (PPE) scandal 112–113
  productivity, impact of on 34
  test and trace system 114–115
  VIP lane contracts 112, 113–114
Cox, Judy 157–158
CRED report *see* Sewell Report
Crerar, Pippa 79
Critical Race Theory (CRT) 14, 155
Crook, Jeremy 84
Crosby, Lynton 55
CRT *see* Critical Race Theory (CRT)
Crumlin, Paddy 124–125
Cullen, Pat 129
cultural identities 4, 19
cultural racism 17, 64

D

Davies, David 55, 168n124, 168n125
Davies, David T.C. 89
Davies, Gareth 118
Debt Issue, Government 142–143, 184n53
de Cordoba Farini, Claudia Fernandez 141–142
Delgado, Richard 14
Dent, Emma 51
Department for Work and Pensions (DWP) 59, 102–103
Department of Health and Social Care (DHSC) 113–114
deportations 6, 46, 57, 59, 74
De Schutter, Olivier 131–132
De Simone, Daniel 151–152
destitution 101, 132
Destitution in the UK 2018 101
Destitution in the UK 2023 132

detention centres 6–7, 77, 85–87, 136–138
Dhaliwal, Sharan 76
Dhesi, Tanmanjeet Singh 37
DHSC *see* Department of Health and Social Care (DHSC)
dinner table test 54–55
discourses 15, 18, 161n36
Disraeli, Benjamin 21–22
divide-and-rule 4, 16
Diwakar, Amar 75–76
Dixon, Jennifer 104
Dowden, Oliver 89, 116
Downie, Matt 119–120
Doyle, Karen 71–72
Drax, Richard 86, 174n109
Duggan, Mark 7, 42, 100
Dunn, Bill 98–99
DWP *see* Department for Work and Pensions (DWP)

E

economic liberalism 162n1
ecosocialism 165n69
Eden, Anthony 23, 173n47
Eisner, Kurt 29–30
elections
  2005 General Election 60
  2009 European Elections 39–40
  2010 General Election 5, 7, 38–39, 40, 97–98
  2017 General Election 55–56
  2019 General Election 60, 64–65, 109, 126
  2024 General Election 8, 69–70, 89, 134, 148, 153, 154
Elliott, Larry 99
emergency Keynesianism 109
Employment Act 1980 32, 130, 182n65
Engels, Friedrich 2, 98, 165n72
English Channel *see* Channel crossings
English Democrats 39
Equality Act 2010 89, 140
ethnic minority groups *see* minority ethnic groups
eugenics 63, 161n27
European Convention on Human Rights 46, 76, 87, 90–91, 154
European Elections *see* elections
European Social Survey (2023) 4, 21
European Union referendum 49–50, 65
  see also Brexit
Evans-Gordon, William 22
Ewing, Keith 131, 182n70
extremism 55, 77, 92, 150, 151–152, 156

F

family migration rules 43–44
Farage, Nigel 39, 44, 58, 60, 148, 149–150, 157, 176n173

far-right riots 8–9, 149–154
Farron, Tim 50, 167n83
Farruku, Leonard 86–87
fascism 8, 46, 63, 152–153
financial crisis (2007–2008) 26, 40, 95–96, 97, 105, 109
Finney, Nissa 20
fire *see* Grenfell Tower
First World War 5, 28–29
Fitzpatrick, Suzanne 101, 102
food banks 101, 105–106, 132
Full Fact 37–38, 165n4

G

Gabrielle, Damian 71
Gallacher, Willie 30–31, 164n56
General Elections *see* elections
genetics 160n12 (chap 1)
Gentleman, Amelia 38, 73, 84, 86
George, Lloyd 30
global financial crisis *see* financial crisis (2007–2008)
Goldsmith, Zac 55, 85
gollywog dolls 81–82
good sense 4, 15–16
Gove, Michael 37, 113
Government Debt Issue 142–143, 184n53
Gramsci, Antonio 15
Grant, Saira 47
Grenfell Tower 5, 50–51, 70, 135, 141–142
grooming gangs 81
GRT *see* anti-Gypsy, Roma and Traveller (GRT) racism
Gurner, Tim 34, 134
Gypsy people 17, 20, 68–69, 89

H

Haldane, Andy 27
Hall, Susan 85
Hancock, Matt 113
Hasan, Mehdi 55–56
hate crimes 81, 139–140, 156
Heath, Allister 117
Heath, Edward 23
Helm, Toby 58
Hemerijck, Anton 26
Hendy, John 131, 182n70
Hillier, Meg 115
'The Historical Roots of the Windrush Scandal' 83–84
Hollobone, Philip 54–55
homelessness 51, 101, 104, 105, 119–121, 175n170
hostile environment
  asylum seekers 48, 52–54, 77–79
  austerity and 135
  author's overview of 1–2, 5–7
  author's suggestions to address 142–146

family migration rules 43–44
'Go home or face arrest' vans 5, 45–46
impact of 52–54
invention of 37–38
for Muslims 54–57
Nationality and Borders Act (2022) 6, 65–67, 79
offshore processing 6, 66–67, 74, 80–81, 88–89, 145
online responses to 52
Police, Crime, Sentencing and Courts Act (2022) 6, 67–70, 127–128
racism of 2–3
the term *hostile environment* 59, 72
see also Windrush generation
hostile environment working group 5, 45
hostility and austerity 1, 8, 135
housing *see* homelessness; mortgages; rents
human rights 44, 46, 52–53, 87–88, 90–91, 137
Human Rights Act 7, 91
Hume, John 4, 25, 162n1
Hungarian Soviet Republic 29
Hungary 29–30
Hunt, Jeremy 8, 60, 74, 118, 119, 127, 129–130, 133–134
hybridist racism 17, 19

I

identities 4, 14–15, 19
ideologies
  austerity ideology 182n48
  Marxism on 3
  New Labour ideology 178n106
  racialization 15
  scientific racism ideology 161n27
  Tory ideology 3, 76, 84, 90, 97, 140–141
IFS *see* Institute for Fiscal Studies (IFS)
illegal immigrants/immigration 3, 18, 42, 46, 77–78, 168n147
Illegal Migration Act 2023 6, 7, 83, 87–88, 144–145
'I LOVE MY FOREIGN SPOUSE' website 52
IMF *see* International Monetary Fund (IMF)
immigrants
  attitudes towards 21
  detention centres 6–7, 77, 85–87, 136–138
  family migration rules 43–44
  leave to remain 43, 44, 46, 54, 168n147
  rights of 52–53
  welfare benefits 44–45
  see also asylum seekers; hostile environment; illegal immigrants/immigration; irregular immigrants; migrants; refugees
immigration
  ConDem Coalition Government on 40–42
  points-based system 41

White Paper on Immigration (2018) 52–54
  see also hostile environment; Tory Party
Immigration Act 1971 23
Immigration Act 2014 5, 46–47
Immigration Act 2016 5, 49
In Defence of Marxism 28, 29
Independents Alliance 154–155
Inman, Phillip 133–134
Institute for Fiscal Studies (IFS) 134
institutional racism 19, 20, 21, 63–64, 76, 85, 140, 155–156
intentional racism 4, 16–17
International Monetary Fund (IMF) 117–118
International Transport Workers' Federation (ITF) 124–125
Irish people 13, 14, 16, 22–23
irregular immigrants 4, 18, 87–88, 145
Islamist (the term) 155
Islamophobia 17, 54–57, 70, 76, 85, 154–155, 156
ITF *see* International Transport Workers' Federation (ITF)

J

Javid, Sajid 6, 57, 59, 60, 72, 116, 172n16
JCWI *see* Joint Council for the Welfare of Immigrants (JCWI)
Jenrick, Robert 9, 82, 86, 154, 155–156, 174n116
Jewish people 13–14, 19, 20, 21–22, 173n47
Johnson, Boris
  2019 General Election 60, 64–65, 109, 126
  Brexit 58, 64–65, 109
  COVID-19 pandemic 7, 109–110
  racism of 6, 60–63, 70
  resignation of 73, 115–116
  on strikes/unions 123
Johnson, Joe 64
Johnson, Paul 134
Johnson Government
  COVID-19 109–112, 112–115
  on immigration 65–70
Joint Council for the Welfare of Immigrants (JCWI) 49, 143–144, 145–146
Jump, Calvert 99

K

Kanagasooriam, James 170n54
Karim, Sajjad 85
Keynes, John Maynard 26, 98
Keynesian economics 7, 96, 109–110, 176n2
Khan, Charlotte 174n116
Khan, Sadiq 55, 56, 85
Kick It Out 17
Kirkup, James 47–48
Kissack, Paul 132
Krugman, Paul 97

Kuenssberg, Laura 155
Kwarteng, Kwasi 117, 118, 125, 180n71

L

Labour Party
  on anti-union legislation 131
  on *Bibby Stockholm* 138
  'Black Sections' 14
  Brexit 58
  financial crisis (2007–2008) 96
  hostile environment 37–38
  on offshore processing 145
  2009 European Elections 39
  2024 election 8, 148
  see also Brown, Gordon; Starmer, Keir
Lamb, Peter 56
Lauber, Kathrin 141–142
Lavery, Ian 159n8
Lawrence, Felicity 113
Lawrence, Stephen 6, 61
leave to remain 43, 44, 46, 54, 168n147
Lee, Phillip 64
Leigh, Edward 75
Lewis, Brandon 57
Lewis, Ed 52–53
Lewontin, Richard 160n12 (chap 1)
Liberal Party 26
life expectancy 103–105
Lineker, Gary 80
Locke, John 4, 25, 162n1
London rally (2024) 148–149
London uprisings (2011) 99–100
Lynch, Mick 122–123, 125, 129

M

Macfarlane, Jenna 71
Macmillan, Harold 23
Mahase, Elisabeth 114
Mahmood, Shabana 156
Major, John 24
Mandelson, Peter 23
Manifesto of the Communist Party (Marx and Engels) 98
Mansfield, Michael 63
Mansour, Adelle 141–142
Marmot, Michael 103, 104
Marmot Report 103–104
Martin, Patrick 34
Marx, Karl 3, 16, 33, 98, 157, 160n10 (intro), 160n12 (intro), 165n68, 187n86
Marxism
  capitalism and 2, 3, 15–16, 32–33, 34, 157–158
  as explanatory theory 2–3
  good sense and 15–16
  ideology 3
  misunderstandings of 159n7
  praxis 160n12 (intro)

on racialization 15
on the state 98–99
the term *Marxism* 2
value theory 165n68, 165n72
Mason, Chris 148
Mason, Rowena 63–64
Mattei, Clara 5, 27–28, 30–31, 32, 33, 99, 108, 142, 165n72, 182n48
Maugham, Jolyon 114
May, Theresa
 on austerity 99
 detentions/deportations under 45–46
 'Go home or face arrest' vans 5, 45–46
 Grenfell Tower 51, 141
 hostile environment policy 5, 38, 42–44, 52
 on immigration 40–41, 47–48
 Islamophobia 55–56
 Labour Party, on nastiness of 38–39
 on London uprisings (2011) 100
 on offshore processing 67
 as Prime Minister 49–50
 resignation of 58
 Yarl's Wood detention centre 136–137
May Government
 on child refugees 50
 White Paper on Immigration (2018) 52–54
McCallig, Elaine 37
McDonald, Mary Lou 23
McDonnell, John 8, 80, 152–153
McGuinness, Alan 116
McLaren, Peter 147
McMurtry, John 147
McVey, Theresa 92
Médecins Sans Frontières 66
Meller Designs 113
Mendez, Ned 151
migrants
 destitution 132
 hostile environment policy and 2–3
 the term *migrants* 1
 see also asylum seekers; immigrants; refugees
Mill, John Stuart 5, 25–26
mini budget and its effects, Truss's 7, 75, 117–121
minority ethnic groups
 austerity on, impacts of 107–108, 138–139
 destitution 132
 detention/deportation of 45–46
 hate crimes against 81, 139–140, 156
 hostile environment policies 48–49
 racism experienced by 20–21
 in Tory Party 39, 60, 75–76
 see also Grenfell Tower; Windrush generation; *specific groups (e.g., Traveller people, Black Caribbean people)*
minority religious groups 20
Mirza, Munira 63–64

Mohammed, Mustafa 113, 114
Monbiot, George 68
Mone, Michelle 113
Moore-Bick, Martin 51, 141
Morgan, Peter 149
mortgages 26, 27, 95–96, 117, 118–119, 120–121
Murray, Simon 84–85
Muslims
 hostile environment for 54–56
 Independents Alliance 154–155
 Tory Party members 85
 see also Islamophobia

N

National Health Service (NHS) 44, 46, 112, 114, 128–129, 144
Nationality and Borders Act (2022) 6, 65–67, 79
National Rail 123, 124
neoliberalism 26, 96, 97, 109, 140, 143
New Labour 61, 106–107, 178n106
New Liberalism 26
NHS *see* National Health Service (NHS)
non-colour-coded racism 6, 17, 22, 68–70, 161n29
Novak, Paul 131
Nowak, Paul 122

O

O'Carroll, Lisa 63–64
offshore processing 6, 66–67, 74, 80–81, 88–89, 145
O'Grady, Frances 123, 124
Onasanya, Fiona 56
O'Neill, Brendan 127
On Liberty (Mill) 25
Operation Vaken 46
Osborne, George 98, 134, 138
Osborne, Peter 56
Owolode, Tomiwa 13
Oxfam 66

P

pandemic *see* COVID-19 pandemic
Pang, Jun 87
Partington, Richard 26, 27, 117, 133–134, 142
Partygate 115–116
Patel, Priti 6, 40, 60, 66–67, 68, 72, 76
Patrick, Andrew 62
Peel, Robert 159n1
Perkins, Stephen 119
personal protective equipment (PPE) 112–113
Peterson, Jordan 157
Pincher, Chris 116
points-based system 41

Police, Crime, Sentencing and Courts Act (2022) 6, 67–70, 127–128
Portes, Jonathan 108
poverty 42, 100–101, 104–106, 110, 131–133
Powell, Enoch 23, 62, 85, 169n18
Powell, Jerome 33
PPE *see* personal protective equipment (PPE)
praxis 160n12 (intro)
prejudice 13, 14, 55
Prince, Rosa 38, 39
Principles of Political Economy (Mill) 25
processing centres *see* detention centres
prorogation 64, 170n50

R

'race' 160n12 (chap 1)
racial identities 4, 19
racialization 3–4, 15
racially or religiously motivated (RRM) crimes 139–140, 156
racism
  author's overview of 3–4
  hate crimes 81, 139–140, 156
  social class and 141–142
  types of 16–18
  see also hostile environment; Johnson, Boris; minority ethnic groups; Tory Party; *specific types of racism (e.g., colour-coded, hybridist, non-colour-coded, scientific)*
Racism and Ethnic Inequality in a Time of Crisis Survey (2023) 4, 20–21
Rail, Maritime and Transport Union (RMT) 122–123, 125, 159n8
Rajina, Fatima 76
Rayner, Tom 116
RCN *see* Royal College of Nursing (RCN)
recession 96
redheads 13, 14
red wall 65, 170n54
Reed, Howard 108
Rees-Mogg, Jacob 56–57, 125, 128
Reeves, Rachel 113, 143
referendum *see* European Union referendum
Reform UK party 69–70, 148, 149, 154, 157
refugees
  child refugees 50
  definitions of 18
  experiences of 48–49
  safe routes for 144–145
  see also asylum seekers; detention centres
Reicher, Stephen 100
religious minority groups *see* minority religious groups
rents 119, 120–121
Resolution Foundation 27
Reynolds, Martin 116
Ricardo, David 5, 25

right wing *see* alt-right movement; extremism; far-right riots
riots *see* far-right riots
Robinson, Tommy 8, 148–149, 151
Roma people 17, 20–21, 68, 89, 161n29
Rose, Hilary 160n12 (chap 1)
Rose, Steven 160n12 (chap 1)
Royal College of Nursing (RCN) 128, 129
RRM *see* racially or religiously motivated (RRM) crimes
Rudd, Amber 59, 64
Russia 22, 28–29, 30, 37, 111, 115
Rwanda 6, 66–67, 74, 80–81, 89
Ryley, Bernice 82

S

Sabisky, Andrew 63
Salter, Ann 86
Salter, Joan 79–80, 173n47
Sanderson, Ginny 159n1
scientific racism 17, 60, 61–62, 63, 161n27
Sewell, Rob 28, 30
Sewell, Tony 63–64
Sewell Report 9, 20, 63–64, 84, 155–156
Shah, Naz 56, 156
Shapps, Grant 63, 124
Simon, Emma 118, 119
Singh, Swaran 85
Singh Report 85
Sitting in Limbo 168n147
Sivanandan, Ambalavaner 17
Smith, Adam 4, 25, 162n1
Smith, Laura 159n8
Soames, Nicholas 40
soccer matches 17
social class
  austerity and 7, 126, 127
  life expectancy and 103–105
  racism and 141–142
social investment paradigm 26
socialism 8, 146–147, 157–158, 160n12 (intro), 185n80
Solomon, Enver 67, 87–88
Southwark, Andy 100
Sowell, Thomas 156
Stacey, Kiran 133–134
Starmer, Keir 8, 65, 143, 153–154, 157
Starmer Government 8–9
Stefancic, Jean 14
Stewart, Bob 91
Stratton, Allegra 115
strikes
  author's overview of 7–8
  Bavarian general strike 29–30
  Britain general strike 32
  Hungarian general strike 29
  hunger strikes 23, 137
  lorry drivers and shunters 127

nurses' strike 128–129
rail transport strikes (UK) 122–125
Scotland (1919) 30
widespread strikes 129
Strikes (Minimum Service Levels)
  Act 2023 8, 32, 128, 130–131
Summers, Larry 117–118
Sunak, Rishi
  anti-union legislation 8, 32, 130–131
  asylum seekers 6
  Braverman, Suella 74, 76, 81, 91–92
  class background of 126–127
  COVID-19 110–111, 116
  'election' of 75, 125
  fiscal and industrial austerity under 7, 125–126, 127, 128, 133–134
  immigration 77–79, 136
  strikes 127–129
Sunak Government 137, 145
surveys 4, 20–21, 42, 100, 120
Sweeney, Sarah 69
Syal, Rajeev 63–64, 67, 74–75

T

taking the knee 68, 155, 157
taxes
  bedroom tax 133
  inequality of system 111–112, 122, 127, 129, 162n1
  tax cuts 117–118, 130, 133–134
  tax havens 108
  on wealthy 5, 34, 142, 143
Taylor, Diane 71
Teather, Sarah 45
Tebbit, Norman 55
Tell MAMA 70, 156, 187n67
test and trace system 114–115
Thatcher, Margaret 23–24, 32, 65, 75, 97, 130, 162n78, 178n106
Thatcher Government 123
Theodoracopulos, Taki 62
there is no alternative (TINA) 97, 98
Thomas, Leslie 50–51
Tomlinson, Sally 46
Tories 159n1
Tory Party
  austerity under 97, 98–99, 100–102, 103–105
  author's overview of 159n1
  Brexit 58
  British Asian people 6, 75–76
  COVID-19 109–112, 112–115
  detention centres 6–7, 77, 85–87, 136–138
  European Convention on Human Rights 46, 76, 87, 90–91, 154
  European Union referendum 49–50
  Grenfell Tower 5, 50–51, 70, 135, 141–142
  ideology of 3, 76, 84, 90, 97, 140–141

immigration stance of 40–41, 47–48, 52–54, 65–67, 77–79, 90
  Islamophobia in 54–57, 70, 85, 154–155
  on protests 67
  racism in 21–24, 38–39, 63–64, 68–69, 89, 91
  see also Badenoch, Kemi; Braverman, Suella; budgets; Cameron, David; elections; Jenrick, Robert; Johnson, Boris; May, Theresa; Sunak, Rishi; Truss, Liz
Toynbee, Polly 106–107
Trades Disputes Act 1927 32
Trades Union Congress (TUC) 122, 131
Traveller people 13, 17, 20, 68–69, 89
Trickett, Jon 159n8
Trotta, Silvano 150
Trump, Donald 60
Truss, Liz 7, 74–75, 117–118, 122, 125
Tsangarides, Natasha 91
TUC see Trades Union Congress (TUC)
Tuckwell, Steve 117
Turnnidge, Sarah 37

U

UK Independence Party (UKIP) 39, 44, 47
Ukraine 37, 111, 115
unintentional racism 4, 16–17
unions see Rail, Maritime and Transport Union (RMT); strikes; Strikes (Minimum Service Levels) Act 2023; Unite union
United Nations Committee on the Elimination of Racial Discrimination (CERD) 152
United Nations High Commissioner for Human Rights 88
United Nations High Commissioner for Refugees 66, 88
United States 99–100, 161n27, 174n102
Unite union 127
Universal Credit 102–103, 106, 111, 128, 130, 131, 133, 178n119
Usborne, Simone 53

V

The Verdict (Toynbee and Walker) 106–107
VIP lane contracts 112, 113–114

W

Walker, Michael 106–107
Warsi, Sayeeda 54–55, 56, 57, 70, 85
wealthy, taxation on the 5, 34, 142, 143
welfare benefits 44–45
Welfare State 7, 26, 109–110, 126
whigs 159n1
White Paper on Immigration (2018) 52–54
Wickham, Alex 56–57
Wildman, John 139–140
Williams, Wendy 72–73, 136
Wilson, Henry 30

Wilson, Paulette 57, 168n147
Windrush generation
  author's update on 145–146
  compensation scheme 6, 71–73
  review recommendations 72–73
  rights of 5, 38
  scandal 57, 59–60, 83–85, 135–136
Windrush Progress Report 72–73, 136
Womack, Amelia 136–137
Woods, Alan 29, 30, 164n37
working class
  austerity measures, impact of 31–32, 33, 106–107, 108
  politicization of 28–29
  the term *working class* 1–2, 3

see also Grenfell Tower; strikes; Universal Credit
working class communities 2, 3
World War I *see* First World War
would-be migrants *see* migrants

X

xeno-racism 17, 78

Y

Yarl's Wood detention centre 136–137
York, Martin 56

Z

Zaranko, Ben 134

www.ingramcontent.com/pod-product-compliance
Lightning Source LLC
Chambersburg PA
CBHW051539020426
42333CB00016B/2001